California County Projections

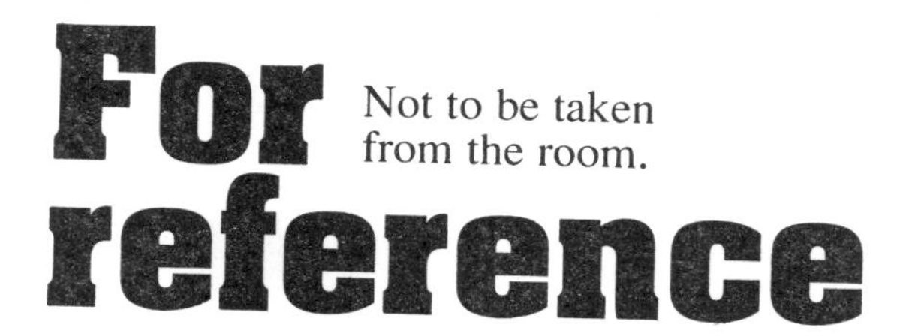

2003 Edition

Center for Continuing Study of the California Economy

California County Projections – 2003 Edition was prepared as part of the research program of the Center for Continuing Study of the California Economy (CCSCE). The project was directed by Stephen Levy, Senior Economist, who was the report's principal author. Estelle Chalfin Champs prepared the text and, with Nancy Levy, handled the report production. CCSCE appreciates the valuable assistance of Robert K. Arnold in providing conceptual guidance to the project.

CCSCE staff specialize in analysis and long term projections of economic and demographic variables in California and subareas of the state. **California County Projections** is the product of an internally financed, ongoing program of CCSCE to provide business and government decision makers with an independent assessment of the growth of California and subareas of the state.

Other publications in the CCSCE Annual Report Series:

CALIFORNIA ECONOMIC GROWTH

by
Center for Continuing Study of the California Economy
610 University Avenue, Palo Alto, CA 94301-2019
Telephone: 650-321-8550
www.ccsce.com

Library of Congress
Catalog Card Number 90-660111

ISBN 1-878316-48-6
ISSN 1050-303X

CALIFORNIA COUNTY PROJECTIONS — 2003 EDITION

Table of Contents

INTRODUCTION

INTRODUCTION

California County Projections – 2003 Edition is the 20th edition of CCSCE's County Projections report series. The objective of these reports is to present a consistent, timely, and credible set of projections for key market variables for each county in California. In this way each county can be ranked and compared with other counties for each key market characteristic.

Nine market characteristics are covered for each county: population, households, total personal income, per capita personal income, average household income, total taxable sales, taxable retail sales, total nonfarm wage and salary jobs and manufacturing jobs. The latest historical data are presented along with projections (except for jobs) for 2010. The dollar denominated variables – income and taxable sales – are discussed both in terms of real growth (measured in 2002 prices) and taking inflation into account.

Organization of the Report

The preface discusses economic and budget issues facing California after the recall election. The first section provides a summary of key findings. The second section looks at the short term outlook for the national and California economy.

Next come four sections with projections, historical analysis, and explanation organized as follows: Population Growth, Household Growth, Trends in Per Capita and Average Household Income, Market Growth – Total Income and Spending. The final section – Job Trends – analyzes 1990-2002 trends but does not include projections.

Appendix A discusses the CCSCE projection methodology. Appendix B presents a discussion of the two different measures of income (money income and total personal income) used by the U.S. Department of Commerce in reporting income data.

Appendix C presents a glossary of key definitions and dates used in **California County Projections.** Appendix D contains additional data from the 2000 Census.

The estimates and projections of California's economic characteristics published in this report are part of an ongoing research program of the Center for Continuing Study of the California Economy (CCSCE). Except where noted, all the detailed estimates and projections in this report were prepared by CCSCE.

COUNTIES BY 9 ECONOMIC REGIONS OF CALIFORNIA

Our work benefited greatly from the continuing assistance of many dedicated people working for local, state and federal agencies involved in data collection and analysis. CCSCE wishes to acknowledge the special assistance of:

Mary Heim, Assistant Chief of the Demographic Research Unit of the California Department of Finance; Howard Roth, Chief Economist of the California Department of Finance; Jeff Reynolds and Joe Fitz of the California Board of Equalization; Ben Bartolotto, Research Director of the Construction Industry Research Board; Richard Holden of EDD and the entire staffs of the U.S. Bureau of Labor Statistics and California Employment Development Department who have responded graciously to numerous requests for data and assistance.

CCSCE also wishes to acknowledge the ongoing support of the many private and public sector clients who have long term relationships with CCSCE. We also wish to acknowledge our loyal subscribers who have affirmed the value of having an independent perspective on the California economy.

AFTER THE RECALL

Recall

November 12, 2003

The recall is over and California has a new governor.

The short and long-term outlook for California's economy will depend primarily on the strength of current and future **national** economic growth and on the ability of California's public policy to play a constructive role in attracting and supporting private sector investment.

Governors and state legislatures do not have the power to create or end recessions nor should they share in the credit or blame for economic cycles. States do not have the power to change interest rates and cannot run deficits to stimulate the economy.

However, governors and legislatures **do** have the power to affect the long-term attractiveness of states for private investment and job creation. The debate over what public policies are needed for creating a "good business climate" will challenge the governor and legislature in the next weeks and months.

California moves toward the future with **a strong set of industries.** California firms are leaders in technology, entertainment, and design. California is the nation's leader in foreign trade, manufacturing, venture capital, agriculture and tourism — not only the leader in terms of size but also in terms of innovation and new products.

And California will start the year with good economic news from the nation. Job losses have stopped and job growth has returned. The strength of near-term job growth remains to be seen as well as when unemployment rates can be reduced. Still, the short-term outlook is better than it was a year ago.

The recall debate raised two questions about the role of public policy in supporting economic growth — two questions which will test Governor Schwarzenegger's ability to create consensus out of contention and gridlock.

-- What policies can lead to a balanced budget while maintaining California's public investment in education, infrastructure and quality of life?

-- Can Californians find a consensus about what makes a "good business climate"?

The Budget

Finding budget solutions is important for two reasons — 1) state and local government agencies need to focus on providing services and not spend endless hours dealing with constantly fluctuating budget deficits and turmoil and 2) California needs a restored credit rating to lower future borrowing costs and to show the world that we can govern ourselves responsibly.

In bold terms, the budget problem facing Californians is easy to describe.

The state faces a long-term "structural" budget deficit of $8 billion as estimated by the independent Legislative Analyst's Office. That **annual and ongoing deficit** rises to $12 billion if the Vehicle License Fee (VLF) is reduced. The ongoing deficit may be shaved by $1 or $2 billion per year if economic growth is strong.

In addition to the ongoing deficit, the state has planned to borrow $15 billion during this fiscal year. There is a possibility that the new governor may seek approval of an even larger bond in March 2004. **The bonds are part of solving past budget deficits and do not directly address the projected ongoing annual deficits.**

The positive effect of borrowing large amounts of money is that it allows more time to develop a consensus about long-term spending and tax priorities. The negative effect of this borrowing is that it does not directly address the gridlock about those choices. Californians have chosen to avoid cutting spending enough to balance the budget and, simultaneously, to avoid raising taxes enough to balance the budget, or to pick a combination of spending cuts and temporary tax increases that does the job.

Until these choices are faced directly, borrowing only postpones the eventual solution and raises the cost of balancing the budget. In addition, the state treasurer has warned that more borrowing will push the state's debt above reasonable levels and that borrowing to pay off the deficit may "crowd out" borrowing for investing in education and infrastructure facilities.

Governor Schwarzenegger hopes to provide part of the solution through identifying "waste" and cutting spending without reducing service levels. As yet, there are no specific solutions on the table and no indication that the gridlock surrounding spending and taxes has been overcome or even reduced.

A "Good" Business Climate

The recall campaign focused attention on the perception that California's business climate has deteriorated and that California is "unfriendly to business".

The challenge facing the new governor and residents is that there is no agreement on what constitutes a good business climate. The recall campaign focused attention on one set of claims:

--Workers' compensation costs in California are out of line with those in other states.

--Energy costs are also higher than in other states.

--The newly-passed state health insurance legislation will be "too costly" to business

--California's unemployment insurance benefits and family leave program are "too costly" to business

--State government does not understand the importance of private sector job creation

However, California has long had a second set of "bad for business" challenges:

--Housing costs are too high for new families and communities are not allowing enough housing to be built.

--California is behind on public investment in infrastructure—roads, public transit, K-12 and higher education facilities, and water-related infrastructure.

--California lags the nation in spending per pupil on K-12 education.

--The quality of life in many communities is falling behind because our system of local finance does not support good land use planning and does not provide enough money to keep up with a growing population.

Reform? Resources?

There is no disagreement that workers' compensation costs are too high. Finding a way to reduce workers' compensation costs will not only address a key complaint of California business owners but will pay a double dividend in helping out government and school district budgets, which are already in fragile condition.

But is there any disagreement that California is behind on infrastructure investment? Congestion is the leading complaint (along with education) in polls of residents, yet recent budget difficulties have led to cuts in pay-as-you-go infrastructure investment. Why would a business create new facilities in California if congestion plagues the movement of people and goods?

There is no disagreement that energy costs are higher in California than in most other states. While there is no consensus yet on how to guarantee that California customers will have access to power, it is reasonable to assume that today's energy costs place the state at a competitive disadvantage.

But housing costs are an even larger competitive disadvantage. Housing affordability and the shortage of new housing affect the lives of California residents but these issues are also part of California's business climate and one of the state's competitive disadvantages. **Housing is a business climate issue.**

One problem in addressing California's business climate is that industries differ greatly in what they seek. There is broad agreement that the California economy is a leader in innovation and the application of creativity to the design of new goods and services. The state economy depends on being able to attract a highly skilled and creative workforce.

So, the discussion of business climate must involve understanding the location choices of creative workers and entrepreneurs. As a result, good schools and universities become business climate issues. Creating great places to live and work is important for a good business climate. And, therefore, California's system of public finance, especially the rules governing local government finance, is a business climate issue.

The public debate today is similar to the debate in California a decade ago during the last recession period. One group is deeply committed to a reform agenda with workers' compensation as the leading symbol of what they feel needs reforming. One group is deeply committed to the ongoing challenges of providing adequate infrastructure, world-class education and great communities for working and living.

And these challenges are complicated by the current budget deficits, just as they were a decade ago.

Some of the components of creating a good business climate will cost more money in the public sector. Some of the components of creating a good business climate point toward reducing costs for private businesses.

Right now the environment is polarized. One side chants WE NEED REFORM. The other side counters WE NEED RESOURCES.

Both sides raise good points.

The challenge for the governor and legislature is to fashion a consensus around reform **and resources** that ends the gridlock and allows the California economy and the state's residents to move forward.

SUMMARY OF FINDINGS

SUMMARY OF FINDINGS

Economic Outlook

Last year's economic forecast was partly right and partly wrong. The correct forecast was that the state and nation would see rising levels of economic growth. This has been true for national GDP and California has experienced modest increases in income and spending as well as a sharp rise in housing construction and prices.

But, the missing ingredient at the national and state level has been job growth. The job growth anticipated a year ago did not happen, not here and not in the nation. GDP, company sales and profits and the stock market have risen in 2003 but job levels have fallen. Measured in terms of job growth, this is the worst recovery period since World War II despite the fact that the last recession was mild by historical standards.

The disconnect between economic growth and job growth is accounted for by the very high levels of productivity growth recorded in recent quarters. Put simply, firms can produce more goods and services with fewer workers.

The first signs of national job growth are still below the 150,000 per month needed to keep pace with labor force growth and well below the levels needed to reduce unemployment rates back toward 4%.

Change in U.S. Nonfarm Jobs
Jan 2001–Oct 2003

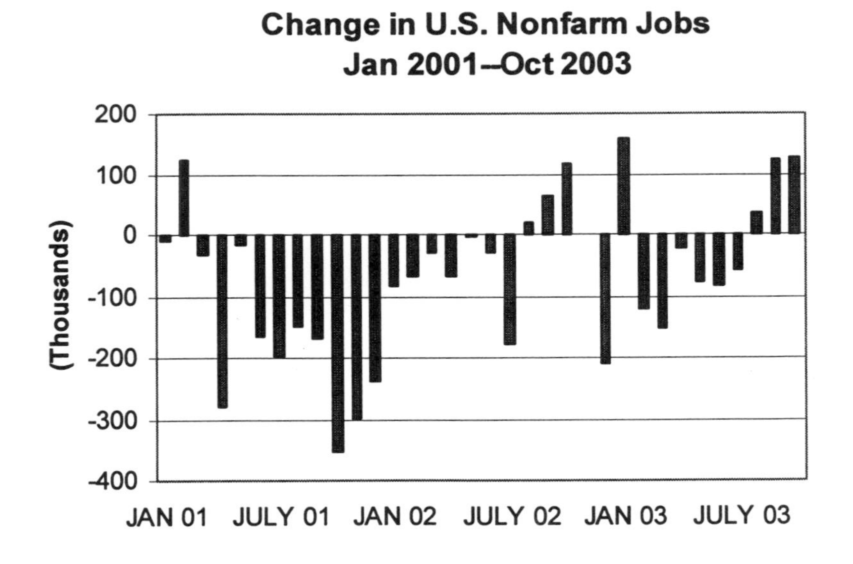

Recently, the press has carried stories filled with assertions about how poorly the California economy was performing and how the state was losing jobs to other states and countries. The papers also carried the actual job comparisons shown below.

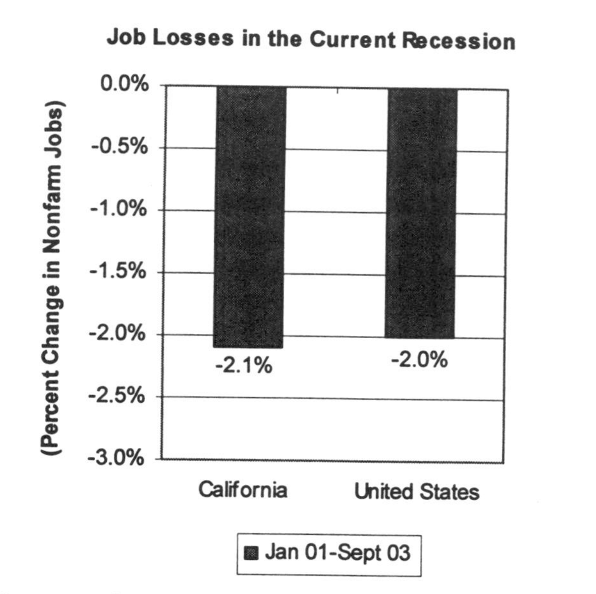

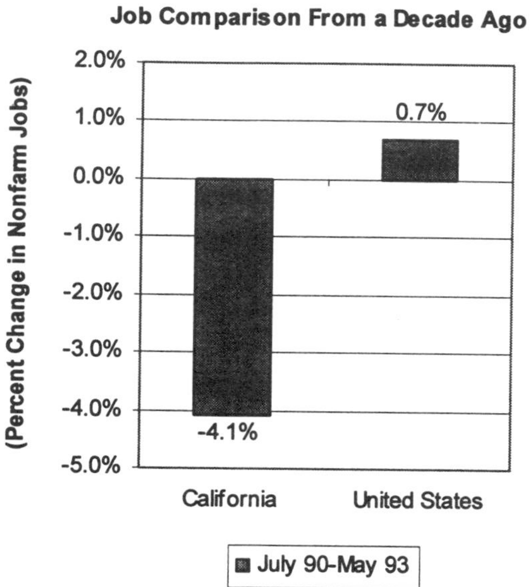

The graphs show, as does the data in Section 2, that the state and national economy are both doing poorly in terms of job creation, both losing near 2% of total jobs since the recession began. Both the state and the nation have also lost approximately 15% of total manufacturing jobs. The current recession, while painful to those involved and to the state budget is, in fact, much milder than the early 90s recession where unemployment rates reached nearly 10% and the state did perform far worse than the nation.

California's job losses are concentrated in the Bay Area. All regions except the Bay Area are doing better than the nation and some regions have recorded job gains during the national recession and subsequent jobless recovery.

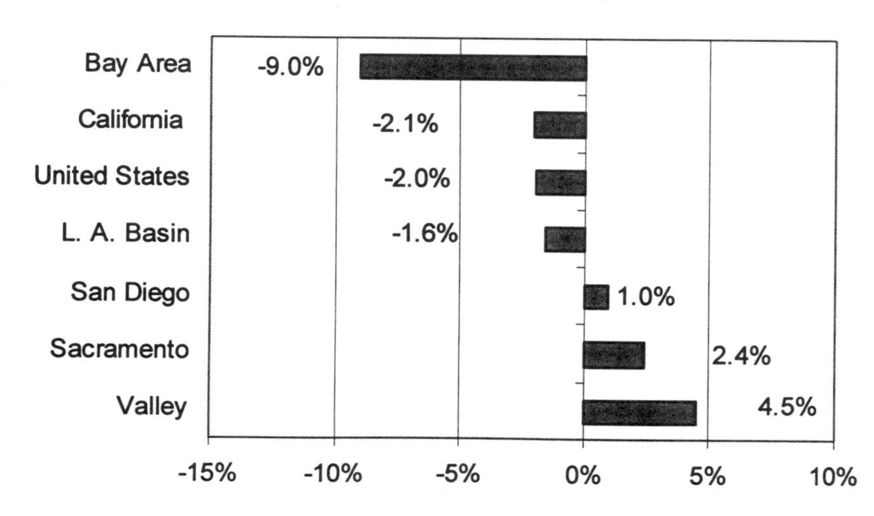

Outlook for 2004

The disconnect to date between the growth in GDP and job growth makes it hard to forecast what is going to happen in the next year.

In normal times, the GDP growth expected for the next twelve months would produce enough job gains to reduce unemployment rates. At this point, however, CCSCE does not expect such high levels of job growth nor do forecasters at UCLA and national economic forecasting centers.

Incomes should rise for those who are employed and there is the possibility that stock option income may rise more than expected as stock prices have risen sharply. To date, income tax receipts in California are running ahead of expectations by about $1 billion for the 2003-2004 budget year.

So, a year of modest economic growth seems likely with the Bay Area recovering later than other regions. But, the reality is that economists are just guessing about short-term trends based on models that may not be applicable to the high productivity growth world of today.

Population

Recent Trends

- Population growth accelerated after 2000. California added 1.8 million residents between January 1, 2000 and January 1, 2003 — an annual growth of 612,700 and far above annual population growth levels in the 1990s. The growth came as a result of natural increase, foreign immigration **and** positive levels of migration from other states.

- Population growth rates were highest in the Sacramento region, the San Joaquin Valley and the Los Angeles Basin. Annual population growth averaged 1.8% per year between 2000 and 2003 — above the 1.2% annual growth for 1990-1996 and 1.6% annual gains from 1996 to 2000.

- Ethnic change continues. Hispanic residents accounted for nearly 80% of California's population growth between 2000 and 2002 with Asian residents accounting for most of the remaining population gains.

California and Economic Regions Population Growth Since 1990						
	Average Annual Growth (Thousands)			Average Annual Growth Rate		
	1990-96	1996-2000	2000-03	1990-96	1996-2000	2000-03
Los Angeles Basin	156.2	245.5	330.7	1.0%	1.5%	2.0%
San Francisco Bay Area	64.1	102.8	76.7	1.0%	1.6%	1.1%
San Diego Region	20.4	50.8	51.9	0.8%	1.9%	1.8%
Sacramento Region	27.7	37.5	48.1	1.8%	2.2%	2.6%
Sacramento Valley Region	8.0	4.1	8.6	1.4%	0.7%	1.4%
Coastal Region	9.8	23.1	15.8	0.8%	1.8%	1.2%
San Joaquin Valley	60.8	50.7	74.6	2.1%	1.6%	2.2%
North Coast Region	3.1	1.3	2.3	1.1%	0.5%	0.8%
Mountain Region	5.2	3.1	4.0	1.5%	0.8%	1.0%
CALIFORNIA	**355.7**	**518.5**	**612.7**	**1.2%**	**1.6%**	**1.8%**

Source: California Department of Finance; 1990-2000, July 1 estimates; 2000-2003 Jan. 1 estimates

Projected Population Growth

California's population is projected to increase from 35.3 million in 2002 to 39.7 million in 2010. The annual projected population growth of 550,000 per year is lower than the recent 600,000+ annual gains but far higher than the 456,100 annual growth since 1990.

California Components of Population Growth (Thousands Per Year)			
	1980-1990	1990-2002	2002-2010
Births	469.4	553.8	558.4
Deaths	190.0	223.3	252.1
Natural Increase	279.4	330.5	306.3
Net Migration	340.0	125.5	243.7
Total Population Growth	619.4	456.1	550.0

Source: DOF, CCSCE; 1990-2002 data based on DOF July 1 estimates

Population growth will be divided evenly between natural increase and net migration in the decade ahead with natural increase accounting for 56% of statewide growth. Between 1990 and 2002, natural increase accounted for the large majority (72%) of population gains as the recession induced substantial domestic out-migration. If future job growth is less than projected, migration will be a smaller component of overall population growth and vice versa.

Population Age Trends

Population growth will be concentrated in the high school and young adult (15-24) age groups and in the 45-64 age groups. Growth in the elementary and middle-school age groups (5-14) will be low compared to recent trends.

California
Population by Age Group
2000 and 2010
(Thousands)

	2000	2003	2010	00-10	% chg
0 to 4	2,525.8	2,637.0	2,906.2	380.4	15.1%
5 to 9	2,686.1	2,598.3	2,767.9	81.9	3.0%
10 to 14	2,609.4	2,790.8	2,680.8	71.4	2.7%
15 to 19	2,426.9	2,571.3	2,892.0	465.1	19.2%
20 to 24	2,380.8	2,572.3	2,899.7	518.9	21.8%
25 to 34	5,115.8	5,208.4	5,526.5	410.7	8.0%
35 to 44	5,450.0	5,543.7	5,577.0	127.0	2.3%
45 to 54	4,457.2	4,823.8	5,572.5	1,115.3	25.0%
55 to 64	2,690.9	3,210.1	4,391.6	1,700.7	63.2%
65 to 74	1,889.0	1,971.8	2,484.3	595.3	31.5%
75-84	1,324.3	1,371.1	1,395.3	71.0	5.4%
85+	480.1	510.5	616.2	136.0	28.3%
Total Population	34,036.4	35,809.1	39,710.1	5,673.7	16.7%

Source: 2000, 2003 – DOF; 2010 – CCSCE total, DOF age distribution

Population Growth in Economic Regions

The Sacramento and San Joaquin Valley regions are projected to be the state's fastest growing regions to 2010. The Sacramento region was the fastest growing region between 1995 and 2002 with an annual growth rate of 2.3%. The region's high rate of growth is projected to continue through 2010 as the region adds more than 360,000 residents.

The Valley will add more than 650,000 residents between 2002 and 2010 – an annual growth rate of 2.2%. The Valley had the second highest regional rate of population growth between 1990 and 2001. The attraction of the region is lower housing costs and fewer "urban ills" than California's coastal regions.

The largest numerical growth, 2.6 million new residents, will locate in the Los Angeles Basin and San Francisco Bay Area. Despite their projected below average growth rates, these regions will still create well over half of the new jobs in California. Though not the fastest growing regions in California, these regions will outpace the projected national population growth rate of 0.8% per year.

Population Growth by Economic Region
1995-2010

	1995-2002		2002-2010	
	Growth (Thousands)	Average Annual Growth Rate	Growth (Thousands)	Average Annual Growth Rate
Sacramento Region	280.7	2.3%	364.5	2.2%
San Joaquin Valley	391.4	1.7%	650.5	2.2%
Coastal Region	129.5	1.4%	202.7	1.7%
Sacramento Valley	36.4	0.9%	83.7	1.6%
San Diego	319.9	1.7%	390.6	1.6%
Mountain Region	25.9	0.9%	50.6	1.5%
Los Angeles Basin	1,777.5	1.6%	2,055.2	1.4%
North Coast	11.1	0.5%	28.6	1.1%
San Francisco Bay Area	611.3	1.3%	588.9	1.0%
CALIFORNIA	3,590.0	1.5%	4,409.1	1.5%

Fastest Growing Counties

Placer County was the fastest-growing larger (more than 150,000 residents) county in California between 1995 and 2002, growing at an annual rate of 3.6%. Other fast-growing larger counties included Riverside, San Joaquin, Sacramento and Yolo.

Imperial is projected to be the fastest-growing larger county to 2010, followed closely by Riverside, Placer, Merced and El Dorado. Of the fastest-growing larger counties, four each are in the San Joaquin Valley and Sacramento regions and two are in the Los Angeles Basin.

San Benito, Madera and Lassen lead the fastest-growing smaller counties in both the 1995-2002 and 2002-2010 periods.

Ten Fastest Growing Large Counties
1995-2010

1995-2002	**Average Annual Growth Rate**	**2002-2010**	**Average Annual Growth Rate**
Placer	3.6%	Imperial	3.0%
Riverside	2.8%	Riverside	2.9%
San Joaquin	2.1%	Placer	2.8%
Sacramento	2.1%	Merced	2.8%
Yolo	2.1%	El Dorado	2.6%
San Bernardino	2.0%	San Joaquin	2.4%
Monterey	1.9%	Kern	2.4%
El Dorado	1.9%	Stanislaus	2.2%
Orange	1.8%	Yolo	2.1%
Stanislaus	1.8%	Sacramento	2.0%
CALIFORNIA	1.5%	**CALIFORNIA**	1.5%

Ten Fastest Growing Smaller Counties 1995-2010			
1995-2002	**Average Annual Growth Rate**	**2001-2010**	**Average Annual Growth Rate**
San Benito	3.4%	San Benito	4.3%
Madera	2.6%	Madera	2.4%
Lassen	2.4%	Lassen	2.3%
Mono	2.3%	Lake	2.2%
Kings	2.2%	Colusa	2.2%
Sutter	1.5%	Calaveras	2.1%
Calaveras	1.4%	Kings	1.9%
Napa	1.4%	Tuolumne	1.8%
Nevada	1.4%	Mariposa	1.8%
Colusa	1.3%	Tehama	1.7%
CALIFORNIA	1.5%	**CALIFORNIA**	1.5%

Households

Short-Term Trends

The past two years (2002 and 2003) have brought **a strong upward trend in the demand for housing in California.**

Housing prices have risen at double-digit levels in all California markets outside the Bay Area and reached record levels. The median resale home price in California is near $400,000 – more than double the national average. The strong demand has been created partly by record-low mortgage rates but has been especially impressive in this period of low job and income growth.

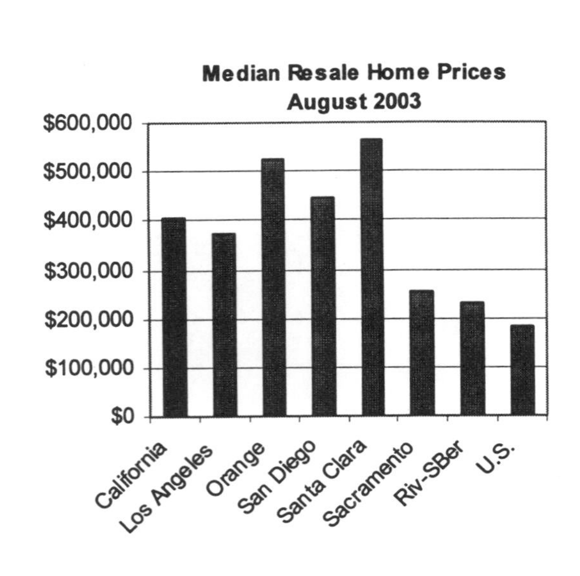

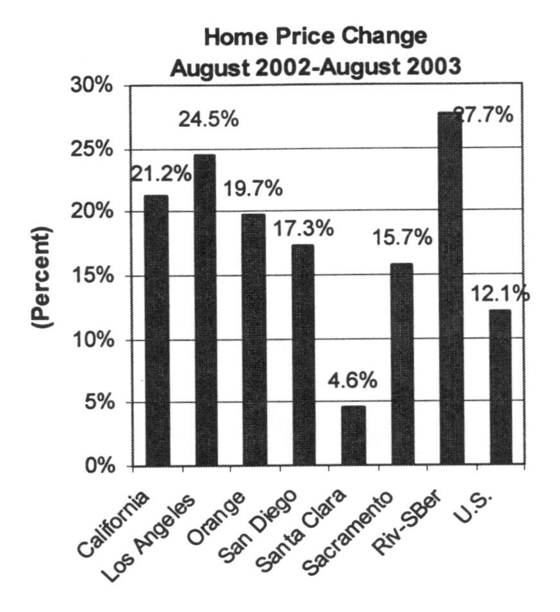

The strong demand for housing has finally brought substantially higher levels of new housing construction in most California markets. Residential permits should reach 185,000 in 2003 – the highest level in California since 1989. Single-family permits are up 12.8% through September 2003 and **multi-family permit levels are up 37.1%.**

Housing construction is being helped by two trends – 1) the conversion of land designated for nonresidential development to housing and 2) the commitment of more communities to find room for and approve new housing developments, especially those involving reuse of existing developed land.

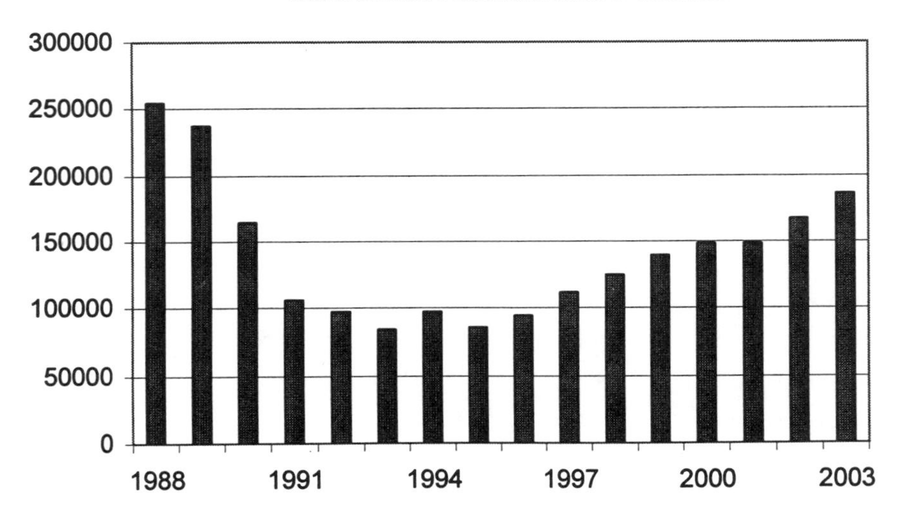

Household Growth Should Increase Substantially To 2010

Four factors should push future household growth well above the 112,000 annual gains of the 1990s:

1) Job growth will be higher.
2) Population growth will be higher.
3) Age trends favor increased household formation.
4) More communities are beginning to allow and plan for infill housing.

Job and Population Growth

CCSCE projects job growth of 2.9 million between 2000 and 2010. The projected growth compares with the 2.1 million jobs gain of the 1990s.

CCSCE projects population growth of 5.7 million residents between 2000 and 2010 – 40% higher than the 4.1 million growth of the 1990s. The annual gains since 2000 are over 600,000 per year but will taper off slightly between 2003 and 2010.

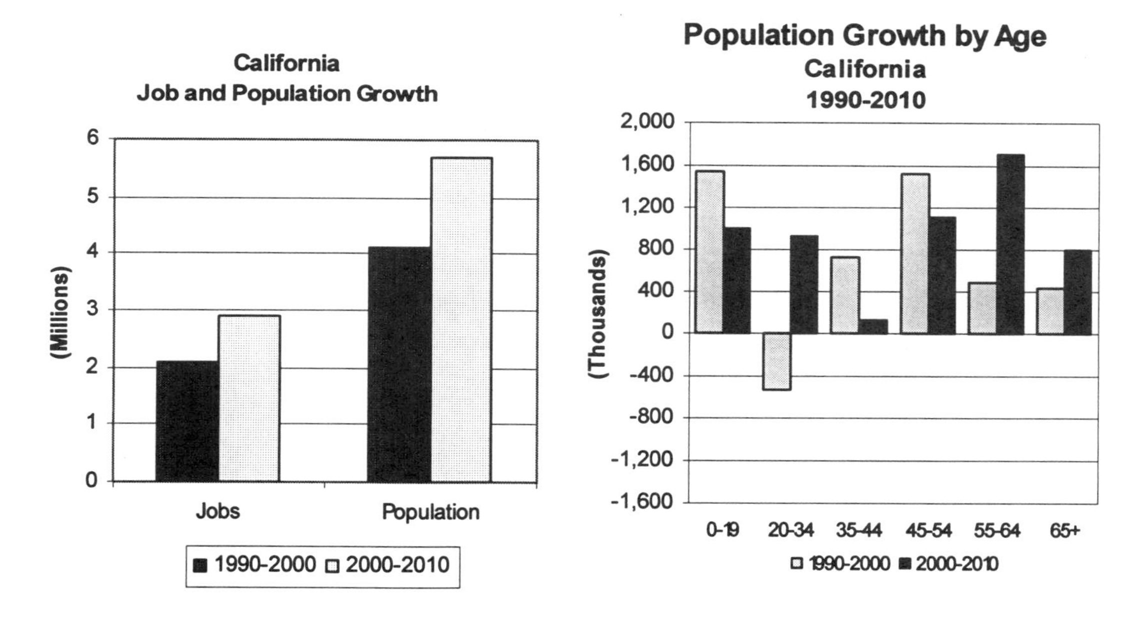

Demographic trends support an increase in household formation, an end to the steady increase in household size, and the beginnings of a change in the type of housing demanded as the population ages.

1) The percentage of children in the total population is expected to decline. Birth rates are falling for all ethnic groups. As a result, an increasing share of the population will be in household-forming age groups.

2) A large share of future population growth will be in the 55+ age groups as shown above and on page 1-6. These groups have a) relatively small

household sizes and b) a different pattern of preferences for the type of housing they desire.

3) The number of residents in the 20-34 age group will rise after falling in the previous decade.

These demographic trends should bring both an increase in the number of households formed as well as potential changes in the type of housing demanded. In particular, the preference for living in smaller units in an urban setting near transit and job sites will increase and provide demand for an increasing number of housing units on existing developed sites.

California
Alternative Household Projections
1990-2010
(Thousands)

Households	1990 Census	2003 Census Jan 1	2010 July	Average Annual Growth 1990-2003	Average Annual Growth 2003-2010
Demographic Trend	10,380.9	11,866.8	13,542.0	116.5	223.4
Current Trend			12,996.6		150.6
Midway Projection			13,263.7		186.3

CCSCE projects that annual household formation between 2003 and 2010 will vary from 150,000 per year to 223,000 per year. CCSCE has prepared a midrange projection of 186,300 additional households per year from 2003 to 2010.

The recent upturn in housing construction gives hope that the midrange projection can be exceeded. A continuation of 2003 permit levels to 2010 will provide close to enough housing to meet CCSCE's midrange household formation projection. If communities and landowners continue the trend toward higher-density reuse of existing sites, the state may be able to accommodate household formation levels above 200,000 for the first time since the mid 1980s.

Housing Permits and Household Growth (Thousands)		
Region	Estimated Permits 2003	Average Household Growth (Midway Projection) Jan. 1,2003-July 1,2010
Los Angeles Basin	78.5	75.4
San Francisco Bay Area	27.1	33.2
San Diego	17.3	17.2
Sacramento	24.1	16.9
San Joaquin Valley	28.2	25.2
California	**186.8**	**186.3**

Source: CCSCE

Much will depend on whether communities and residents recognize the importance of housing in creating a positive climate for economic growth in California. Housing is, truly, one of the most critical components of a "good business climate".

Income

Short-Term Trends

Total personal income, adjusted for inflation, declined in California in 2001 and 2002 after outpacing the national growth rate during the late 1990s. All of the income losses occurred in the San Francisco Bay Area where large job losses and a sharp decline in stock option income pushed per capita incomes down in most Bay Area counties.

Income growth, while modest, kept pace with national trends in counties outside the Bay Area.

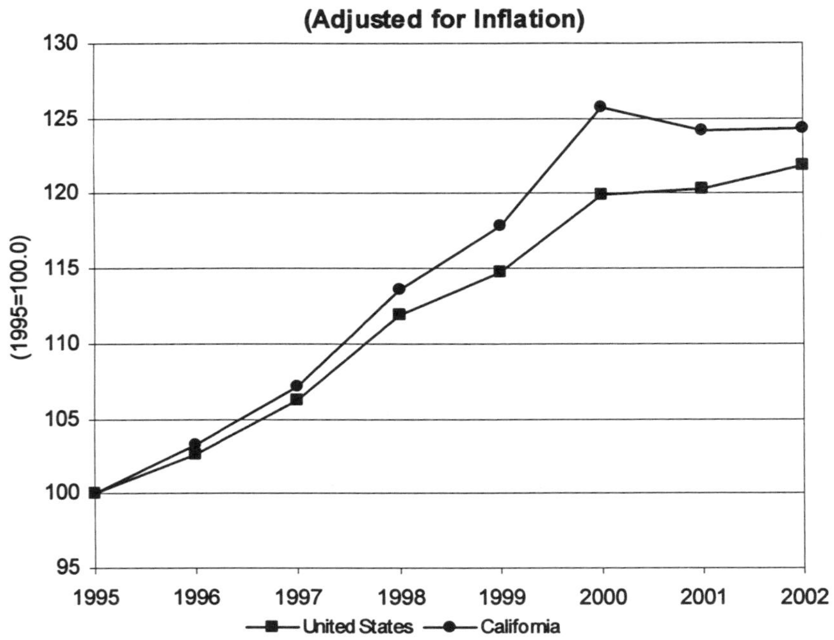

Income Growth to 2010

Continuing strong productivity growth and the eventual rebound from the current slow-growth period will push per capita and total income sharply higher to 2010. Real income is projected to grow by 4.0% annually from the recession-depressed levels of 2002.

California
Components of Real Income Growth
Average Annual Growth

			2002-2010		
	1980-1990	1995-2002	Low Growth	Moderate Growth	High Growth
Total Personal Income	3.4%	3.2%	3.5%	4.0%	4.6%
Per Capita Income	1.1%	1.6%	2.0%	2.5%	3.0%
Population	2.3%	1.5%	1.5%	1.5%	1.5%

County Income Trends

The highest per capita incomes will continue to be in the Bay Area, Orange and Placer counties. Even including the sharp losses in 2001 and 2002, the highest wage and income gains since 1995 were in the Bay Area. Most counties outside of the Bay Area, Los Angeles, San Diego, Sacramento and Coastal regions remain well below the national average in per capita income.

Ten Counties With Largest Per Capita Income 1995-2010

1995	(2002$)	2002	(2002$)	2010 Moderate	(2002$)
Marin	$52,520	Marin	$61,897	Marin	$76,692
San Francisco	43,851	San Mateo	54,160	San Francisco	67,387
San Mateo	43,802	Santa Clara	50,137	San Mateo	66,949
Santa Clara	39,407	San Francisco	53,851	Santa Clara	61,478
Contra Costa	37,489	Contra Costa	41,781	Contra Costa	51,292
Orange	33,159	Alameda	38,376	Orange	46,620
Alameda	33,148	Napa	37,603	Napa	46,519
Napa	33,125	Orange	37,376	Santa Cruz	46,248
Placer	31,500	Santa Cruz	37,351	Alameda	45,771
Santa Cruz	31,299	Placer	37,064	Placer	45,116
CALIFORNIA	$29,581	**CALIFORNIA**	$32,831	**CALIFORNIA**	$40,072

Fastest-Growing County Markets

Placer County had the highest real income growth between 1995 and 2002 — 50.5% or 6.0% per year — followed by Santa Clara County with a gain of 39.0% despite two years of income losses in 2001 and 2002. San Benito is projected to have the fastest income growth rate to 2010 (83.2%) while four San Joaquin Valley counties are in the top ten. Riverside and San Joaquin counties are the fastest-growing large county markets.

Ten Fastest Growing Large Counties 1995-2010 (2002$)			
1995-2002	**Percent Growth in Total Income**	**2002-2010**	**Percent Growth in Total Income**
Placer	50.5%	San Benito	83.2%
Santa Clara	39.0%	Imperial	66.9%
Nevada	36.6%	Merced	65.5%
Riverside	35.4%	Colusa	62.2%
El Dorado	34.8%	Riverside	58.9%
San Benito	34.4%	San Joaquin	54.9%
San Diego	33.6%	Madera	53.8%
San Francisco	31.1%	Placer	52.1%
San Mateo	30.6%	Stanislaus	51.6%
Alameda	29.2%	El Dorado	51.4%
CALIFORNIA	24.4%	**CALIFORNIA**	37.3%

Taxable Sales

Short Term Trends

Real taxable sales fell sharply in 2001 and 2003 following six years of strong growth. The taxable sales losses were concentrated in the Bay Area. Counties outside the Bay Area had sales growth that generally kept pace with or exceeded the rate of inflation.

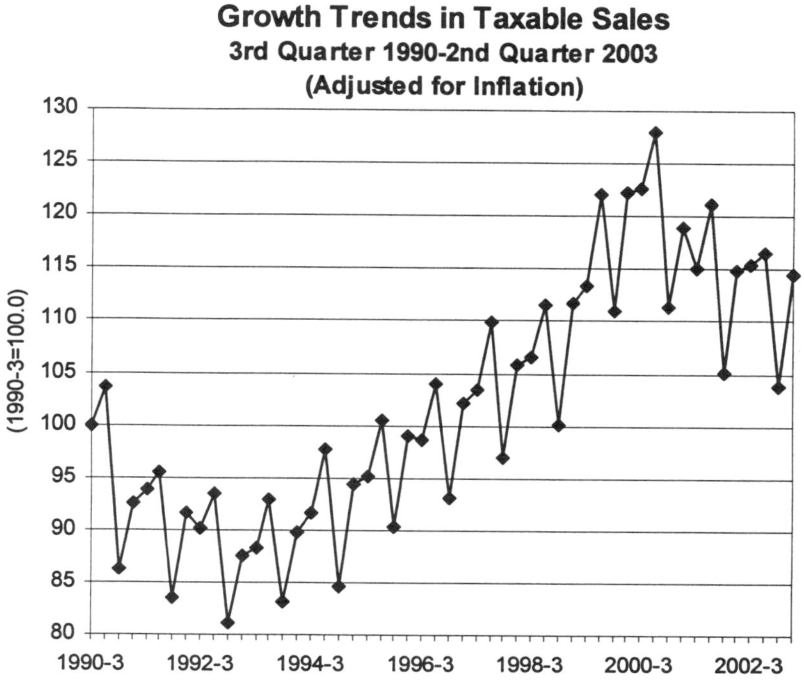

Growth Trends in Taxable Sales
3rd Quarter 1990-2nd Quarter 2003
(Adjusted for Inflation)

(1990-3=100.0)

130
125
120
115
110
105
100
95
90
85
80

1990-3 1992-3 1994-3 1996-3 1998-3 2000-3 2002-3

The San Diego and Sacramento regions led the state in taxable sales growth since 1995 and both regions posted above average gains in the 2000-2002 period. The San Joaquin Valley recorded the largest growth since 2000 while the Los Angeles Basin kept pace with the statewide average since 1995.

Average Taxable Sales by Economic Region
1995-2002

	1995	2002	2002$	1995-2002 (in Curr$)	2000-2002 (in Curr$)
San Diego Region	$23,452.0	$38,631.8	36.4%	64.7%	6.6%
Sacramento Region	16,452.6	26,885.4	35.3%	63.4%	7.2%
Coastal Region	10,537.2	16,300.5	28.1%	54.7%	1.6%
San Joaquin Valley	24,159.2	36,701.6	25.8%	51.9%	8.2%
Los Angeles Basin	139,043.6	203,730.5	21.3%	46.5%	3.2%
Sacramento Valley Region	4,691.1	6,870.7	21.3%	46.5%	6.9%
Mountain Region	2,681.2	3,856.3	19.1%	43.8%	5.8%
North Coast Region	2,166.0	2,987.4	14.2%	37.9%	4.4%
San Francisco Bay Area	75,633.6	100,447.1	10.0%	32.8%	-15.4%
California	300,914.3	437,907.0	20.5%	45.5%	-0.9%
California exc. Bay Area	$225,280.7	$337,459.9	24.0%	49.8%	4.4%

The fastest growing markets to 2010 include San Benito, Placer and the Inland Empire (Riverside and San Bernardino) counties.

Ten Fastest Growing Counties 1995-2010 (2002$)

1995-2002	Percent Growth in Taxable Sales	Moderate 2002-2010	Percent Growth in Taxable Sales
Placer	82.4%	San Benito	75.4%
Riverside	55.7%	Riverside	62.4%
Napa	48.4%	Placer	61.7%
Solano	47.8%	Merced	61.0%
Sierra	44.2%	Alpine	58.6%
San Joaquin	44.0%	Santa Clara	57.7%
San Benito	42.7%	San Bernardino	56.9%
San Luis Obispo	41.3%	Colusa	55.4%
Mono	39.8%	Madera	47.7%
San Bernardino	36.6%	Yolo	45.8%
CALIFORNIA	20.5%	**CALIFORNIA**	38.1%

Baseline Growth Projections to 2010

CCSCE's statewide projections are summarized below. These projections all start from the job and population projections published in **California Economic Growth – 2003 Edition.**

California Growth Indicators 1990-2010

	1990	1995	2002	Baseline Growth Projections 2010
Population (Millions)	29.8	31.7	35.3	39.3
Households (Millions)	10.4		11.9	13.6
Total Personal Income (Billions of 2002$)	$903	$932	$1,159	$1,591
Per Capita Personal Income (2002$)	$30,281	$29,383	$32,831	$40,072
Average HH Income (2002$)	$85,832	$83,003	$97,640	$118,449
Total Taxable Sales (Billions of 2002$)	$387	$363	$438	$605
Taxable Retail Sales (Billions of 2002$)	$250	$235	$302	$390

The baseline projections include the demographic trend projection for household growth (the highest of three alternatives prepared by CCSCE) and the middle growth alternative for all income and spending variables.

Alternative Projections

- Growth in population, households, income and spending will vary 1) if U.S. growth rates are different than projected and 2) if California gets a different share of U.S. job growth.

- However, growth in households, income and spending **may vary even if job and population growth match CCSCE's projections**. The low and high series projections presented below are based on CCSCE's middle series job and population projections.

- Variations in the rate of household growth should be evaluated seriously by affected decision makers in California. A detailed analysis in the *Household* section concludes that household growth could range from 150,000 per year to 223,000 per year based on the same amount of job and population growth.

Average Annual Growth Rates for Major Indicators
1980-2010

				2002-2010	
	1980-1990	**1995-2002**	**Low**	**Moderate**	**High**
Population (Millions)	2.3%	1.5%	1.5%	1.5%	1.5%
Households (Millions)	1.9%	1.0%	1.2%	1.4%	1.8%
Total Personal Income (Billions of 2002$)	3.4%	3.2%	3.5%	4.0%	4.5%
Per Capita Personal Income (2002$)	1.1%	1.6%	2.0%	2.5%	3.0%
Average HH Income (2002$)	1.5%	2.3%	1.9%	2.4%	2.9%
Total Taxable Sales (Billions of 2002$)	2.0%	2.7%	3.1%	4.1%	4.8%
Taxable Retail Sales (Billions of 2002$)	1.8%	3.7%	2.2%	3.3%	3.9%

- Real income growth will depend on gains in productivity. The moderate growth alternative assumes annual productivity gains of 2.0% per year — well below recent productivity growth rates.

- The growth in real (i.e., inflation adjusted) income and spending will vary with productivity growth.

- Total personal income will vary from a low projection of 3.5% per year to a high of 4.5% per year from the recession-depressed levels of 2002.
- Taxable sales will vary between a low projection of 3.1% per year and a high of 4.8% annually (higher than normal because the 2002 base year level is abnormally low) and growth will be further restricted if e-commerce transactions remain mostly untaxed.

- California will add substantial numbers of people and households after 2010. California's population should grow to 45 million by 2020 and then to 50 million sometime in the next 30 to 35 years.

Average Annual Growth Rates for Major Indicators 1980-2010

			2000-2010		
	1980-1990	**1995-2002**	**Low**	**Moderate**	**High**
Population (Millions)	2.3%	1.5%	1.5%	1.5%	1.5%
Households (Millions)	1.9%	1.0%	1.2%	1.4%	1.8%
Total Personal Income (Billions of 2002$)	3.4%	3.2%	3.5%	4.0%	4.5%
Per Capita Personal Income (2002$)	1.1%	1.6%	2.0%	2.5%	3.0%
Average HH Income (2002$)	1.5%	2.3%	1.9%	2.4%	2.9%
Total Taxable Sales (Billions of 2002$)	2.0%	2.7%	3.1%	4.1%	4.8%
Taxable Retail Sales (Billions of 2002$)	1.8%	3.7%	2.2%	3.3%	3.9%

OUTLOOK FOR THE CALIFORNIA ECONOMY

OUTLOOK FOR THE CALIFORNIA ECONOMY

The U.S. Economy in 2003 and 2004

The national economy turned up during the past three months. Gross Domestic Product (GDP) rose by 7.2%. Business capital spending surged, led by a 15.4% increase in spending on equipment and software. Personal consumption rose by 6.6% above the rate of inflation, buoyed by tax cuts and moderate wage gains.

And, finally, after 30 months, job levels rose for three months in a row.

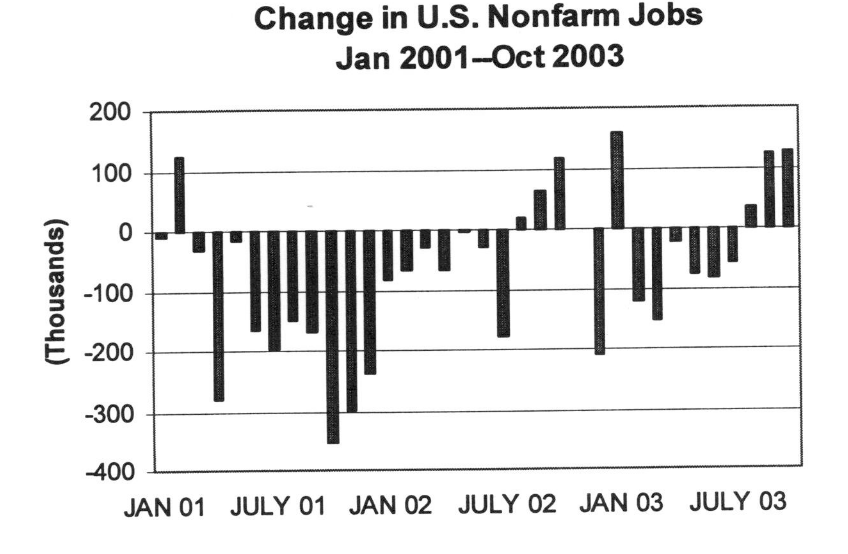

Productivity Growth – Is it a Blessing or Curse?

Strong productivity growth has allowed GDP to rise so far without creating job growth. For example, the third quarter GDP gain of 7.2% was matched by a 7.4% gain in productivity. Put simply, productivity growth at these levels allows firms to produce substantially more goods and services without adding workers and, in some cases, with fewer workers.

Economists, including CCSCE, argue that productivity growth is good and, indeed, productivity growth should eventually lead to job gains. Here is how it is supposed to work.

Productivity growth holds down costs and raises profits. Increased profits allow businesses to increase capital spending **and** to pay higher wages because they are based on increased worker productivity. The higher wages create income growth that supports higher levels of consumer spending. At some point, the higher business and consumer spending creates enough new demand that companies add workers.

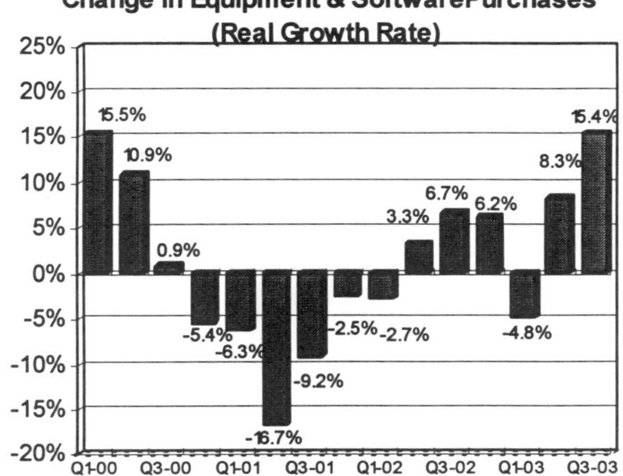
United States
Change in Equipment & SoftwarePurchases
(Real Growth Rate)
25%
20%
15%
10%
5%
0%
-5%
-10%
-15%
-20%
15.5%
10.9%
0.9%
-5.4%
-6.3%
-16.7%
-9.2%
-2.5%
-2.7%
3.3%
6.7%
6.2%
-4.8%
8.3%
15.4%
Q1-00
Q3-00
Q1-01
Q3-01
Q1-02
Q3-02
Q1-03
Q3-03

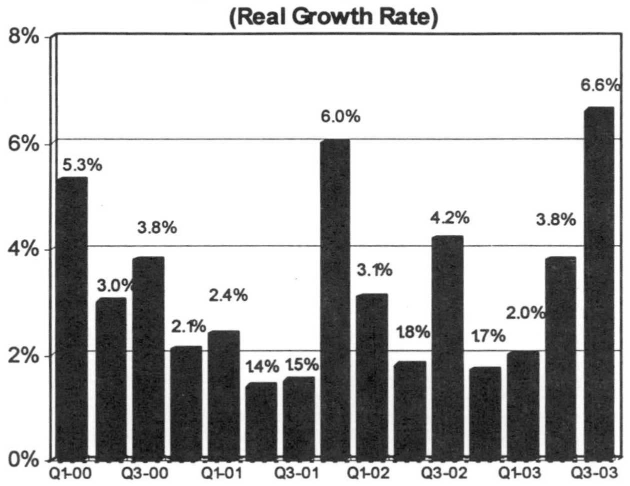
United States
Change in Consumption Purchases
(Real Growth Rate)
8%
6%
4%
2%
0%
5.3%
3.0%
3.8%
2.1%
2.4%
1.4%
1.5%
6.0%
3.1%
1.8%
4.2%
1.7%
2.0%
3.8%
6.6%
Q1-00
Q3-00
Q1-01
Q3-01
Q1-02
Q3-02
Q1-03
Q3-03

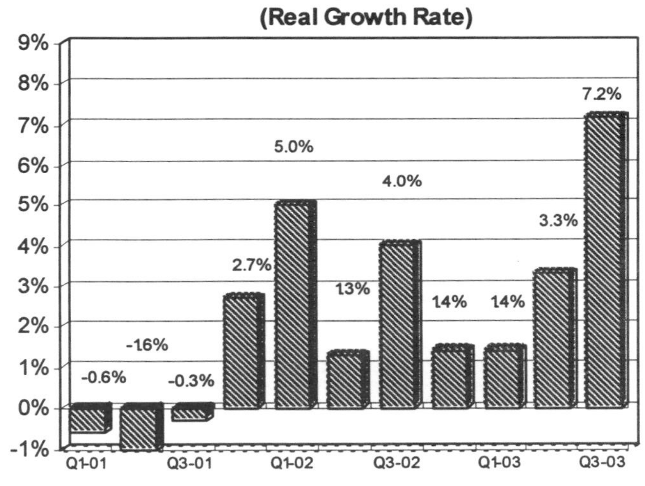
United States
Change in G.D.P.
(Real Growth Rate)
9%
8%
7%
6%
5%
4%
3%
2%
1%
0%
-1%
-0.6%
-1.6%
-0.3%
2.7%
5.0%
1.3%
4.0%
1.4%
1.4%
3.3%
7.2%
Q1-01
Q3-01
Q1-02
Q3-02
Q1-03
Q3-03

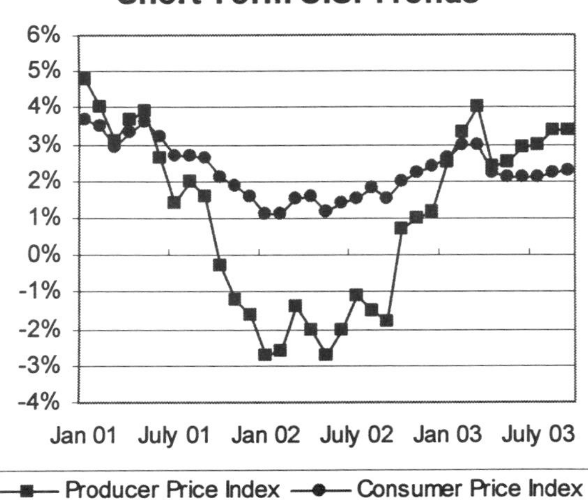
Consumer and ProducerPrices
Short Term U.S. Trends
6%
5%
4%
3%
2%
1%
0%
-1%
-2%
-3%
-4%
Jan 01
July 01
Jan 02
July 02
Jan 03
July 03
Producer Price Index
Consumer Price Index

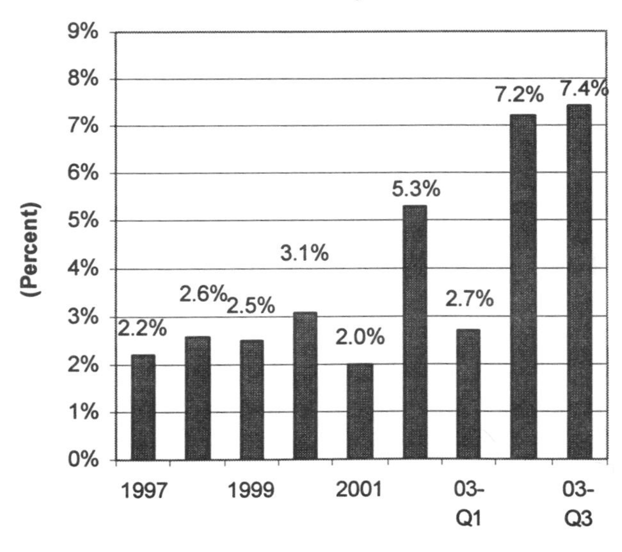
U. S. Productivity Growth Rate
(Percent)
9%
8%
7%
6%
5%
4%
3%
2%
1%
0%
2.2%
2.6%
2.5%
3.1%
2.0%
5.3%
2.7%
7.2%
7.4%
1997
1999
2001
03-Q1
03-Q3

While this reasoning is correct, it does not completely answer the question of how the nation can create enough jobs to keep pace with labor force growth **and** reduce unemployment. As shown on the graph on page 2-2, job levels have fallen in most months since January 2001. This job performance is the worst since World War II.

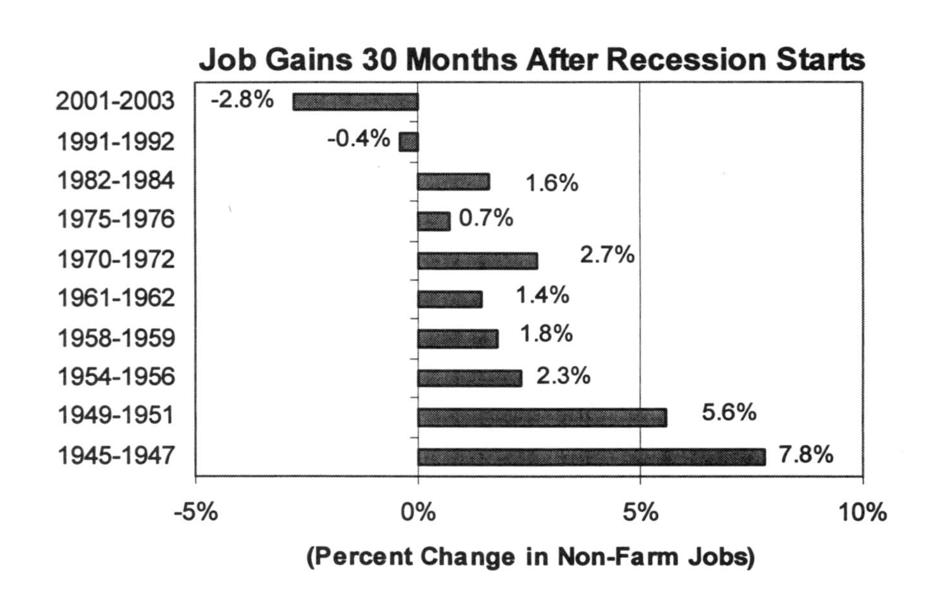

The national labor force grows by approximately 150,000 per month and that many jobs are needed to keep unemployment rates constant. In addition, unemployment levels have risen by more than 2 million **and** another 2 million workers left the labor force when jobs were scarce.

So, a considerable amount of job growth is needed just to return to the pre-recession level of employment.

Moreover, while it is reasonable to expect productivity growth to fall back from the recent levels, it is still possible that productivity growth could remain above 2.5% per year. Such productivity growth would require GDP growth of near 4% per year to sustain job gains. With defense spending likely to fall, housing unlikely to match the current pace, state and local governments under pressure to cut spending and interest rates soon to rise, it is not clear how the economy can easily sustain 4% GDP growth for more than a few quarters.

Such high levels of productivity growth are a blessing but they also may pose new challenges to the people charged with managing the national economy.

Prices and Interest Rates

Interest rates are unusually low for this point in an economic recovery. The Federal Funds rate remains at 1% and the Federal Reserve Bank has no immediate plans to raise rates. Mortgage rates have been under 6% for almost a year and have stimulated increased housing sales and construction.

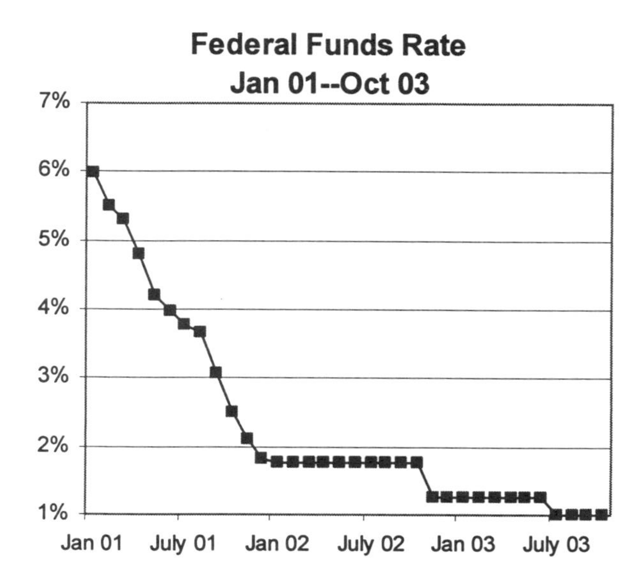

Consumer and producer price increases remain moderate but the days of 1% annual inflation appear gone. Prices today are rising at between 2% and 3% per year.

The expected level of GDP growth will put upward pressure on prices unless productivity growth continues at these record levels. The upward price pressure will, in turn, push interest rates higher. The Federal Reserve Bank may be unable to keep interest rates low in a high-growth environment. The traditional concerns of an inflationary environment may reemerge before job growth can be sustained for very long.

The rapid growth of GDP plus the very high and ongoing federal budget deficits create substantial risks as the recovery proceeds.

The California Economy in 2003 and 2004

The recent economic outlook in California can be summarized in five points:

1) Job levels have fallen and unemployment rates have risen since late 2000. The state and nation have seen approximately the same percentage losses in total jobs **and** manufacturing jobs.

2) Job losses were concentrated in the Bay Area. Regions outside the Bay Area did better than the nation and some regions **added jobs** during the recession.

3) Income and spending fell, led by the recession and drop in stock option income following the Internet bubble of the late 1990s. The drop in stock option income, capital gains and taxable sales created a drop in state revenue of upwards of $10 billion in each of the past three years.

4) Residential construction levels are surging and have kept total construction activity strong despite a drop in nonresidential building. This is a dramatic difference from the early 90s recession where construction fell by two thirds.

5) The state experienced an 80% drop in venture capital funding as well as substantial losses in high-tech jobs. **Nevertheless, the state's share of venture capital funding and high-tech jobs did not drop.**

Job Growth Will Start Again — How Much is Uncertain

Job growth has been on hold for nearly three years in California and the nation.

The nation started the year weak and finally achieved job growth in August as shown on page 2-2. California started the year stronger but posted job losses as the year progressed.

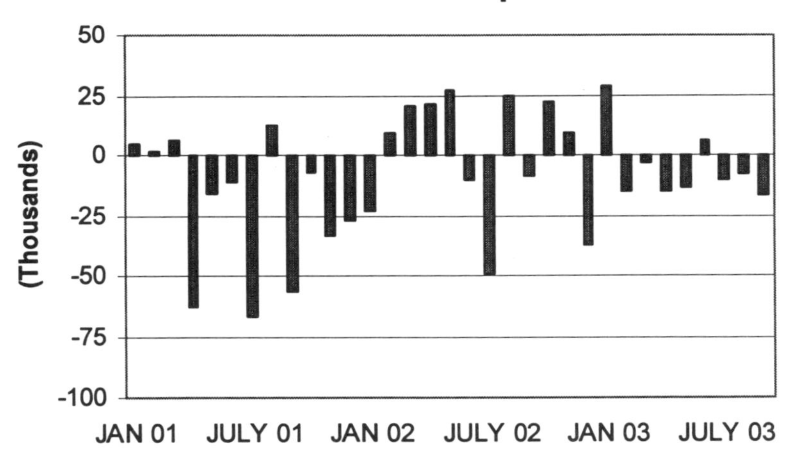

In contrast to the early 90s, California is not faring worse than the nation, except in the Bay Area, which has lost more than 300,000 jobs — more, in fact, than the total state. For the year to date, both the state and nation posted slight job losses through September. The nation added jobs in October and added more jobs in the revised September estimates. The California data for October was not available as **County Projections** went to press.

				January-September		
	2000	2001	2002	2002	2003	% Change
United States	131,799	131,829	130,376	130,388	130,040	-0.3%
California	14,488	14,603	14,476	14,472	14,456	-0.1%

Nonfarm Wage & Salary Jobs
(Thousands; Seasonally Adjusted)

Source: U.S. Bureau of Labor Statistics; California Employment Development Department

The longer-term picture since 1994 shows California outpacing the nation between 1994 and 2000, followed by three years in which both areas lost approximately 2% of total jobs.

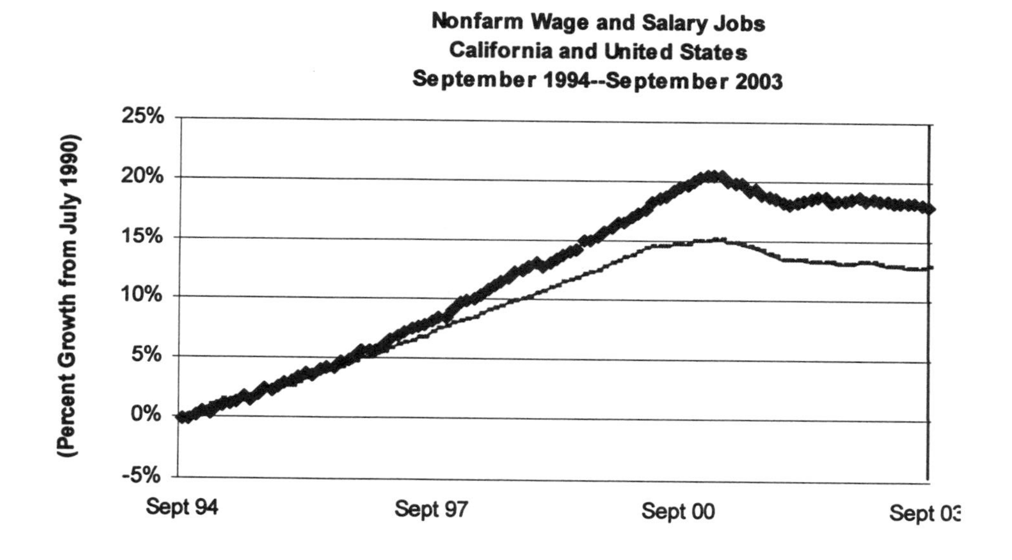

Both the state and nation lost approximately 15% of total manufacturing jobs during the recent recession. Productivity gains were the major cause of these job losses. With manufacturing productivity growing by more than 5%, sales gains must be even higher to produce job growth. Manufacturing sales did not grow during the recession and productivity growth allowed firms to produce the same level of output (or even slight increases) with fewer workers.

The movement of jobs overseas has been a factor in the state and nation's manufacturing climate for more than two decades. While these movements have probably accelerated, the real change since 2000 has been the decline in high-tech and new manufacturing startups.

The longer-term picture shows that California outperformed the nation in manufacturing since 1994, led by high-tech job gains in the late 1990s. What is surprising is that China heads the list of areas with large percentage losses in manufacturing jobs.

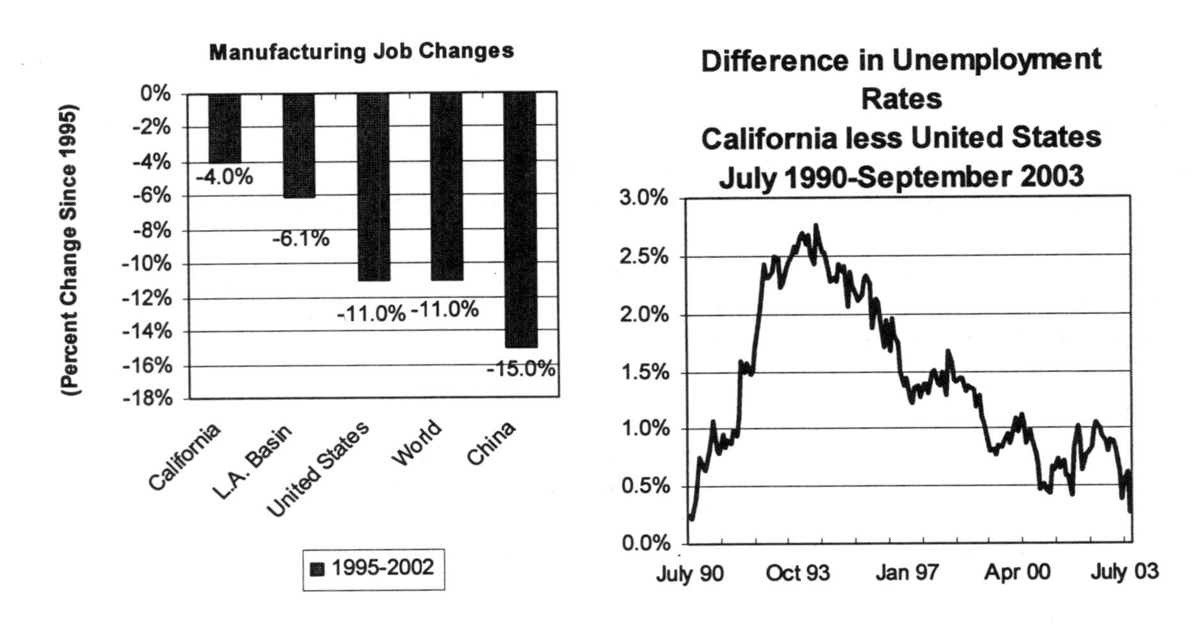

Unemployment rates have risen in both the state and the nation. In September 2003, California's unemployment rate was 6.4% compared to the 6.1% national average. As shown above, in the early 90s recession, California's unemployment rate was as much as 2.8% above the national average. In September 2003, the unemployment rate "gap" had shrunk to 0.3%, the smallest difference in more than a decade.

Unemployment Rates: Then and Now

Where is the state in comparison to the early 90s recession? While unemployment rates have risen sharply, they started from very low levels and are unlikely to even approach the levels seen throughout California in 1992 and 1993, except in Santa Clara County, the heart of the tech downturn.

	Sept. 03	Recession Peak	Early 90's
United States	6.1%	6.4%	7.8%
California	6.4%	6.8%	9.7%
Los Angeles County	6.8%	7.6%	10.8%
Santa Clara County	7.5%	8.9%	7.3%
San Diego County	4.1%	4.7%	8.9%
Sacramento County	5.5%	6.0%	9.3%

In 2000 and 2001, state and national unemployment rates reached near all-time lows and remained below 5%. It is important to remember that in this downturn, unemployment rates are **rising** to levels that used to be considered full employment.

Regional Economic Update

The California recession is a Bay Area recession. Job levels in the Bay Area fell by 8.9% (316,000 jobs) between September 2000 and September 2003. Job levels in California fell by just 191,100 (1.3%) during the same period. Note that the Sept 00 – Sept 03 comparisons are slightly different from the January 01 – September 03 comparisons shown on page 1-3.

The San Joaquin Valley recorded a 5.1% job **increase, far outpacing the 1.6% national job loss.** The Sacramento and San Diego regions also recorded job increases.

The 2000-2003 picture is the mirror image of the 1990-1994 recession in California where nearly all job losses occurred in the Los Angeles Basin and, by 1994, all other regions were showing positive job growth.

Both examples show that it is informative to look at the California economy in terms of regional trends. Because regions have different key industries, they will often move in different directions or at different rates in terms of short-term job trends.

In the longer term, the Sacramento, San Diego and San Joaquin Valley regions all outpaced the state and nation in job growth as shown on the graphs on page 2-11.

Nonfarm Wage and Salary Jobs
(Thousands)

Region	Sept 2000	Sept 2002	Sept 2003	2000-2003 % Change
Los Angeles Basin	6,726	6,775	6,740	0.2%
L.A. County	4,083	4,034	3,994	-2.2%
Orange County	1,406	1,404	1,403	0.2%
Riv-San Bern Metro Area	995	1,058	1,070	7.5%
San Francisco Bay Area	3,561	3,300	3,245	-8.9%
Oakland Metro Area	1,054	1,043	1,042	-1.1%
San Fran Metro Area	1,096	986	972	-11.3%
San Jose (Silicon Valley)	1,046	898	860	-17.8%
San Diego	1,199	1,222	1,228	2.4%
Sacramento	804	835	826	2.7%
San Joaquin Valley (1)	837	874	880	5.1%
California	14,610	14,470	14,419	-1.3%
United States	132,129	130,289	130,006	-1.6%

Source: California Employment Development Department; U.S. Bureau of Labor Statistics; (1) Fresno, Kern, San Joaquin, Stanislaus counties

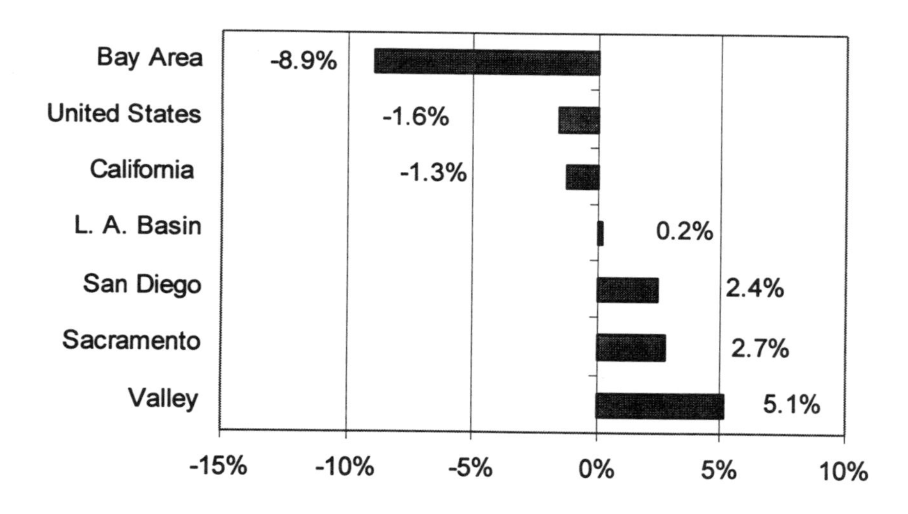

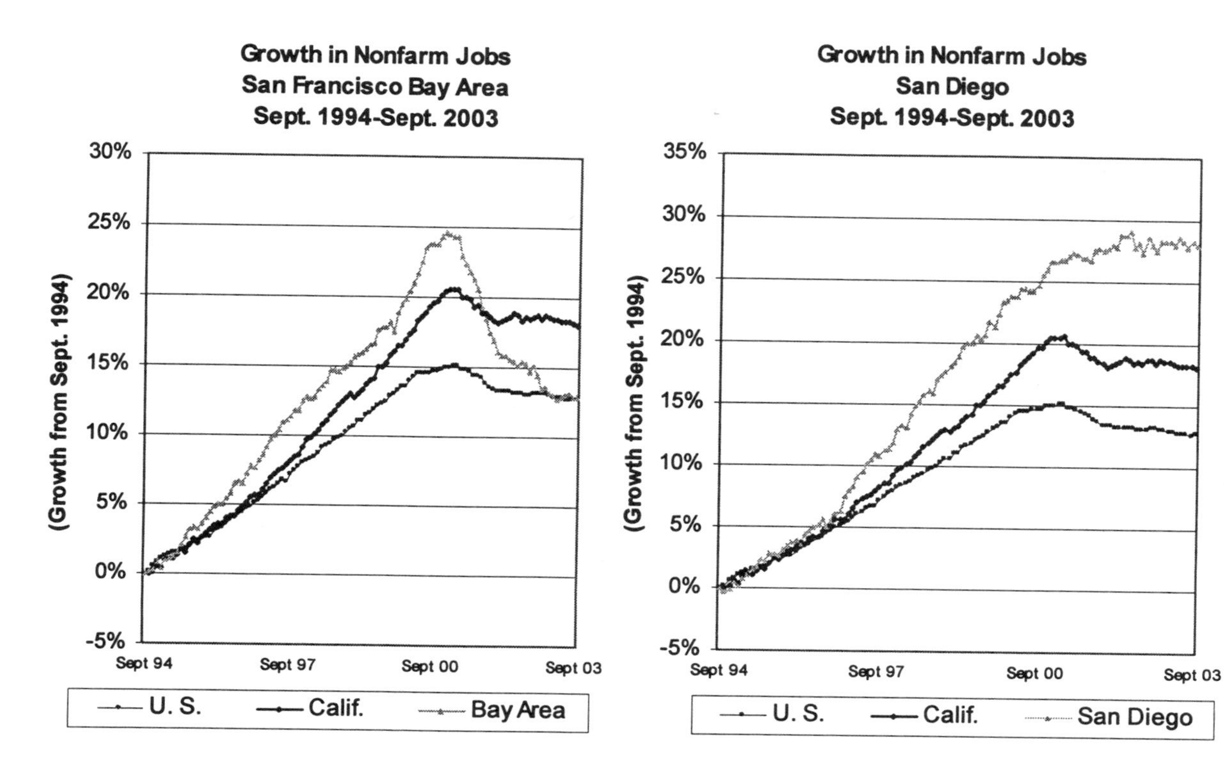
Growth in Nonfarm Jobs
San Francisco Bay Area
Sept. 1994-Sept. 2003
30%
25%
20%
15%
10%
5%
0%
-5%
(Growth from Sept. 1994)
Sept 94
Sept 97
Sept 00
Sept 03
U. S.
Calif.
Bay Area
Growth in Nonfarm Jobs
San Diego
Sept. 1994-Sept. 2003
35%
30%
25%
20%
15%
10%
5%
0%
-5%
(Growth from Sept. 1994)
Sept 94
Sept 97
Sept 00
Sept 03
U. S.
Calif.
San Diego

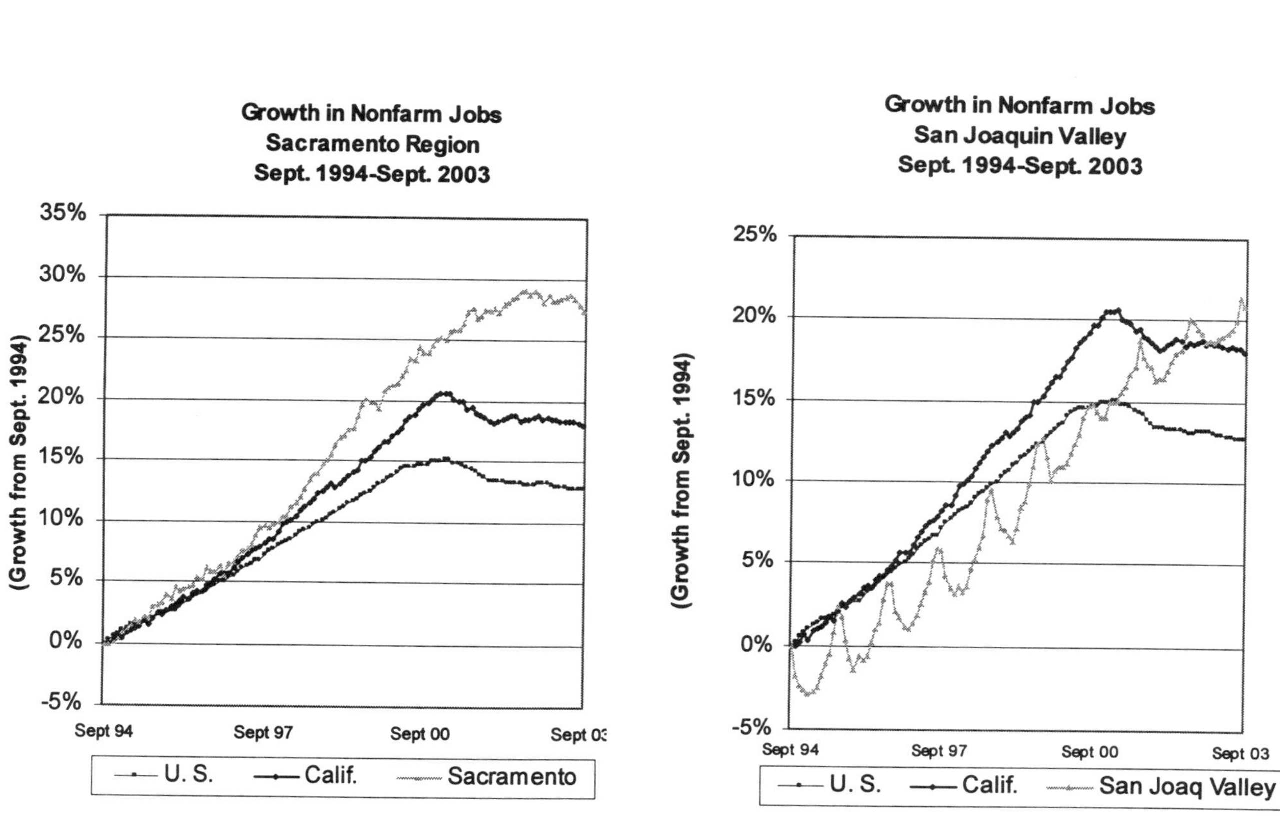
Growth in Nonfarm Jobs
Sacramento Region
Sept. 1994-Sept. 2003
35%
30%
25%
20%
15%
10%
5%
0%
-5%
(Growth from Sept. 1994)
Sept 94
Sept 97
Sept 00
U. S.
Calif.
Sacramento
Growth in Nonfarm Jobs
San Joaquin Valley
Sept. 1994-Sept. 2003
25%
20%
15%
10%
5%
0%
-5%
(Growth from Sept. 1994)
Sept 94
Sept 97
Sept 00
Sept 03
U. S.
Calif.
San Joaq Valley

The Los Angeles Basin

Job levels have remained flat during the past three years. Strong job growth in the Riverside-San Bernardino area was offset by a corresponding job decline in Los Angeles County. Job levels in Orange and Ventura counties remain near 2000 levels as of September 2003.

Los Angeles Basin
Nonfarm Wage & Salary Jobs
(Thousands)

				January-Sept		
Metro Area	**2000**	**2001**	**2002**	**2002**	**2003**	**% Change**
Los Angeles County	4,072.1	4,073.6	4,033.5	4,025.2	3,999.5	-0.6%
Orange County	1,388.9	1,413.7	1,403.0	1,398.6	1,400.1	0.1%
Riverside-San Bernardino	988.4	1,029.7	1,057.8	1,053.4	1,067.6	1.3%
Ventura County	275.1	279.9	280.3	279.9	274.4	-2.0%
Los Angeles Basin	6,724.5	6,796.9	6,774.6	6,757.2	6,741.6	-0.2%

The region is following the national trends with a decline in manufacturing jobs caused by strong productivity gains and a drop in exports in 2001 and 2002. Manufacturing job losses are concentrated in Los Angeles and Orange counties.

Foreign trade volumes are up by 7.3% so far in 2003 after declines from peak 2000 levels. Tourism is recovering and the region continues to add and upgrade major attraction centers with the latest addition being the opening of the Disney Concert Hall.

Foreign Trade by Customs District
($Billions)

	1990	**2000**	**2002**	**Jan-Aug 03**
Los Angeles	$106.7	$230.0	$214.3	+7.3%
San Francisco	57.3	127.2	79.6	-3.0%
San Diego	7.8	35.0	35.9	-0.4%
California	165.7	392.2	329.8	4.6%
United States	$888.2	$2,028.8	$1,934.3	6.6%

Source: U.S. Department of Commerce

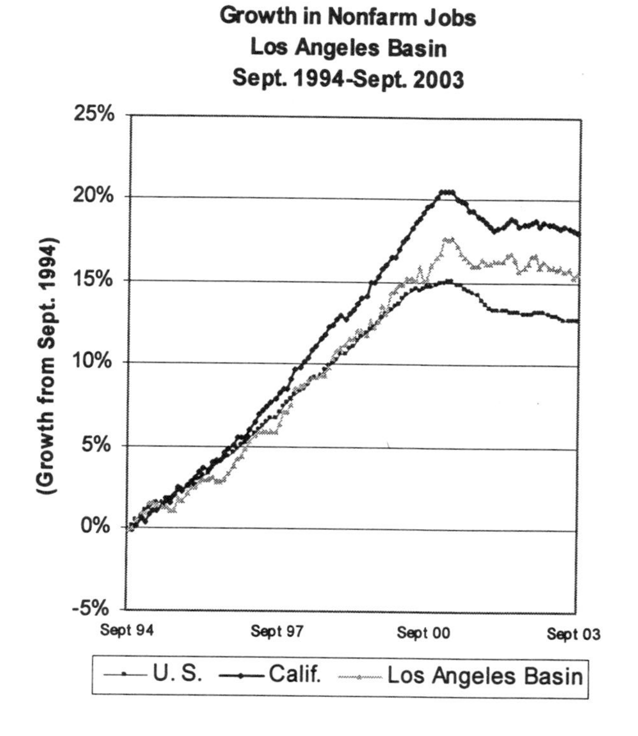
Growth in Nonfarm Jobs
Los Angeles Basin
Sept. 1994-Sept. 2003
25%
20%
15%
10%
5%
0%
-5%
(Growth from Sept. 1994)
Sept 94
Sept 97
Sept 00
Sept 03
U. S.
Calif.
Los Angeles Basin

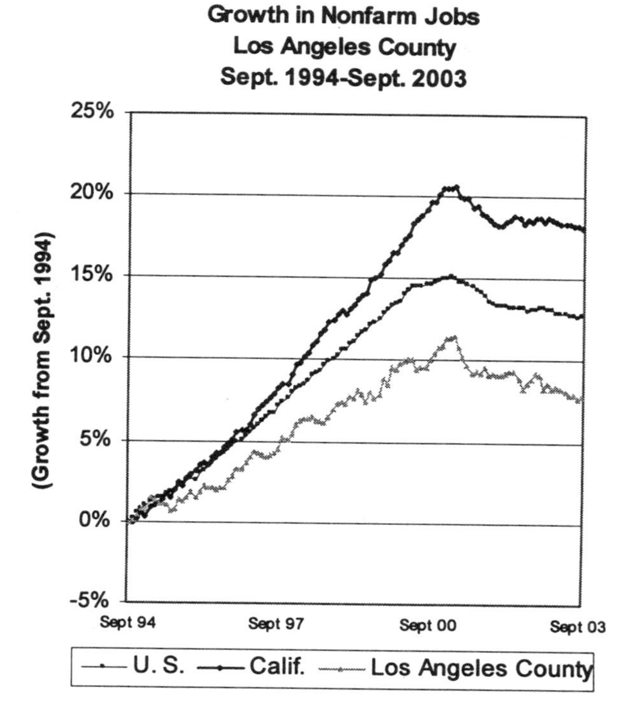
Growth in Nonfarm Jobs
Los Angeles County
Sept. 1994-Sept. 2003
25%
20%
15%
10%
5%
0%
-5%
(Growth from Sept. 1994)
Sept 94
Sept 97
Sept 00
Sept 03
U. S.
Calif.
Los Angeles County

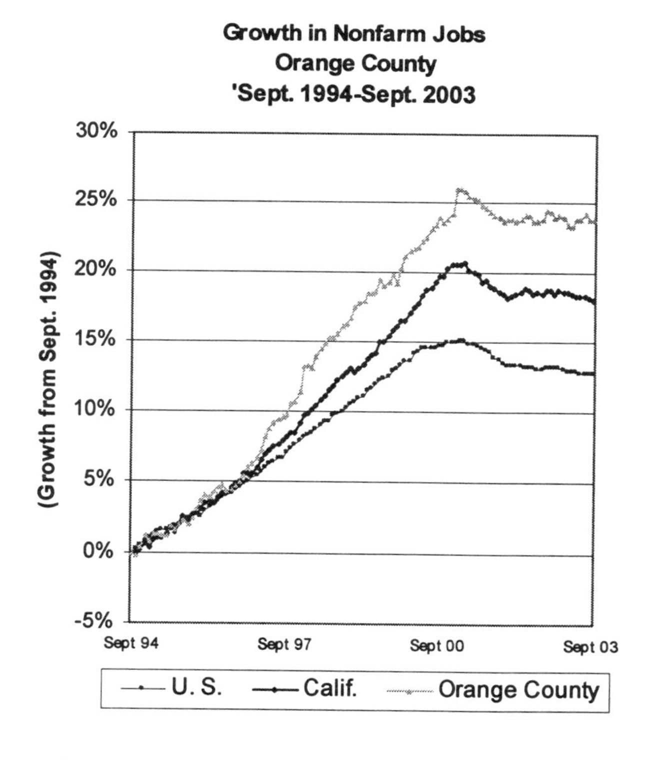
Growth in Nonfarm Jobs
Orange County
'Sept. 1994-Sept. 2003
30%
25%
20%
15%
10%
5%
0%
-5%
(Growth from Sept. 1994)
Sept 94
Sept 97
Sept 00
Sept 03
U. S.
Calif.
Orange County

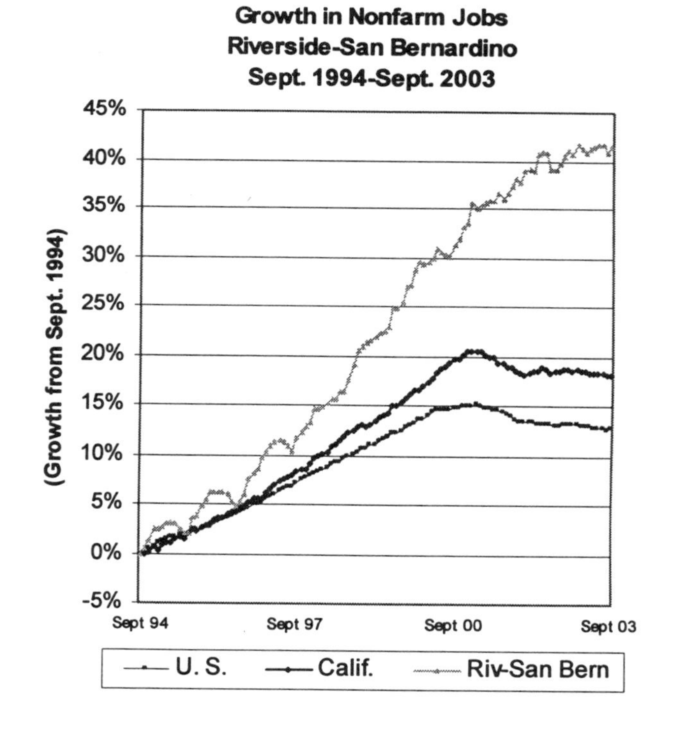
Growth in Nonfarm Jobs
Riverside-San Bernardino
Sept. 1994-Sept. 2003
45%
40%
35%
30%
25%
20%
15%
10%
5%
0%
-5%
(Growth from Sept. 1994)
Sept 94
Sept 97
Sept 00
Sept 03
U. S.
Calif.
Riv-San Bern

Over the longer term, the region has outpaced the nation in job growth while trailing the state average. Los Angeles County remains below the state and national average for job growth, even disregarding the poor 1990-1994 performance. Orange County and the Inland Empire have added jobs faster than the state and nation.

San Francisco Bay Area

The Bay Area has experienced the state's sharpest downturn in jobs, income and spending. The reason – tech is the dominant sector in the region's economic base and high tech manufacturing led the national economic slowdown.

Not only are domestic tech purchases down, but tech exports were down 35% compared to 2000. And the decline continued in the 1st half of 2003 with an additional 16% drop. The Bay Area also had the largest drop in air traffic and hotel occupancy with both business and tourism markets declining.

The largest job declines are in Santa Clara and San Francisco. The East Bay and North Bay markets have avoided serious job losses since 2000.

San Francisco Bay Area
Nonfarm Wage & Salary Jobs
(Thousands)

				January-Sept		
Metro Area	**2000**	**2001**	**2002**	**2002**	**2003**	**% Change**
Oakland	1,044.6	1,054.8	1,042.6	1,056.7	1,038.3	-1.7%
San Francisco	1,082.1	1,053.9	988.6	989.7	969,1	-2.1%
San Jose	1,030.0	1,003.5	909.5	914.1	868.9	-4.9%
Santa Rosa	186.1	189.8	187.4	186.9	184.5	-1.3%
Vallejo-Napa	172.2	178.1	181.2	180.3	182.7	1.3%
San Francisco Bay Area	3,515.0	3,480.1	3,309.3	3,309.3	3,245.7	-1.9%

Source: California Employment Development Department

The Bay Area now trails the state and just equals the nation in job growth since 1994. The Santa Clara and San Francisco metro areas trail the state and nation while the North Bay and East Bay have recorded much larger percentage job gains.

Silicon Valley depends on startups for job growth. Venture capital funding has plummeted as shown on page 2-16. This decline has meant that the region has not been able to replace jobs lost to productivity with a continuing stream of new companies as was true in 1999 and 2000.

Growth in Nonfarm Jobs
Santa Clara County
Sept.1994-Sept. 2003

35%
30%
25%
20%
15%
10%
5%
0%
-5%

(Growth from Sept. 1994)

Sept 94
Sept 97
Sept 00
Sept 03

U. S.
Calif.
Santa Clara

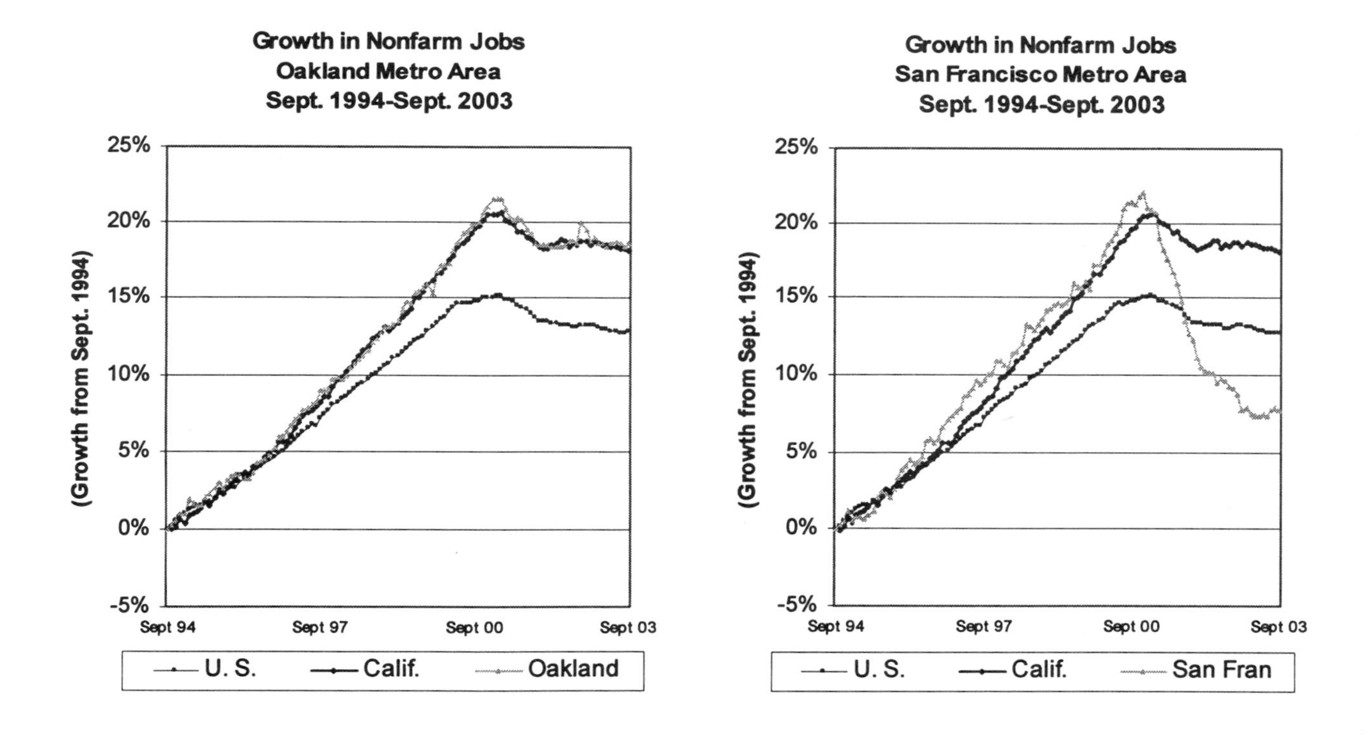

Venture Capital, Stock Prices and the California Economy

Venture capital funding in Silicon Valley fell to approximately $1.5 billion in each of the past four quarters from a peak of $9.7 billion in the 2nd quarter of 2000. Nationally, VC funding fell to $4.5 billion in the second quarter of 2003 from $28.6 billion at the peak.

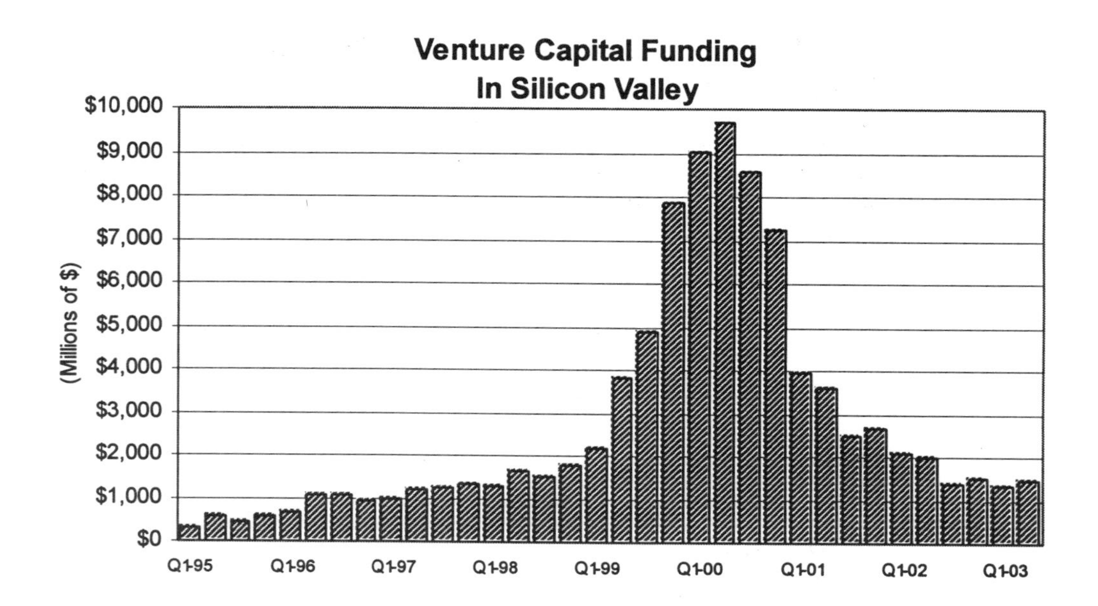

However, the tech boom is not over in terms of goods and services, which reduce costs and improve daily life. In time good ideas will be funded and great opportunities will emerge although there may be fewer instant millionaires. Even with the sharp drop in funding, there are signs that higher stock prices and the passage of time are setting the stage for an uptick in VC funding.

Silicon Valley and California have maintained their high shares of U.S. venture capital funding through the nationwide downturn. Silicon Valley's share of new funding has varied between 30% and 35% during recent quarters. The state's share of national funding has varied between 40% and 45% during the same time period.

The problem is not loss of share but, rather, the sharp decline in funding for new startups since 2000.

Exports

Exports of goods manufactured in California fell in 2001. In fact, California has temporarily fallen slightly behind Texas as the leading export state.

In 2002, exports fell 13.5% from $106.8 billion to $92.4 billion. All major trading partners bought fewer California goods in 2002.

California
Top Export Markets
2000-2003
($Billions)

	2000	2001	2002	1st H 2003	% Chg 2002-2003
Mexico	$17.5	$16.3	$16.1	$7.1	-9.5%
Canada	14.1	11.8	10.1	5.6	12.5%
Japan	16.4	14.6	11.1	5.6	-2.3%
South Korea	6.9	5.0	4.7	2.5	3.3%
China	3.5	4.7	4.5	2.4	10.9%
U. K.	6.0	5.6	4.3	2.2	2.3%
Taiwan	7.4	5.7	5.4	2.1	-22.5%
Hong Kong	4.1	3.9	3.7	1.9	8.3%
Germany	5.3	4.7	3.5	1.8	4.5%
Singapore	5.0	4.2	3.3	1.6	-3.1%
Total Exports	**$119.9**	**$106.8**	**$92.4**	**$44.7**	**-3.2%**

In the first half of 2003, exports are down just 3% and an export turnaround is expected going forward. Exports to Canada, China and Hong Kong are up in 2003 while exports to Mexico, Japan and Taiwan are down. China is now the state's 5th largest export market.

High tech exports account for more than half of the state's total exports. Tech exports were down 21% in 2002 and an additional 16% for the first half of 2002. Other machinery exports were also down substantially.

Exports of chemicals, miscellaneous manufacturing, crops and food products increased in 2002 and are up again in the first six months of 2003.

California Top Export Industries 2000-2003 ($Billions)	2000	2001	2002	1st H 2003	%Chg
Computers, Elec. Products	$61.4	$50.3	$39.7	$17.3	-16.0%
Machinery, except Elec.	13.8	10.7	9.5	4.4	-4.1%
Transportation Equipment	8.2	8.4	7.1	4.0	16.0%
Chemicals	4.8	5.2	5.4	2.9	12.2%
Misc. Manufacturing	4.1	4.4	4.5	2.4	8.7%
Crops	3.6	3.9	4.0	2.1	15.9%
Food Products	3.4	3.9	3.6	1.8	3.9%
Electrical Equipment	4.0	3.3	3.0	1.4	-4.5%
Total Exports	**$119.6**	**$106.8**	**$92.2**	**$44.7**	**-3.2%**

Foreign trade volumes, including imports, are up in Los Angeles and statewide as shown on page 2-12.

Construction

Home prices have continued to set records in most areas of the state despite more than a year of economic slowdown. Residential construction levels are surging compared to a year earlier. Total construction spending is up 8.0% so far in 2003, fueled by a 18% gain in residential construction. The state's median resale price reached $400,000 in August 2003 – an all-time high – and most regional markets posted new records as shown below.

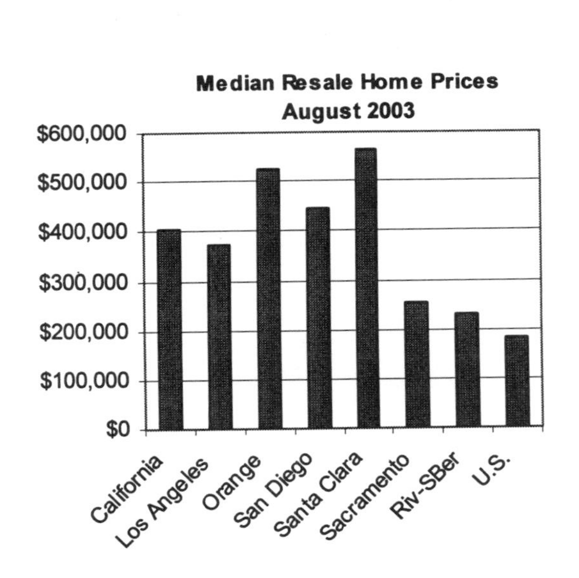

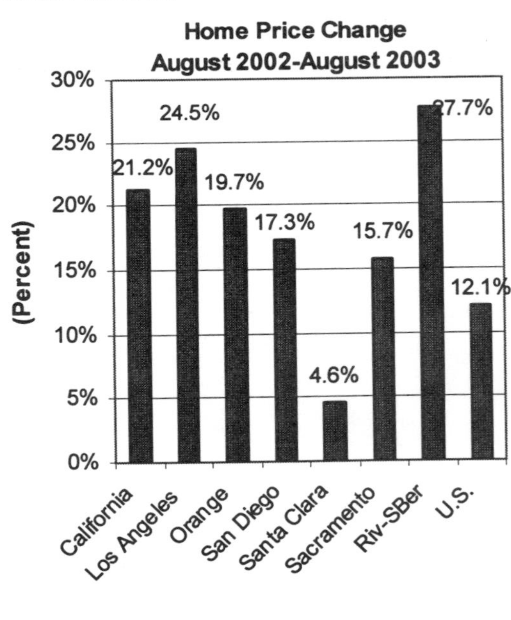

Residential Construction
New Housing Permits

				January-September		
	2000	**2001**	**2002**	**2002**	**2003**	**% Change**
California	148,540	148,757	167,761	122,477	145,411	+18.7%
Los Angeles County	17,071	18,107	19,364	13,452	15,367	+14.2%
Orange County	12,367	8,646	12,020	7,963	6,933	-12.9%
Riverside-San Bernardino	21,990	27,541	33,280	24,834	33,227	+33.8%
San Diego County	15,927	15,650	15,738	12,162	14,029	+15.4%
Santa Clara County	7,054	5,960	4,513	3,725	5,653	+51.8%
San Joaquin Valley	19,.287	19,559	23,504	16,893	22,298	+32.0%

Source: Construction Industry Research Bureau

Residential construction permits are up. The Inland Empire posted double digit gains in 2002 and again in the first nine months of 2003. San Joaquin Valley building levels were up 20% in 2002 and another 32% so far in 2003. Los Angeles and San Diego counties are recording higher levels of residential construction coming in 2003 and multi-family permits are up 37.5% in 2003 compared to a gain of 12.8% in single-family permits.

Nonresidential construction is down 3.4% in the first nine months of 2003 after falling 13% in 2002. The economic slowdown has resulted in surging vacancy rates and falling rents, particularly in the Bay Area. In 2003, nonresidential construction is up in two fast-growing areas – the Inland Empire and San Joaquin Valley.

Nonresidential Construction
($Billions)

				January-September		
	2000	**2001**	**2002**	**2002**	**2003**	**% Change**
California	$18,624.9	$16,653.3	$14,529.1	$10,873.8	$10,508.2	-3.4%
Los Angeles County	3,295.9	3,551.3	2,920.3	2,214.7	2,157.6	-2.6%
Orange County	1,762.1	1,349.6	1,208.6	886.2	769.5	-13.1%
Riverside-San Bernardino	1,536.3	1,423.0	1,267.0	1,095.1	1,306.4	+19.3%
San Diego County	1,391.5	1,189.9	1,168.9	912.7	916.7	+0.4%
Santa Clara County	2,865.9	2,254.8	1,330.5	1,055.3	743.9	-29.5%
San Joaquin Valley	$1,.285.9	$1,325.9	$1,341.3	$1,030.4	$1,186.9	+15.2%

Source: Construction Industry Research Board

Real (i.e. inflation adjusted) public works spending is in a long-term up trend. Public works spending in 2002 was $16 billion (out of $64 billion in total construction spending) up 20% from the levels of the late 1990s. Public works spending is off 1.1% in the first nine months of 2003 because some transportation projects have been delayed or canceled. The recent and expected passage of bonds for school and other construction will provide support for California's construction markets in the long term. However, budget deficits have resulted in short-term cuts in some projects.

California
Total Construction Valuations
($Millions)

	Jan-Sept 2003	Jan-Sept 2002	% Change
Residential	$29,015.5	$24,639.5	+18.7%
Nonresidential	10,308.2	10,873.8	-3.4%
Public Buildings	7,084.8	5,457.7	+29.8%
Heavy Construction	5,765.9	7,530.4	-23.4%
Total Construction	$52,374.4	$48,501.4	8.0%

Source: Construction Industry Research Board

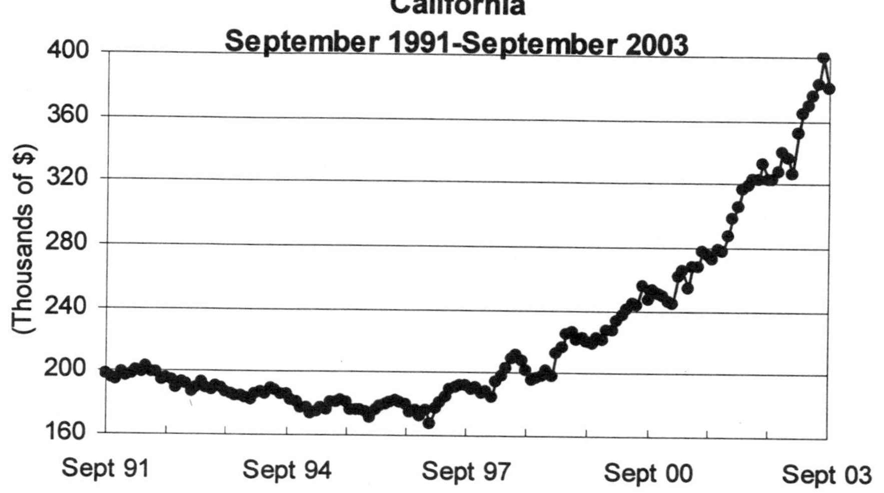

Median Existing Home Sales Price
California
September 1991-September 2003
(Thousands of $)
400
360
320
280
240
200
160
Sept 91
Sept 94
Sept 97
Sept 00
Sept 03

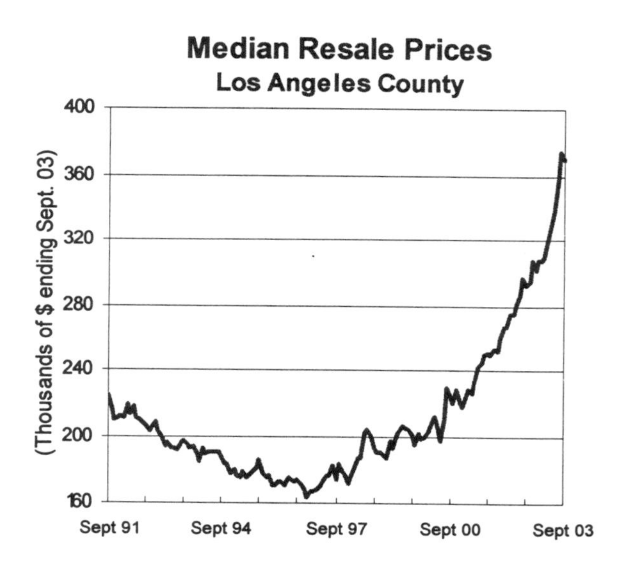

Median Resale Prices
Los Angeles County
(Thousands of $ ending Sept. 03)
400
360
320
280
240
200
160
Sept 91
Sept 94
Sept 97
Sept 00
Sept 03

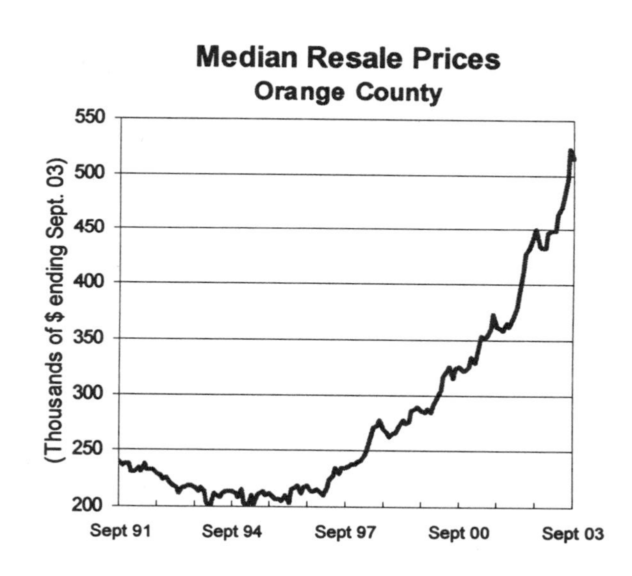

Median Resale Prices
Orange County
(Thousands of $ ending Sept. 03)
550
500
450
400
350
300
250
200
Sept 91
Sept 94
Sept 97
Sept 00
Sept 03

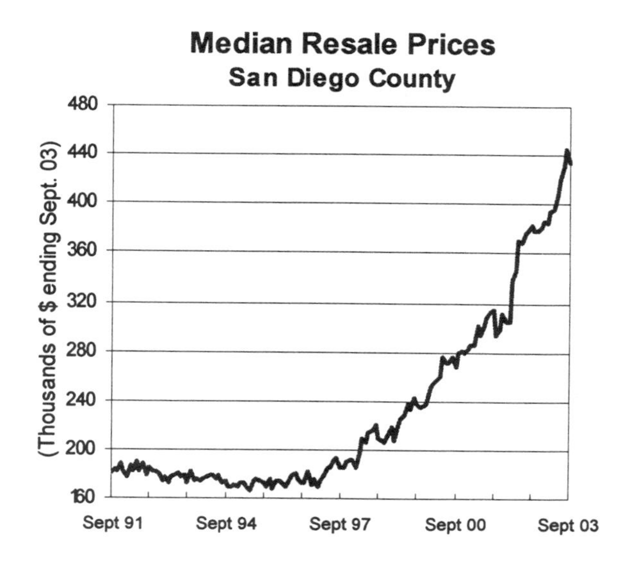

Median Resale Prices
San Diego County
(Thousands of $ ending Sept. 03)
480
440
400
360
320
280
240
200
160
Sept 91
Sept 94
Sept 97
Sept 00
Sept 03

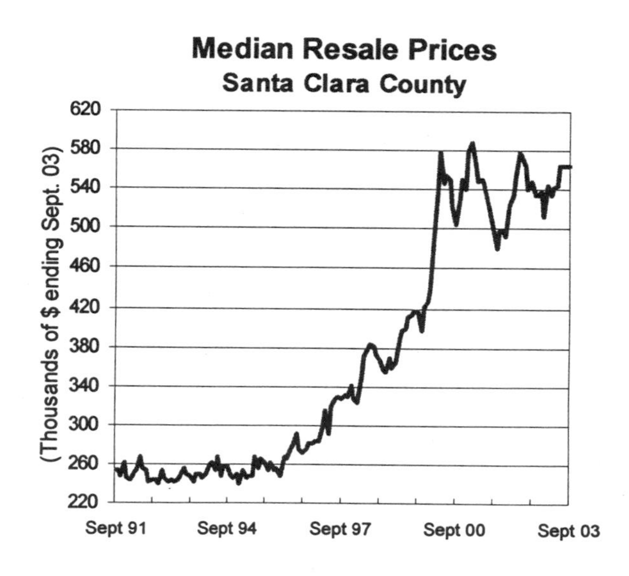

Median Resale Prices
Santa Clara County
(Thousands of $ ending Sept. 03)
620
580
540
500
460
420
380
340
300
260
220
Sept 91
Sept 94
Sept 97
Sept 00
Sept 03

Income and Spending

The growth in personal income and spending declined sharply at the end of 2000 and turned negative in mid 2001. Modest growth in income and taxable sales returned in the first half of 2003 and the outlook is for slowly rising growth rates.

Personal income growth in California trailed the national average primarily because stock option income fell sharply in 2001 and 2002. As shown in Section 5, all of the income losses were concentrated in the Bay Area. Outside of the Bay Area, wage and income growth kept pace with or exceeded the national average.

Taxable sales growth also trailed the national average. Again, the losses were concentrated in the Bay Area as a result of falling income **and** because non-retail (business to business) sales fell during the high-tech slump.

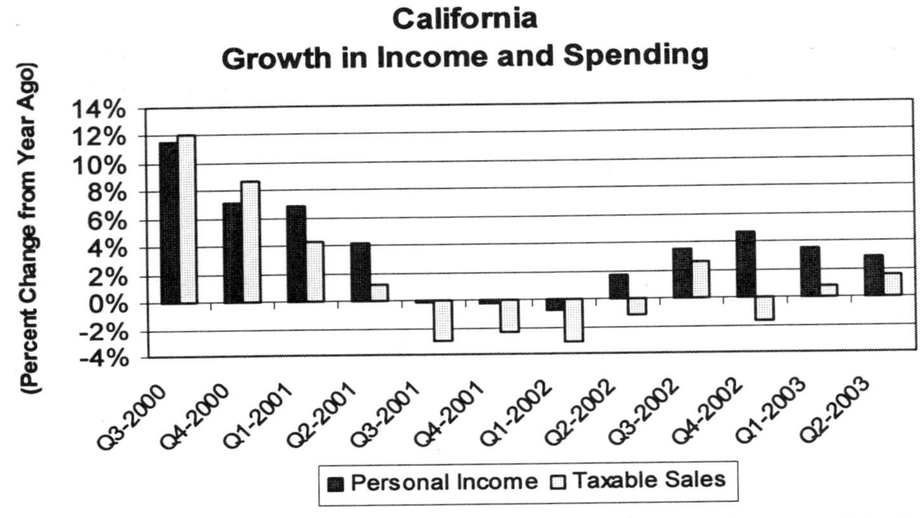

The sharp drop in stock option income and taxable sales, along with the drop in capital gains, has cost the state upwards of $10 billion in revenue in each of the past three years.

Personal income rose by approximately 3% in the first half of 2003 and income growth has picked up in the 2nd half as evidenced by the fact that income tax receipts are running ahead of expectations. The October 2003 consensus of California economists was that personal income would grow by 4.6% in 2004. However, this expectation was formed before the good news about GDP and job growth published in the past two weeks.

Taxable sales were up slightly year over year in the 1st half of 2003. It is reasonable to assume that both income and spending will rise as the economy produces job growth.

An upturn in income and spending will make a modest contribution to reducing the state budget deficit but legislators should not expect the economy to produce nearly enough gains to avoid the tough budget choices facing the state.

POPULATION GROWTH – THE OUTLOOK TO 2010

TOTAL POPULATION

Summary

Recent Events

- Population growth accelerated after 2000. California added 1.8 million residents between January 1, 2000 and January 1, 2003 — an annual growth of 612,700 and far above annual population growth levels in the 1990s. The growth came as a result of natural increase, foreign immigration **and** positive levels of migration from other states.

- Population growth rates were highest in the Sacramento region, the San Joaquin Valley and the Los Angeles Basin. Annual population growth averaged 1.8% per year between 2000 and 2003 — above the 1.2% annual growth for 1990-1996 and 1.6% annual gains from 1996 to 2000.

- The Census Bureau published population estimates for 2002 for California that were slightly lower than those published by the California Department of Finance and used by CCSCE. The difference is that the Census Bureau estimates that domestic migration was slightly negative after 2000.

- These population estimates do **not** incorporate estimates for potential undercount in the 2000 Census. The estimates of annual undocumented immigration into California have been **lowered** from 99,000 per year to 73,000 per year.

- Ethnic change continues. Hispanic residents accounted for nearly 80% of California's population growth between 2000 and 2002 with Asian residents accounting for most of the remaining population gains.

Projections

- Population growth is expected to decrease to 550,000 per year (1.5% annual growth) between 2002 and 2010, when the state is projected to have 39.7 million residents.

- The Sacramento region is projected to be the state's fastest growing region followed by the San Joaquin Valley. Still, 60% of overall population growth will occur in the Los Angeles and Bay Area regions.

- Natural increase and foreign immigration will be the largest components of growth. In the long term, the level of population growth depends on the nation's growth and the **state's share of national job growth.**

Recent Population Growth

Population growth rose to 612,700 between January 2000 and January 2003. Between 1996 and 2000 population growth averaged near 518,500 per year compared to 355,700 annually for the 1990-96 period.

California and Economic Regions
Population Growth Since 1990

	Average Annual Growth (Thousands)			Average Annual Growth Rate		
	1990-96	**1996-2000**	**2000-03**	**1990-96**	**1996-2000**	**2000-03**
Los Angeles Basin	156.2	245.5	330.7	1.0%	1.5%	2.0%
San Francisco Bay Area	64.1	102.8	76.7	1.0%	1.6%	1.1%
San Diego Region	20.4	50.8	51.9	0.8%	1.9%	1.8%
Sacramento Region	27.7	37.5	48.1	1.8%	2.2%	2.6%
Sacramento Valley Region	8.0	4.1	8.6	1.4%	0.7%	1.4%
Coastal Region	9.8	23.1	15.8	0.8%	1.8%	1.2%
San Joaquin Valley	60.8	50.7	74.6	2.1%	1.6%	2.2%
North Coast Region	3.1	1.3	2.3	1.1%	0.5%	0.8%
Mountain Region	5.2	3.1	4.0	1.5%	0.8%	1.0%
CALIFORNIA	**355.7**	**518.5**	**612.7**	**1.2%**	**1.6%**	**1.8%**

Source: California Department of Finance; 1990-2000, July 1 estimates; 2000-2003 Jan. 1 estimates

Highlights from comparing the three periods – 1990/96, 1996/2000 and 2000/2003 are listed below:

- In the Los Angeles Basin annual growth rose from 156,200 (1.0% per year) to 245,500 (1.5% annually) and then surged to 330,700 (2.0%) between 2000 and 2003.
- Bay Area annual population gains fell to 76,700 (1.1% per year) after averaging near 100,000 per year (1.6% annually) between 1996 and 2000. More Bay Area job holders are now residing in adjacent counties including San Joaquin and Stanislaus.
- In San Diego population growth levels more than doubled from 20,400 (0.8% annually in the early 1990s) to 50,800 – 1.9% per year and then to 51,900 (1.8% per year) after 2000.
- In the Sacramento region, population growth started the 1990s high and grew even higher as time passed. The region's annual growth

accelerated from 27,700 annually to 1996 to 37,500 (2.2% per year) between 1996 and 2000 and 48,100 (2.6% per year) after 2000.

- The San Joaquin Valley followed a different pattern. The Valley was California's population growth leader between 1990 and 1996 – averaging gains of 2.1% annually. Then, as the coastal economies surged, Valley growth declined between 1996 and 2000 when the Valley just matched the state's growth rate. After 2000, growth has increased to 74,600 (2.2%) annually.

- The Sacramento Valley, North Coast and Mountain regions have posted below average population growth rates since 1996.

The Components of Population Growth

The state's population growth has four main sources:

- Natural Increase – Births minus deaths

- Legal Foreign Immigration – Including an estimate of emigration (people leaving California to reside in foreign countries)

- Undocumented Immigration – Estimated by the U.S. Census Bureau and California Department of Finance

- Domestic Migration – The movement of people between California and other states

Components of Population Growth (Thousands)

	Natural Increase	Net Legal Immigration	Undocumented Immigration	Domestic Migration	Population Growth
2001-2002	295	159	73	76	603
2000-2001	298	153	73	102	662
1999-2000	298	105	73	143	619
1998-99	293	130	73	59	555
1997-98	296	127	73	-86	410
1996-97	309	138	73	-30	490
1995-96	319	102	73	-243	251
1994-95	337	145	73	-367	188
1993-94	356	189	73	-410	209
1992-93	372	187	73	-305	327

Source: California Department of Finance; INS, CCSCE

Natural Increase

Natural increase fell from 400,000 new residents in 1990 and 1991 to near 300,000 per year between 1996 and 2002. Natural increase fell because the annual level of births fell from near 600,000 in 1990 to near 525,000 during the past five years. Population growth from natural increase will remain near current levels to 2010 as increases in births are matched by increases in the number of deaths.

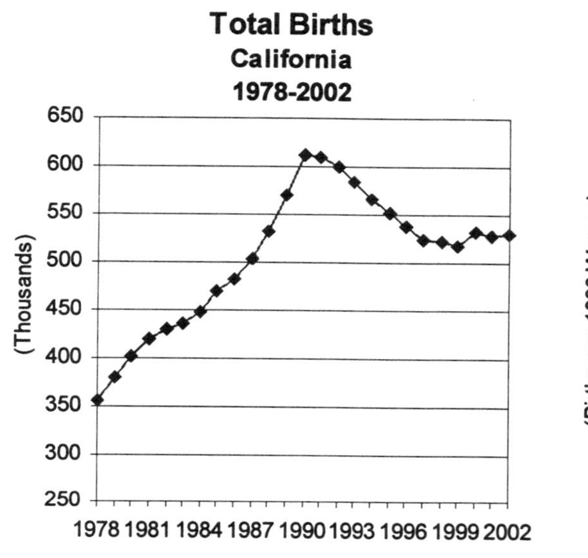

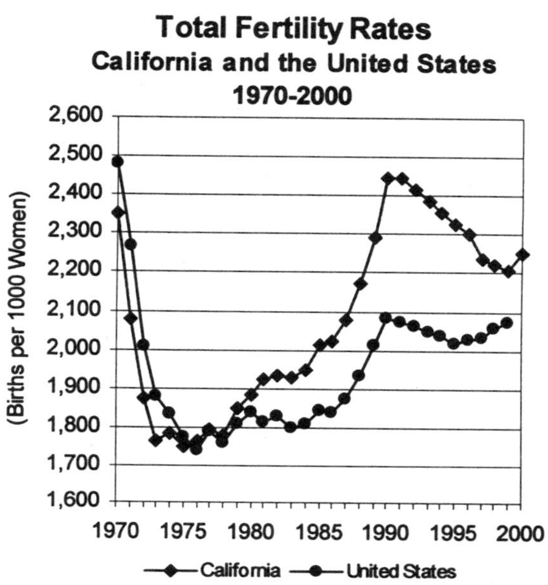

As shown on the graphs, both fertility rates and the level of births in California have dropped in recent years. Moreover, state fertility rates are now closer to national rates than since the mid 1980s. Lower fertility rates mean that a given level of job gains will result in lower overall population growth.

Natural increase accounted for all of the state's population growth in the early 90s. During the past five years, natural increase accounted for 50% of the state's gain primarily because domestic migration turned positive after 1997.

The California Department of Finance projects that the number of births will start rising in the decade ahead but will not reach the high level of the early 90's despite a rise in the number of women in childbearing age groups. For more information, see www.dof.ca.gov/HTML/DEMOGRAP/whatsnew.htm.

Foreign Immigration

There are three main kinds of foreign immigration into California — 1) people who come new as legally admitted immigrants each year, 2) people already living here who were granted legal status and 3) new undocumented immigrants. Some of the people adjusting status (category 2) came originally as undocumented immigrants but have been granted amnesty and allowed to become legal immigrants.

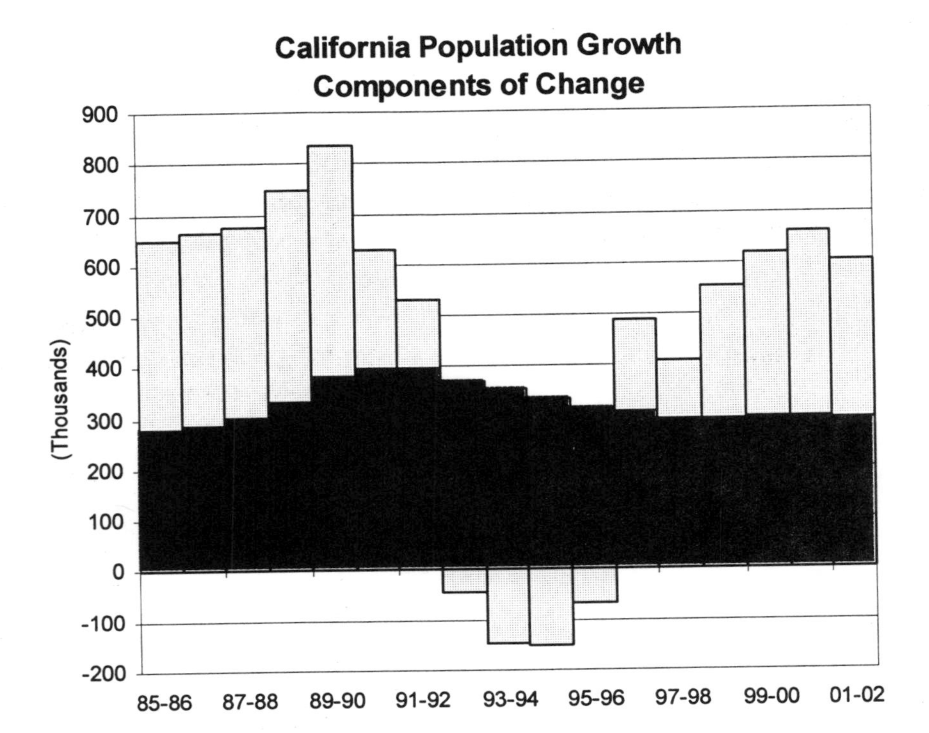

Legal Immigration

Statistics on legal immigration are collected by the Bureau of Citizenship and Immigration Services of the Department of Homeland Security and reported by the California Department of Finance (www.dof.ca.gov/HTML/DEMOGRAP/repndat.htm). Since 1990, the number of legal immigrants has averaged 212,000 per year with a high of 291,000 in 2002.

However, the number of **new** legal immigrants actually dropped in 2002, responding to the post 9/11 slowdown in immigration. The number of new arrivals has averaged near 100,000 per year as shown below while the number of adjustments in status surged as the backlog of previous immigration applications was finally reduced.

California
Immigrant by Type
1999 - 2002
(Thousands)

	Adjustments	New Arrivals	Total
2002	202.5	88.7	291.2
2001	179.9	102.8	282.7
2000	121.3	96.2	217.6
1999	60.8	100.4	161.2

Source: DOF

The Department of Finance adjusts the immigration data to reflect 1) their estimate of when people actually came to California and 2) to include an adjustment for people leaving to live in foreign countries. The DOF annual estimates of legal immigration are shown on page 3-4.

Mexico is, by far, the largest country of origin for legal immigrants to California. In 2002, 105,678 immigrants came from Mexico--36% of all immigrants that year. The next largest group came from the Philippines—21,971.

Foreign immigration levels should fall during the next few years. Tighter immigration screening after 9/11 should reduce the number of new arrivals. The number of status adjustments should decline as the backlog has been reduced.

Undocumented Immigration

Estimates of undocumented immigration are based on the ongoing work of Robert Warren of the Bureau of Immigration and Citizenship Services. His latest report, published in January 2003, is available at their website: www.uscis.gov, under Immigration Statistics.

The latest estimate of annual undocumented immigration into the United States is 350,000 for 1990-2000. This represents an upward revision from the previous estimate of 275,000 per year. On the other hand, the estimate for California was revised downward from 99,000 per year to 73,000 per year. Part of the downward revision is the result of amnesties that allowed undocumented immigrants to obtain legal immigrant status.

With the revisions, California accounted for just over 20% of the nation's undocumented immigrant flow, down from a previous estimate of 35%. Texas had the second largest undocumented immigrant flow at 60,000 per year.

Domestic Migration

Domestic migration is the most volatile component of state population growth responding with a lag to changes in the relative rates of job growth between California and the rest of the nation. Migration trends **do** respond to short term fluctuations in job growth. The principal reason for long distance migration (in contrast to moves **within** a metropolitan area) is for job opportunities. Workers (and their families) migrate to regions with good job prospects.

Domestic migration **responded sharply** to the early 1990s California recession. It was the change in the direction and amount of interstate migration flows that caused the decline in California's population growth between 1990 and 1996. As the graph indicates, net domestic migration into California moved from a significant plus in the late 1980s to an estimated out-migration of between 250,000 and 400,000 per year in the 1992-96 fiscal years.

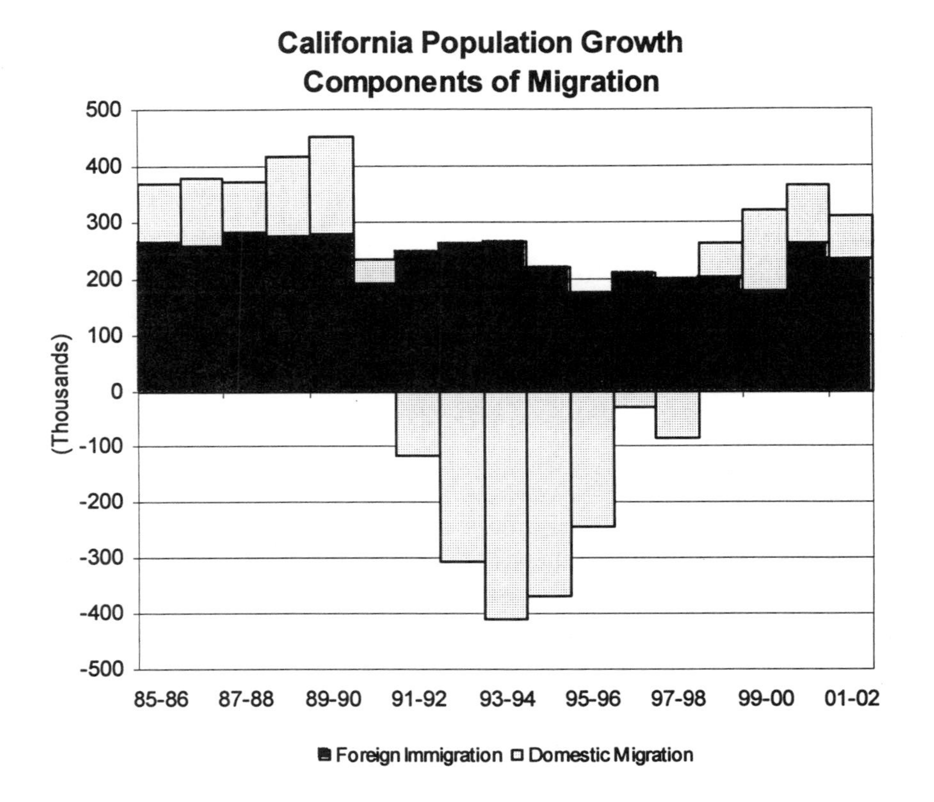

Six years of strong job growth and falling unemployment rates reversed the trend in domestic migration. For the past four years domestic migration was positive as shown on the graph above and on page 3-4. For additional discussion of domestic migration trends, see www.ccsce.com/irus_cbe.htm.

Domestic Migration and Population Growth – DOF Versus Census Bureau Estimates

The current published DOF estimate of California's population on July 1, 2002 is 35,301,000. The Census Bureau estimates that California has 185,000 fewer residents. Both begin with the Census estimate of 33,871,600 on April 1, 2000. The two sets of estimates of California's population and domestic migration trends are shown on Table 1E.

The primary reason for the difference in population estimates is a difference in estimates of recent domestic migration trends. For the 2000-2002 fiscal years, DOF estimated that domestic migration **into** California was 177,800. The Census Bureau estimates that domestic migration was **out of** California totaling 69,500.

Major differences, as shown in Table 1E, occurred in the Los Angeles Basin and San Francisco Bay Area and, in particular in Los Angeles and Santa Clara counties. The Census Bureau estimates that out-migration from Los Angeles County in 2000-02 was 169,700 – more than 125,000 higher than reported by

DOF. For Santa Clara County, the Census Bureau estimates out-migration of 96,700 versus 39,800 for DOF. Outside of these two regions, differences between DOF and Census were much smaller.

Census Bureau population estimates were slightly **higher** than DOF's in the San Joaquin Valley and San Diego regions.

Population Growth by Ethnic Group Since 1990

Virtually all of the state's growth in the 1990s was the result of increases in California's Hispanic and Asian populations and residents who marked two or more race categories on the 2000 Census. California had nearly 11 million Hispanic residents in 2000, approximately one-third of the state's total population, and representing a 42.6% increase in Hispanic population in the 1990s.

This was the first Census in which residents could mark more than one race category. Just over 900,000 residents, 2.7% of California's total population, marked two or more race categories on the 2000 Census. Hispanic is considered an ethnic group, not a racial identity. Anyone who marked Hispanic is included under the Hispanic category in the tables in **County Projections**, regardless of whether they marked another group also on the Census form.

The Census Bureau and DOF have adjusted the tabulated Census estimates for the 2 or more races group. Some of the respondents who marked Other as their primary race category were reclassified as Non Hispanic White, Black or Asian. The result was a reduction in the estimate for 2 or more races from 903,100 to 628,300 with most of these respondents reclassified as Non Hispanic White.

Table 1E
California, Economic Regions and Counties
COMPARISON OF DOF AND CENSUS ESTIMATES
2000 – 2002
(Thousands)

	July 1,2002 Population		2000-02 Domestic Mig	
	DOF	Census	DOF	Census
Imperial	151.9	146.2	-3.2	-2.6
Los Angeles	9,902.7	9,806.6	-43.9	-169.7
Orange	2,954.5	2,938.5	-4.7	-42.6
Riverside	1,677.1	1,699.1	80.2	92.7
San Bernardino	1,811.7	1,816.1	43.1	41.4
Ventura	785.7	783.9	-2.7	2.9
Los Angeles Basin	17,283.6	17,190.4	68.8	-77.9
Alameda	1,490.0	1,472.3	-4.6	-38.2
Contra Costa	987.0	992.4	12.7	11.9
Marin	249.1	247.6	-2.0	-5.2
Napa	128.9	130.3	1.9	3.2
San Francisco	789.8	764.0	-8.5	-35.9
San Mateo	713.8	703.2	-18.8	-34.3
Santa Clara	1,718.5	1,683.5	-39.8	-96.7
Solano	408.7	411.1	4.4	2.7
Sonoma	470.2	468.4	2.6	-2.3
San Francisco Bay Area	6,956.0	6,872.8	-52.1	-194.8
San Diego	2,935.1	2,906.7	24.3	-7.2
San Diego Region	2,935.1	2,906.7	24.3	-7.2
El Dorado	165.2	165.7	5.2	6.5
Placer	270.7	278.5	18.2	22.9
Sacramento	1,297.6	1,305.1	39.9	37.7
Yolo	179.0	180.9	5.5	4.6
Sacramento Region	1,912.5	1,930.2	68.8	71.7
Butte	208.8	209.2	3.9	4.1
Colusa	19.6	19.3	-0.4	-0.4
Glenn	26.9	26.6	-0.5	-0.3
Shasta	171.1	171.8	6.3	7.1
Sutter	82.5	82.6	1.1	1.1
Tehama	57.3	57.5	0.9	1.1
Yuba	62.4	62.3	0.5	0.4
Sacramento Valley Region	628.5	629.3	11.8	13.1

	July 1,2002 Population		2000-02 Domestic Mig	
	DOF	Census	DOF	Census
Monterey	412.0	413.4	-7.5	-9.6
San Benito	56.0	55.9	0.0	-0.1
San Luis Obispo	254.5	253.4	4.7	3.1
Santa Barbara	407.8	403.1	-4.0	-9.2
Santa Cruz	259.0	253.8	-5.7	-9.4
Coastal Region	1,389.3	1,379.6	-12.5	-25.2
Fresno	835.4	834.6	1.2	2.0
Kern	697.1	694.1	10.2	7.3
Kings	134.7	135.0	0.0	0.6
Madera	131.8	130.3	0.7	1.8
Merced	222.7	225.4	3.3	5.1
San Joaquin	605.5	614.3	21.4	26.7
Stanislaus	470.2	482.4	14.6	18.6
Tulare	382.0	381.8	-3.0	-1.9
San Joaquin Valley	3,479.4	3,497.9	48.4	60.2
Del Norte	27.9	27.5	0.2	-0.2
Humboldt	127.5	127.2	0.4	0.3
Lake	61.1	62.0	2.5	3.6
Mendocino	87.9	87.2	0.0	-0.2
North Coast Region	304.4	303.9	3.1	3.5
Alpine	1.2	1.2	0.0	0.0
Amador	36.4	36.7	1.3	1.7
Calaveras	42.3	43.0	1.6	2.2
Inyo	18.3	18.2	0.3	0.2
Lassen	34.2	34.0	-0.2	0.1
Mariposa	17.4	17.2	0.3	0.1
Modoc	9.3	9.3	-0.1	-0.1
Mono	13.4	13.1	0.2	-0.1
Nevada	95.7	95.0	3.4	2.5
Plumas	21.0	20.9	0.2	0.3
Sierra	3.5	3.6	0.0	0.0
Siskiyou	44.3	44.1	-0.2	-0.2
Trinity	13.1	13.2	0.2	0.2
Tuolumne	56.2	55.8	1.7	1.5
Mountain Region	406.1	405.3	8.7	8.4
California	**35,301.0**	**35,116.0**	**177.8**	**-69.5**

Domestic migration from April 1, 2000 to July 1, 2002

The adjusted Census estimates for 2000 are shown on Table 1A.

The Census Bureau has published estimates of population by ethnic group and county for 2002. Estimates of the change in population by ethnic group between 2000 and 2002 are shown on Table 1B.

California
Population by Ethnic Group
(Thousands)

	1990	2000 (as adjusted)	2002	Change	% Change
Hispanic	7,687.9	10,966.6	11,936.7	970.4	8.8%
Non Hispanic – One Race					
White	17,084.4	16,059.6	16,032.0	-27.6	-0.2%
Black	2,092.0	2,210.8	2,248.0	37.2	1.7%
Asian & Other	2,894.0	4,006.6	4,252.1	245.5	6.1%
Two or More Races		625.3	647.2	18.9	3.5%
Total Population	29,758.2	33,871.6	35,116.0	1,244.4	3.7%

Source: Census Bureau

Nearly 80% of California's recent population growth was in Hispanic residents and most of the remaining increase was Asian. If the estimate of 73,000 undocumented immigrants per year into California is accurate, then it is likely that less than 10% of the Hispanic population increase came from undocumented immigrants, as not all undocumented immigrants are Hispanic.

In 2002, Hispanics were the largest population group in one region – the Los Angeles Basin. Hispanics represented 42.3% of the Basin's population in 2002. In two other regions the Hispanic population share also exceeded the state average – the San Joaquin Valley (41.9%) and Coastal Region (35.4%).

California and Economic Regions
Population by Ethnic Group
July 1, 2002
(Percent)

	Hispanic	Non-Hispanic White	Black	Asian & Other	Two + Races	Total
Los Angeles Basin	42.3%	38.0%	7.2%	11.2%	1.4%	100.0%
San Francisco Bay Area	20.4%	48.8%	7.2%	21.2%	2.5%	100.0%
San Diego Region	28.4%	54.0%	5.4%	9.9%	2.3%	100.0%
Sacramento Region	16.7%	62.4%	7.1%	10.7%	3.2%	100.0%
Sacramento Valley Region	14.9%	75.3%	1.3%	6.0%	2.6%	100.0%
Coastal Region	35.4%	55.9%	2.2%	4.8%	1.7%	100.0%
San Joaquin Valley	41.9%	44.5%	4.8%	7.2%	1.7%	100.0%
North Coast Region	12.1%	78.2%	1.4%	5.5%	2.9%	100.0%
Mountain Region	8.8%	84.4%	1.9%	3.0%	2.0%	100.0%
California	34.0%	45.7%	6.4%	12.1%	1.8%	100.0%

Source: Census Bureau

The Asian population exceeded the number of Hispanics in only one region – the Bay Area. Asians represented 21.2% of the Bay Area population. Asians were about 10% of regional population totals in the Los Angeles, San Diego and Sacramento regions.

The African American population share was near 7% in the Los Angeles Basin, Bay Area and Sacramento region and much less in other regions.

The White Non-Hispanic population share was above 75% in three mostly rural and mountain regions – the Sacramento Valley, North Coast and Mountain regions.

Table 1A
California, Economic Regions and Counties
POPULATION BY ETHNIC GROUP
2000
(Thousands)

	Hispanic	Non Hispanic White	Black	Asian & Other	Two + Races	Total
Imperial	102.9	29.2	5.2	4.4	0.7	142.4
Los Angeles	4,242.2	3,040.3	912.8	1,194.4	129.7	9,519.3
Orange	875.6	1,476.5	43.6	405.6	45.0	2,846.3
Riverside	559.6	796.8	93.5	70.5	25.1	1,545.4
San Bernardino	669.4	763.1	152.0	95.3	29.7	1,709.4
Ventura	251.7	430.6	13.7	44.8	12.4	753.2
Los Angeles Basin	**6,701.4**	**6,536.4**	**1,220.7**	**1,814.9**	**242.7**	**16,516.0**
Alameda	273.9	603.2	213.6	311.8	41.2	1,443.7
Contra Costa	167.8	556.9	87.8	111.9	24.4	948.8
Marin	27.4	195.8	7.1	12.3	4.7	247.3
Napa	29.4	86.7	1.5	4.6	2.1	124.3
San Francisco	109.5	345.3	59.5	246.2	16.3	776.7
San Mateo	154.7	358.5	24.1	153.6	16.2	707.2
Santa Clara	403.4	756.8	45.4	442.6	34.4	1,682.6
Solano	69.6	196.7	58.0	55.4	14.8	394.5
Sonoma	79.5	344.5	6.3	18.7	9.6	458.6
San Francisco Bay Area	**1,315.1**	**3,444.2**	**503.4**	**1,357.3**	**163.8**	**6,783.8**
San Diego	751.0	1,566.0	157.9	277.3	61.7	2,813.8
San Diego Region	751.0	1,566.0	157.9	277.3	61.7	2,813.8
El Dorado	14.6	133.4	0.7	4.7	2.8	156.3
Placer	24.0	208.4	1.9	9.3	4.8	248.4
Sacramento	195.9	716.2	119.4	153.1	38.8	1,223.5
Yolo	43.7	99.3	3.2	18.6	3.9	168.7
Sacramento Region	**278.1**	**1,157.3**	**125.3**	**185.8**	**50.4**	**1,796.9**
Butte	21.3	163.8	2.7	10.7	4.7	203.2
Colusa	8.8	9.1	0.1	0.6	0.2	18.8
Glenn	7.8	16.8	0.1	1.3	0.4	26.5
Shasta	9.0	141.7	1.2	7.3	4.0	163.3
Sutter	17.5	47.9	1.4	10.4	1.7	78.9
Tehama	8.8	44.3	0.3	1.5	1.1	56.0
Yuba	10.4	39.7	1.8	6.1	2.2	60.2
Sacramento Valley Region	**83.7**	**463.3**	**7.7**	**37.9**	**14.3**	**606.9**

	Hispanic	Non Hispanic White	Black	Asian & Other	Two + Races	Total
Monterey	188.0	164.1	14.5	27.1	8.1	401.8
San Benito	25.5	24.9	0.5	1.6	0.8	53.2
San Luis Obispo	40.2	189.1	4.8	8.3	4.3	246.7
Santa Barbara	136.7	228.9	8.5	18.8	6.5	399.3
Santa Cruz	68.5	169.6	2.2	10.2	5.1	255.6
Coastal Region	**458.8**	**776.7**	**30.5**	**65.9**	**24.8**	**1,356.6**
Fresno	351.7	322.9	40.9	72.9	11.0	799.4
Kern	254.1	330.6	38.2	28.8	10.0	661.6
Kings	56.5	55.0	10.5	5.5	2.0	129.5
Madera	54.5	58.5	4.8	3.5	1.9	123.1
Merced	95.5	87.8	7.7	16.1	3.4	210.6
San Joaquin	172.1	271.7	36.4	70.1	13.3	563.6
Stanislaus	141.9	260.8	10.7	24.5	9.2	447.0
Tulare	186.9	156.6	5.2	15.2	4.2	368.0
San Joaquin Valley	**1,313.1**	**1,543.8**	**154.4**	**236.6**	**55.0**	**3,302.8**
Del Norte	3.8	19.4	1.2	2.2	0.8	27.5
Humboldt	8.2	104.3	1.1	9.0	4.0	126.5
Lake	6.6	47.2	1.2	2.0	1.3	58.3
Mendocino	14.2	65.2	0.5	4.6	1.9	86.3
North Coast Region	**32.8**	**236.1**	**3.9**	**17.9**	**7.9**	**298.6**
Alpine	0.1	0.9	0.0	0.2	0.0	1.2
Amador	3.1	29.1	1.4	0.9	0.6	35.1
Calaveras	2.8	35.7	0.3	1.0	0.9	40.6
Inyo	2.2	13.5	0.0	1.9	0.4	17.9
Lassen	4.7	24.2	3.1	1.4	0.6	33.8
Mariposa	1.3	14.6	0.1	0.7	0.4	17.1
Modoc	1.1	7.7	0.1	0.4	0.2	9.4
Mono	2.3	9.9	0.1	0.4	0.2	12.9
Nevada	5.2	83.6	0.2	1.5	1.6	92.0
Plumas	1.2	18.5	0.1	0.6	0.4	20.8
Sierra	0.2	3.2	0.0	0.1	0.1	3.6
Siskiyou	3.3	37.1	0.6	2.2	1.1	44.3
Trinity	0.5	11.3	0.1	0.7	0.5	13.0
Tuolumne	4.4	46.6	1.1	1.3	1.1	54.5
Mountain Region	**32.4**	**335.9**	7.2	**13.0**	**7.9**	**396.3**
California	**10,966.3**	**16,059.6**	**2,210.8**	**4,006.6**	**628.3**	**33,871.7**

Source: DOF adjustment of 2000 Census estimates

Table 1B
California, Economic Regions and Counties
POPULATION CHANGE BY ETHNIC GROUP
2000 – 2002
(Thousands)

	Hispanic	White Non Hispanic	Black	Asian & Other	Two + Races	Total
Imperial	5.9	-1.2	-0.1	-0.5	-0.2	3.9
Los Angeles	300.2	-54.4	2.1	53.0	-13.7	287.2
Orange	62.1	-6.2	0.4	35.1	0.7	92.2
Riverside	91.2	43.5	8.8	7.8	2.5	153.7
San Bernardino	86.9	1.5	11.2	5.3	1.6	106.6
Ventura	21.9	5.5	0.4	3.0	0.0	30.7
Los Angeles Basin	**568.2**	**-11.2**	**22.8**	**103.6**	**-9.0**	**674.4**
Alameda	22.2	-19.6	-6.5	29.7	2.8	28.6
Contra Costa	26.0	-0.5	2.9	11.5	3.6	43.5
Marin	1.6	-2.0	-0.2	0.8	0.0	0.3
Napa	3.8	0.4	0.5	1.3	0.1	6.0
San Francisco	-1.6	-13.4	-2.9	6.4	-1.2	-12.7
San Mateo	2.9	-13.2	-2.2	8.7	-0.1	-4.0
Santa Clara	11.0	-42.8	-3.4	35.6	0.5	0.9
Solano	9.4	-0.5	3.0	2.7	1.9	16.5
Sonoma	9.0	-1.6	0.0	1.4	0.9	9.8
San Francisco Bay Area	**84.4**	**-93.2**	**-8.8**	**98.0**	**8.6**	**89.0**
San Diego	75.5	3.4	-0.4	10.1	4.2	92.8
San Diego Region	**75.5**	**3.4**	**-0.4**	**10.1**	**4.2**	**92.8**
El Dorado	2.3	6.1	0.3	0.3	0.4	9.4
Placer	4.3	20.9	0.9	2.3	1.6	30.1
Sacramento	31.9	14.9	9.2	16.9	8.6	81.6
Yolo	5.2	4.3	0.4	1.7	0.5	12.2
Sacramento Region	**43.8**	**46.3**	**10.8**	**21.2**	**11.1**	**133.3**
Butte	2.1	2.8	0.1	0.1	0.9	6.0
Colusa	0.7	-0.1	0.0	0.0	-0.1	0.5
Glenn	0.5	-0.2	0.0	-0.1	-0.1	0.2
Shasta	1.9	5.8	0.2	-0.4	1.0	8.5
Sutter	2.0	1.2	0.0	0.4	0.0	3.6
Tehama	1.2	0.3	0.0	-0.1	0.0	1.4
Yuba	1.5	0.5	0.2	-0.3	0.2	2.1
Sacramento Valley Region	**10.0**	**10.4**	**0.5**	**-0.4**	**1.9**	**22.5**

	Hispanic	White Non Hispanic	Black	Asian & Other	Two + Races	Total
Monterey	14.9	-2.6	-0.2	0.7	-1.2	11.6
San Benito	2.3	0.3	0.0	0.2	-0.1	2.7
San Luis Obispo	2.9	3.3	0.0	0.2	0.3	6.7
Santa Barbara	7.4	-3.3	-0.2	-0.1	-0.1	3.7
Santa Cruz	1.8	-3.1	-0.1	0.0	-0.4	-1.8
Coastal Region	**29.4**	**-5.4**	**-0.4**	**1.0**	**-1.6**	**23.0**
Fresno	29.7	1.1	2.0	2.2	0.2	35.2
Kern	28.0	2.0	1.3	0.9	0.1	32.4
Kings	4.5	0.8	0.5	0.0	-0.2	5.6
Madera	5.9	1.6	-0.1	0.2	-0.4	7.2
Merced	13.5	1.1	0.3	0.0	0.0	14.8
San Joaquin	28.0	4.2	6.2	9.6	2.7	50.7
Stanislaus	26.5	4.9	1.6	1.6	0.9	35.4
Tulare	15.7	-1.5	0.3	-0.3	-0.4	13.8
San Joaquin Valley	**151.8**	**14.4**	**12.0**	**14.2**	**2.8**	**195.1**
Del Norte	0.2	0.0	0.0	-0.2	0.0	0.0
Humboldt	1.0	-0.2	0.1	-0.9	0.7	0.6
Lake	1.4	2.0	0.2	0.0	0.0	3.7
Mendocino	1.5	-0.3	0.0	-0.3	0.0	1.0
North Coast Region	**4.0**	**1.6**	**0.3**	**-1.3**	**0.7**	**5.3**
Alpine	0.0	0.0	0.0	0.0	0.0	0.0
Amador	0.4	1.2	0.1	0.0	0.0	1.6
Calaveras	0.4	1.8	0.1	0.1	0.1	2.4
Inyo	0.4	0.0	0.0	-0.1	0.0	0.3
Lassen	0.3	0.0	0.1	-0.2	0.0	0.2
Mariposa	0.1	0.1	0.0	-0.1	0.0	0.1
Modoc	0.0	-0.1	0.0	0.0	0.0	-0.2
Mono	0.5	-0.2	0.0	0.0	-0.1	0.3
Nevada	0.6	2.3	0.0	0.0	0.1	3.0
Plumas	0.1	0.1	0.0	-0.1	0.0	0.1
Sierra	0.0	0.0	0.0	0.0	0.0	0.0
Siskiyou	0.3	-0.2	0.0	-0.3	0.0	-0.2
Trinity	0.0	0.1	0.0	-0.1	0.0	0.2
Tuolumne	0.4	0.9	0.0	-0.1	0.1	1.3
Mountain Region	**3.4**	**6.1**	**0.3**	**-1.0**	**0.1**	**9.0**
California	**970.4**	**-27.6**	**37.2**	**245.5**	**18.9**	**1,244.4**

Source: Census Bureau

California had 20 counties in 2002 where the White Non-Hispanic population share was 50% or below. Five were in the Los Angeles Basin – every county except Ventura; five in the Bay Area – Alameda, San Francisco, San Mateo, Santa Clara and Solano; seven in the San Joaquin Valley – all Valley counties except Stanislaus; and Colusa, Monterey and San Benito.

Imperial County had the highest Hispanic concentration (74.4%) followed by Tulare (54.0%). San Francisco had the largest Asian concentration (33.1%) followed by Santa Clara (28.4%).

Solano had the highest Black population share – 14.9% followed by Alameda (14.1%). Nineteen counties had White Non-Hispanic concentrations of over 75% including 11 in the Mountain region.

California has a majority of minorities in the state's K-12 school system.

California
K-12 Enrollment by Ethnic Group
1990-2003
(Thousands)

	1990-91	2002-2003	Change	% of Total in 2002-03
Hispanic	1,702.4	2,819.5	1,117.1	45.2%
White Non Hispanic	2,259.3	2,106.0	-153.3	33.7%
Black	426.4	515.8	89.4	8.3%
Asian & Other	562.4	803.1	240.7	12.9%
Total	4,950.5	6,244.4	1,293.9	100.0%

Source: California Department of Education

Approximately 1.3 million students have been added to the state's K-12 enrollment since 1990. All of the growth was in minority students with the largest gain, 1.1 million, in Hispanic K-12 enrollment.

In the 2002-2003 school year, Hispanic students represented 45.2% (2.8 million) of California's 6.2 million K-12 students. White Non Hispanic students accounted for 33.7% (2.1 million) of total enrollment followed by Asian and Other (12.9%) and Black (8.3%). All of the minority groups have higher shares of K-12 enrollment than they represent in the total population.

Future Population Growth

CCSCE projects that California's population will increase by 5.7 million between 2000 and 2010 – an average of 567,000 new residents per year. Based on the projected population growth, California will have 39.7 million residents in 2010.

California
Total Population
(Thousands)

	Population at End of Decade	Annual Growth	Average Annual Growth Rate	% of U.S. Growth
1980s	29,828.0	609.1	2.3%	27.4%
1990s	34,036.0	417.2	1.3%	13.8%
2000s	39,710.0	567.0	1.5%	20.1%

California Population as of July 1

Annual population growth between 2002 and 2010 is well above the level of the 1990s and just below the 609,000 annual gains in the 1980s. Measured by annual percentage growth rates, however, growth to 2010 (1.5% per year) is just slightly faster than in the 1990s (1.3% per year) and well below the 2.3% annual gains of the 1980s.

Population Growth Primarily Dependent on Job Gains

CCSCE population projections depend significantly on the state's projected job growth and the nation's projected population growth.

Below is a list of the principal reasons why California's population growth will reach or exceed 5.7 million in the decade ahead as well as significant events which would result in a lower rate of population growth.

Reasons for Growth of 5.7 Million or More

- CCSCE projects that California will add approximately 2.9 million jobs and capture approximately 17% of the nation's job growth – projections that continue the strong competitive performance of the late 1990s. The projected job growth will cause substantial migration into the state.

- New Census projections of U.S. population growth to 2010, scheduled for publication at the end of the year, are expected to show increased levels of population growth.

  — The recent job losses do not reflect any loss in California's share of U.S. jobs. Even the tech downturn, unlike the decade earlier aerospace job losses, is **not** the result of a loss in the state's share of national jobs and production. It is the national population level and California's **share** of U.S. job growth that primarily determine the state's population growth.

Reasons for Lower State Population Growth

- To house 5.7 million new residents California will need nearly 2 million new homes and apartments. To build this many units will require policy changes, higher densities, and creative and attractive new developments.

  Failure to build the needed dwelling units or failure to build units that are affordable and located near job growth areas will eventually have a negative impact on California's competitive position for job growth.

- Other factors could result in lower than projected job growth. A failure to provide adequate infrastructure will reduce California's economic competitiveness. An unexpected decline in the long-term growth potential of key sectors like foreign trade, technology or entertainment would also result in lower long-term job and population growth.

Components of Change

Natural increase and net migration will both contribute to California's population growth in the decade ahead.

The number of births each year will average just over 550,000 according to DOF projections – close to the 1990s average. Annual birth levels will rise throughout the decade. A slight decline in fertility rates will be combined with a rise in the number of women of childbearing age.

California
Components of Population Growth
(Thousands Per Year)

	1980-1990	1990-2002	2002-2010
Births	469.4	553.8	558.4
Deaths	190.0	223.3	252.1
Natural Increase	279.4	330.5	306.3
Net Migration	340.0	125.5	243.7
Total Population Growth	619.4	456.1	550.0

Source: DOF, CCSCE; 1990-2002 data based on DOF July 1 estimates

Net migration will average 243,700 per year – below the 1980s average but much higher than the 125,500 annual gains between 1990 and 2002.

Population growth will be divided evenly between natural increase and net migration in the decade ahead with natural increase accounting for 56% of statewide growth. Between 1990 and 2002, natural increase accounted for the large majority (72%) of population gains as the recession induced substantial domestic out-migration. If future job growth is less than projected, migration will be a smaller component of overall population growth and vice versa.

Components of Net Migration

Legal migration, undocumented immigration and domestic migration each accounted for roughly one-third of California's net migration in the 1980s.

California
Components of Net Migration
(Thousands Per Year)

	1980-1990	1990-2002	2001-2010
Net Legal Immigration	130.6	148.5	140.0
Undocumented Immigration	100.0	73.0	73.0
Domestic Migration	109.4	-96.0	30.7
Net Migration	340.0	125.5	243.7

Source: DOF, INS, CCSCE

Between 1990 and 2002 legal **and** undocumented immigration were close to 1980s levels. On the other hand domestic migration turned sharply negative as the number of migrants moving to California from other states declined after the recession started and more existing residents moved out.

The components of net migration in the decade ahead cannot be known with certainty. If foreign immigration continues at current levels, the implication is that domestic migration will be close to 0.

Other possible outcomes include reduced immigration levels for legal or undocumented immigrants. Immigrants who were going to California may go in larger numbers to other states. Recent immigrants may also move in response to changing labor market conditions. If foreign immigration is reduced, higher domestic migration levels are likely.

Population By Age Group

California's population growth in the 1990s was concentrated in two major groups:

- School age population (5 –19) with an increase of 1.5 million or 23.8%
- The baby boomers (35 –54) with an increase of 2.3 million or 30.2%

Between 2000 and 2010, population growth will be concentrated in slightly different groups as shown below

- College ages and young adults (15 –24) with an increase of 1.0 million or 20.5%
- The baby boomers (45 – 64) with an increase of 2.8 million or 39.4%.

California
Population by Age Group
2000 and 2010
(Thousands)

	2000	2003	2010	00-10	% chg
0 to 4	2,525.8	2,637.0	2,906.2	380.4	15.1%
5 to 9	2,686.1	2,598.3	2,767.9	81.9	3.0%
10 to 14	2,609.4	2,790.8	2,680.8	71.4	2.7%
15 to 19	2,426.9	2,571.3	2,892.0	465.1	19.2%
20 to 24	2,380.8	2,572.3	2,899.7	518.9	21.8%
25 to 34	5,115.8	5,208.4	5,526.5	410.7	8.0%
35 to 44	5,450.0	5,543.7	5,577.0	127.0	2.3%
45 to 54	4,457.2	4,823.8	5,572.5	1,115.3	25.0%
55 to 64	2,690.9	3,210.1	4,391.6	1,700.7	63.2%
65 to 74	1,889.0	1,971.8	2,484.3	595.3	31.5%
75-84	1,324.3	1,371.1	1,395.3	71.0	5.4%
85+	480.1	510.5	616.2	136.0	28.3%
Total Population	34,036.4	35,809.1	39,710.1	5,673.7	16.7%

Source: 2000, 2003 – DOF; 2010 – CCSCE total, DOF age distribution

The number of children under the age of 15 will increase by just over 500,000 compared with a gain of 1.2 million in the 1990s. The 25 – 44 year age group will experience very little growth, gaining just over 500,000, or approximately 5%, during the decade. The 65 + population will grow by nearly 800,000 from 3.7 million to almost 4.5 million by 2010.

Population Growth by Economic Region

CCSCE projects county population in two steps. First regional population totals are projected based primarily on job growth trends.

- In the Los Angeles Basin and San Francisco Bay Area the regional growth is allocated to counties based on land use, housing price, and commuting trends. Local analyses by the regional councils of government (SCAG and ABAG) are integrated into the projections.

- In other regions historical trends and analyses of special factors e.g., new prison and specific residential development plans, are used. CCSCE also examines DOF projections of the share of regional growth allocated to specific counties.

Although regional growth is heavily influenced by job trends, other factors do matter. One factor in Bay Area and San Joaquin Valley projections is the anticipated level of inter-regional commuting. New prisons and new campuses are other special factors – particularly in small counties.

Population Growth by Economic Region
1995-2010

	1995-2002		2002-2010	
	Growth (Thousands)	Average Annual Growth Rate	Growth (Thousands)	Average Annual Growth Rate
Sacramento Region	280.7	2.3%	364.5	2.2%
San Joaquin Valley	391.4	1.7%	650.5	2.2%
Coastal Region	129.5	1.4%	202.7	1.7%
Sacramento Valley	36.4	0.9%	83.7	1.6%
San Diego	319.9	1.7%	390.6	1.6%
Mountain Region	25.9	0.9%	50.6	1.5%
Los Angeles Basin	1,777.5	1.6%	2,055.2	1.4%
North Coast	11.1	0.5%	28.6	1.1%
San Francisco Bay Area	611.3	1.3%	588.9	1.0%
CALIFORNIA	3,590.0	1.5%	4,409.1	1.5%

The Sacramento region was the fastest growing region between 1995 and 2002 and will remain the fastest growing region to 2010 — slightly ahead of the San Joaquin Valley. The region will add more than 360,000 residents to grow at 2.2% per year. The Sacramento region has been able to accommodate large residential and nonresidential growth. Although residential prices are now rising rapidly, the region still has land available for growth and is engaged in a regional effort to organize future growth.

The San Joaquin Valley is projected to be the state's 2nd fastest growing region to 2010. The Valley will add 650,000 residents between 2002 and 2010 – an annual growth rate of 2.2%. The Valley had the second highest regional rate of population growth between 1990 and 2002. The attraction of the region is lower housing costs and fewer "urban ills" than California's coastal regions.

The largest numerical growth, 2.6 million new residents, will locate in the Los Angeles Basin and San Francisco Bay Area. Despite their projected below average growth rates, these regions will still create well over half of the new jobs in California. Though not the fastest growing regions in California, both regions will outpace the projected national population growth rate of 0.8% per year.

The Coastal, San Diego and Sacramento Valley regions will be the next fastest growing regional areas.

County Population Projections

Population projections by county for the year 2010 are shown on Table 1 along with DOF estimates for July 1, 2002.

Total population in California will increase by 1.5% annually to 2010. This is above the 1990s growth rate but represents a slowing in the rate of growth from the 2.3% annual population increase in the 1980s.

The fastest growing larger counties (more than 150,000 residents) since 1995 were led by Placer County which maintained a 3.6% annual growth rate.

Riverside County grew by 2.8% per year, followed by eight counties that increased between 1.8% and 2.1% annually.

Imperial, Riverside, Placer and Merced are projected to be the fastest growing larger counties to 2010 — all growing close to 3.0% annually. The next six fast-growing larger counties are all in the San Joaquin Valley and Sacramento regions.

Seven counties — Placer, Riverside, San Joaquin, Sacramento, Yolo, Stanislaus, and El Dorado — are among the ten fastest growing larger counties for both periods.

Ten Fastest Growing Large Counties 1995-2010			
1995-2002	**Average Annual Growth Rate**	**2002-2010**	**Average Annual Growth Rate**
Placer	3.6%	Imperial	3.0%
Riverside	2.8%	Riverside	2.9%
San Joaquin	2.1%	Placer	2.8%
Sacramento	2.1%	Merced	2.8%
Yolo	2.1%	El Dorado	2.6%
San Bernardino	2.0%	San Joaquin	2.4%
Monterey	1.9%	Kern	2.4%
El Dorado	1.9%	Stanislaus	2.2%
Orange	1.8%	Yolo	2.1%
Stanislaus	1.8%	Sacramento	2.0%
CALIFORNIA	1.5%	**CALIFORNIA**	1.5%

San Benito, Madera and Lassen led the smaller counties in population growth between 1995 and 2002. Smaller counties generally had **lower** growth rates than larger counties during this time period, which is a reversal of the usual pattern of growth.

San Benito, Madera and Lassen are projected to lead the smaller counties in population growth rates to 2010, repeating their 1995-2002 performance.

Ten Fastest Growing Smaller Counties 1995-2010			
1995-2002	**Average Annual Growth Rate**	**2001-2010**	**Average Annual Growth Rate**
San Benito	3.4%	San Benito	4.3%
Madera	2.6%	Madera	2.4%
Lassen	2.4%	Lassen	2.3%
Mono	2.3%	Lake	2.2%
Kings	2.2%	Colusa	2.2%
Sutter	1.5%	Calaveras	2.1%
Calaveras	1.4%	Kings	1.9%
Napa	1.4%	Tuolumne	1.8%
Nevada	1.4%	Mariposa	1.8%
Colusa	1.3%	Tehama	1.7%
CALIFORNIA	1.5%	**CALIFORNIA**	1.5%

Table 1
California, Economic Regions, and Counties
TOTAL POPULATION
1995 – 2010
(Thousands)

	1995	2002	2010	Average Annual Growth Rate	
				1995-2002	2002-2010
Imperial	136.2	151.9	191.9	1.6%	3.0%
Los Angeles	9,101.1	9,902.7	10,771.4	1.2%	1.1%
Orange	2,604.5	2,954.5	3,272.1	1.8%	1.3%
Riverside	1,378.8	1,677.1	2,101.8	2.8%	2.9%
San Bernardino	1,580.4	1,811.7	2,123.4	2.0%	2.0%
Ventura	705.1	785.7	878.2	1.6%	1.4%
Los Angeles Basin	**15,506.1**	**17,283.6**	**19,338.8**	**1.6%**	**1.4%**
Alameda	1,335.1	1,490.0	1,609.4	1.6%	1.0%
Contra Costa	872.8	987.0	1,086.8	1.8%	1.2%
Marin	238.4	249.1	265.9	0.6%	0.8%
Napa	117.3	128.9	140.8	1.4%	1.1%
San Francisco	739.9	789.8	815.9	0.9%	0.4%
San Mateo	675.9	713.8	757.6	0.8%	0.7%
Santa Clara	1,573.5	1,718.5	1,865.0	1.3%	1.0%
Solano	367.5	408.7	476.7	1.5%	1.9%
Sonoma	424.3	470.2	526.8	1.5%	1.4%
San Francisco Bay Area	**6,344.7**	**6,956.0**	**7,544.9**	**1.3%**	**1.0%**
San Diego	2,615.2	2,935.1	3,325.7	1.7%	1.6%
San Diego Region	**2,615.2**	**2,935.1**	**3,325.7**	**1.7%**	**1.6%**
El Dorado	144.9	165.2	202.8	1.9%	2.6%
Placer	211.6	270.7	338.3	3.6%	2.8%
Sacramento	1,120.7	1,297.6	1,524.2	2.1%	2.0%
Yolo	154.6	179.0	211.7	2.1%	2.1%
Sacramento Region	**1,631.8**	**1,912.5**	**2,277.0**	**2.3%**	**2.2%**
Butte	197.5	208.8	239.1	0.8%	1.7%
Colusa	17.9	19.6	23.2	1.3%	2.2%
Glenn	26.4	26.9	30.3	0.2%	1.5%
Shasta	159.7	171.1	190.5	1.0%	1.3%
Sutter	74.2	82.5	93.9	1.5%	1.6%
Tehama	54.6	57.3	65.6	0.7%	1.7%
Yuba	61.9	62.4	69.6	0.1%	1.4%
Sacramento Valley Region	**592.2**	**628.5**	**712.2**	**0.9%**	**1.6%**

	1995	2002	2010	Average Annual Growth Rate 1995-2002	2002-2010
Monterey	360.4	412.0	478.0	1.9%	1.9%
San Benito	44.4	56.0	78.2	3.4%	4.3%
San Luis Obispo	230.2	254.5	297.9	1.4%	2.0%
Santa Barbara	383.7	407.8	451.4	0.9%	1.3%
Santa Cruz	241.2	259.0	286.4	1.0%	1.3%
Coastal Region	**1,259.9**	**1,389.3**	**1,592.0**	**1.4%**	**1.7%**
Fresno	756.0	835.4	958.0	1.4%	1.7%
Kern	619.0	697.1	842.4	1.7%	2.4%
Kings	115.9	134.7	157.0	2.2%	1.9%
Madera	109.9	131.8	159.0	2.6%	2.4%
Merced	199.0	222.7	277.1	1.6%	2.8%
San Joaquin	522.1	605.5	734.4	2.1%	2.4%
Stanislaus	415.3	470.2	558.9	1.8%	2.2%
Tulare	350.8	382.0	443.0	1.2%	1.9%
San Joaquin Valley	**3,088.0**	**3,479.4**	**4,129.9**	**1.7%**	**2.2%**
Del Norte	27.9	27.9	29.9	0.0%	0.9%
Humboldt	125.0	127.5	133.2	0.3%	0.5%
Lake	56.6	61.1	72.9	1.1%	2.2%
Mendocino	83.8	87.9	96.9	0.7%	1.2%
North Coast Region	**293.3**	**304.4**	**332.9**	**0.5%**	**1.1%**
Alpine	1.2	1.2	1.4	0.7%	1.6%
Amador	33.4	36.4	38.7	1.2%	0.8%
Calaveras	38.4	42.3	49.8	1.4%	2.1%
Inyo	18.3	18.3	19.4	0.0%	0.8%
Lassen	28.9	34.2	40.9	2.4%	2.3%
Mariposa	16.5	17.4	20.0	0.8%	1.8%
Modoc	10.0	9.3	10.0	-1.0%	1.0%
Mono	11.4	13.4	14.9	2.3%	1.4%
Nevada	87.1	95.7	109.5	1.4%	1.7%
Plumas	20.8	21.0	21.7	0.1%	0.4%
Sierra	3.6	3.5	3.5	-0.2%	0.0%
Siskiyou	45.0	44.3	48.0	-0.2%	1.0%
Trinity	13.5	13.1	14.0	-0.4%	0.8%
Tuolumne	52.2	56.2	64.7	1.1%	1.8%
Mountain Region	**380.1**	**406.1**	**456.7**	**0.9%**	**1.5%**
California	**31,711.0**	**35,301.0**	**39,710.1**	**1.5%**	**1.5%**

Source: 1995 and 2002 – DOF; 2010 – CCSCE

Los Angeles Basin

The Los Angeles Basin will add 1.9 million residents between 2002 and 2010 to reach a total population of 19.3 million people in the region – 11.9% more residents than in 2002.

The Basin is more able to accommodate projected growth than either the Bay Area or San Diego. There is more land availability relative to projected growth. The geography of the Basin allows for many ways to site jobs and housing and link them with roads and public transit. The ability for the region's job growth to move toward the Inland Empire opens up additional options for accommodating projected growth.

The region's population growth will be driven by a 16.5% increase in total jobs between 2000 and 2010. As discussed in **California Economic Growth—2003 Edition**, job growth in California will be less than expected last year. National job growth to 2010 will be less as labor force growth has slowed as people have left the labor force in response to the long jobless recovery. While the recession job losses will be recovered and job growth will return, it will be lower than anticipated a year ago. The jobless recovery is discussed in more detail in Section 2.

The lower job growth will **not** result in lower population growth in the region or state. What will happen is that unemployment will be slightly higher in 2010 and fewer of the region's residents will be in the labor force.
Within the region, individual counties will grow at very different rates. The Inland Empire (Riverside and San Bernardino counties) will experience rapid growth – 25.3% and 17.2% respectively by 2010 when the Inland Empire will have more than 4.2 million residents. Both counties have recently experienced very rapid growth with Riverside adding 160,000 residents and San Bernardino nearly 125,000 residents between April 1, 2000 and January 1, 2003.

County by County Population Growth
1995-2010

	Average Annual Growth Rate		**Growth in**	**Pop in 2010**	**% Growth**
	1995-2002	**2002-2010**	**2002-2010**	**(Thousands)**	**2002-2010**
Imperial	1.6%	3.0%	40.0	191.9	26.3%
Los Angeles	1.2%	1.1%	868.7	10,771.4	8.8%
Orange	1.8%	1.3%	317.6	3,272.1	10.8%
Riverside	2.8%	2.9%	424.7	2,101.8	25.3%
San Bernardino	2.0%	2.0%	311.7	2,123.4	17.2%
Ventura	1.6%	1.4%	92.5	878.2	11.8%
Los Angeles Basin	1.6%	1.4%	2,055.2	19,338.8	11.9%

Regional Planning Agency Projections

Regional planning agencies prepare long-term job, population and household projections for many regions within California. These agencies prepare projections at the regional and sub-regional level. They are the major source of information for smaller area data within each region. The regional planning agencies are continually working to improve the quality of their land use database, which gives them a unique advantage in preparing sub-regional projections.

In the Los Angeles Basin, projections are prepared by the Southern California Association of Governments (SCAG @ www.scag.ca.gov). In the Bay Area, see the Association of Bay Area Governments (ABAG @ www.abag.ca.gov). In San Diego, see the San Diego Association of Governments (SANDAG @ www.sandag.com). In Sacramento, see the Sacramento Area Council of Governments @ www.sacog.org).

CCSCE has recently prepared regional projections for SCAG and SACOG.

The regional agency projections all have a technical phase and a policy phase. Unfortunately, in many California regions, there is intense local pressure to avoid higher household growth projections. These pressures reflect both concerns of residents about the implications of growth for their communities and the desire of local policy leaders to minimize the pressures to meet state-mandated fair-share housing targets.

The technical projections are often changed (mostly lowered) during the final adoption phase to respond to local political pressures. Local pressures to reduce housing targets are currently strongest in the SCAG, ABAG and SANDAG regions.

As a result, CCSCE's long-term projections are sometimes higher, particularly for household growth, than those published by the regional planning agencies. In terms of sub-regional projections, the regional planning agencies usually try to honor the projections submitted to them by local communities, which also raises the possibility of political considerations influencing the projections.

Los Angeles County will have a lower growth rate (8.8%) but add the most people – nearly 900,000. Orange and Ventura counties' growth will be near the regional average but higher than the U.S. growth rate. Orange County, with nearly 3.3 million residents, will be the third largest county in California – barely behind 2nd place San Diego

There are a number of trends which affect each county's growth. Comparatively lower housing prices and land availability have pushed the region's growth outward since the late 1940s. In recent decades Riverside and San Bernardino counties have absorbed an increasing share of new growth. The Inland Empire, with 20.2% of the region's 2002 population, will receive 35.8% of the projected growth.

All areas in the Basin are experiencing significant increases in median resale home prices. The Inland Empire "advantage" remains strong as median prices are far below most other Basin markets, but are now moving further above the national average.

Median Home Price
Detached Homes and Condos
August 2003

County	Price	Change from 2002
Los Angeles	$335,000	+24.8%
Orange	$420,000	+18.3%
Riverside	$259,000	+20.5%
San Bernardino	$191,500	+21.6%
Ventura	$389,000	+15.3%

Source: California Association of Realtors

Nearly all of the region's growth since 1990 came from natural increase as shown on Table 1C. Net migration was 29,500 per year or just 13.5% of overall population growth.

CCSCE expects that migration will be a more significant factor in regional growth – particularly in the Inland Empire – in the decade ahead. The 1997-2002 trends are more indicative of future population growth trends than the trends for the entire 1990s.

Recent Population Growth Trends 1997-2002 (Thousands Per Year)				
	Natural Increase	**Net Migration**	**Foreign Immigration**	**Domestic Migration**
Imperial	1.7	0.9	2.7	-1.8
Los Angeles	97.0	46.4	92.4	-46.0
Orange	29.8	21.1	21.1	0.1
Riverside	12.3	35.9	7.4	28.5
San Bernardino	17.6	19.5	6.8	12.7
Ventura	6.8	6.0	4.3	1.7
Los Angeles Basin	165.2	129.8	134.7	-4.8

Source: California Department of Finance

Approximately 56% of the region's growth came from natural increase between 1997 and 2002. Natural increase was the primary cause of growth in Los Angeles County but net migration has been positive since 1999. Net migration accounted for 75% of the growth in Riverside County, 40% in Orange and approximately half of total growth in San Bernardino and Ventura.

The region received approximately 150,000 foreign immigrants per year since 1990. As shown on Table 1D, most of the foreign immigrants located in Los Angeles (107,500 per year) and Orange (22,100 per year). The growth in Riverside and San Bernardino counties normally comes from migration but **not** primarily foreign immigration.

The foreign immigration trends for the past five years are similar to those for the entire decade and a good guide to future trends. However, the same is not true with regard to domestic migration.

Domestic migration was significantly negative (-119,400 per year) since 1990 driven by large out-migration in the early part of the 1990s when the region experienced a deep recession. Domestic migration was close to zero (-4,800 per year) for the 1997-2002 period.

A substantial portion of domestic migration and population growth in the Inland Empire comes from people moving in from elsewhere in the region.

The ethnic composition of Los Angeles Basin counties continues to change as shown in Tables 1A, 1B and on page 3-36. Hispanic and Asian population gains accounted for the total population growth in the region between 2000 and 2002. Orange County now has the second largest Hispanic population and third largest Asian population among California counties.

Table 1C
California, Economic Regions and Counties
COMPONENTS OF POPULATION CHANGE
1990 – 2002
(Thousands Per Year)

	Natural Increase	Net Migration	Total Change	Migration as % of Change
Imperial	1.8	1.8	3.6	49.4%
Los Angeles	112.9	-26.0	86.9	-29.9%
Orange	32.8	12.4	45.2	27.4%
Riverside	13.4	27.3	40.7	67.1%
San Bernardino	19.8	11.8	31.6	37.3%
Ventura	7.5	2.2	9.7	22.7%
Los Angeles Basin	**188.2**	**29.5**	**217.7**	**13.5%**
Alameda	11.9	5.9	17.8	33.2%
Contra Costa	6.5	8.6	15.1	57.0%
Marin	0.9	0.9	1.8	47.5%
Napa	0.3	1.2	1.5	80.8%
San Francisco	1.4	4.1	5.5	74.5%
San Mateo	5.4	0.0	5.4	0.1%
Santa Clara	18.3	0.3	18.6	1.6%
Solano	3.6	1.9	5.5	34.5%
Sonoma	2.0	4.7	6.7	70.1%
San Francisco Bay Area	**50.3**	**27.6**	**77.8**	**35.4%**
San Diego	27.6	8.3	35.9	23.1%
San Diego Region	**27.6**	**8.3**	**35.9**	**23.1%**
El Dorado	0.7	2.4	3.1	77.4%
Placer	1.2	6.8	8.0	85.0%
Sacramento	10.1	10.8	20.9	51.7%
Yolo	1.2	1.9	3.1	61.3%
Sacramento Region	**13.2**	**21.9**	**35.1**	**62.4%**
Butte	0.3	1.8	2.1	84.2%
Colusa	0.2	0.1	0.3	33.6%
Glenn	0.2	0.0	0.2	-18.0%
Shasta	0.4	1.5	1.9	77.0%
Sutter	0.6	1.0	1.6	63.1%
Tehama	0.1	0.5	0.6	82.3%
Yuba	0.6	-0.3	0.3	-104.4%
Sacramento Valley Region	**2.5**	**4.5**	**7.0**	**64.4%**

	Natural Increase	Net Migration	Total Change	Migration as % of Change
Monterey	4.9	-0.3	4.6	-6.5%
San Benito	0.6	1.0	1.6	63.1%
San Luis Obispo	0.7	2.4	3.1	77.4%
Santa Barbara	3.2	0.0	3.2	0.0%
Santa Cruz	2.0	0.5	2.5	20.0%
Coastal Region	**11.4**	**3.6**	**15.0**	**24.0%**
Fresno	9.7	4.1	13.8	29.5%
Kern	7.6	4.8	12.4	38.7%
Kings	1.5	1.2	2.7	44.4%
Madera	1.2	2.4	3.6	66.7%
Merced	2.7	0.9	3.6	25.0%
San Joaquin	5.2	5.1	10.3	49.5%
Stanislaus	4.1	4.5	8.6	52.3%
Tulare	4.6	1.1	5.7	19.3%
San Joaquin Valley	**36.6**	**24.1**	**60.7**	**39.7%**
Del Norte	0.1	0.2	0.3	70.0%
Humboldt	0.4	0.3	0.7	43.1%
Lake	-0.1	1.0	0.8	115.6%
Mendocino	0.3	0.3	0.6	51.2%
North Coast Region	**0.6**	**1.8**	**2.4**	**73.6%**
Alpine	0.0	0.0	0.0	50.0%
Amador	-0.1	0.6	0.5	115.1%
Calaveras	0.0	0.8	0.8	102.6%
Inyo	0.0	0.0	0.0	-25.0%
Lassen	0.1	0.4	0.5	78.6%
Mariposa	0.0	0.3	0.3	100.4%
Modoc	0.0	0.0	0.0	90.3%
Mono	1.0	0.2	1.2	14.8%
Nevada	0.0	1.4	1.4	98.3%
Plumas	0.0	0.1	0.1	131.3%
Sierra	0.0	0.0	0.0	114.8%
Siskiyou	0.0	0.1	0.1	124.1%
Trinity	0.0	0.0	0.0	300.0%
Tuolumne	0.0	0.7	0.6	107.0%
Mountain Region	**0.9**	**4.5**	**5.4**	**82.9%**
California	**330.6**	**125.5**	**456.1**	**27.5%**

Source: California Department of Finance

Table 1D
California, Economic Regions and Counties
COMPONENTS OF FOREIGN IMMIGRATION
1990 – 2002
(Thousands Per Year)

	Net Migration	Foreign Immigration	Domestic Migration
Imperial	1.8	2.2	-0.5
Los Angeles	-26.0	107.5	-133.5
Orange	12.4	22.1	-9.7
Riverside	27.3	6.4	20.9
San Bernardino	11.8	6.7	5.1
Ventura	2.2	4.1	-1.9
Los Angeles Basin	**29.5**	**148.9**	**-119.4**
Alameda	5.9	8.2	-2.3
Contra Costa	8.6	3.5	5.1
Marin	0.9	0.7	0.1
Napa	1.2	0.6	0.6
San Francisco	4.1	8.4	-4.3
San Mateo	0.0	5.4	-5.4
Santa Clara	0.3	13.5	-13.2
Solano	1.9	1.2	0.7
Sonoma	4.7	1.3	3.4
San Francisco Bay Area	**27.6**	**42.9**	**-15.3**
San Diego	8.3	15.9	-7.6
San Diego Region	**8.3**	**15.9**	**-7.6**
El Dorado	2.4	0.2	2.2
Placer	6.8	0.3	6.5
Sacramento	10.8	4.5	6.3
Yolo	1.9	0.9	1.0
Sacramento Region	**21.9**	**5.8**	**16.1**
Butte	1.8	0.4	1.4
Colusa	0.1	0.2	-0.1
Glenn	0.0	0.1	-0.2
Shasta	1.5	0.0	1.5
Sutter	1.0	0.5	0.5
Tehama	0.5	0.1	0.4
Yuba	-0.3	0.3	-0.6
Sacramento Valley Region	**4.5**	**1.7**	**2.8**

	Net Migration	Foreign Immigration	Domestic Migration
Monterey	-0.3	3.0	-3.3
San Benito	1.0	0.3	0.7
San Luis Obispo	2.4	0.5	1.9
Santa Barbara	0.0	2.4	-2.4
Santa Cruz	0.5	1.8	-1.3
Coastal Region	**3.6**	**7.9**	**-4.3**
Fresno	4.1	5.2	-1.2
Kern	4.8	3.1	1.7
Kings	1.2	0.6	0.6
Madera	2.4	0.7	1.7
Merced	0.9	1.6	-0.7
San Joaquin	5.1	2.8	2.3
Stanislaus	4.5	2.0	2.5
Tulare	1.1	2.4	-1.3
San Joaquin Valley	**24.1**	**18.4**	**5.6**
Del Norte	0.2	0.0	0.2
Humboldt	0.3	0.1	0.2
Lake	1.0	0.2	0.8
Mendocino	0.3	0.2	0.1
North Coast Region	**1.8**	**0.5**	**1.3**
Alpine	0.0	0.0	0.0
Amador	0.6	0.0	0.5
Calaveras	0.8	0.0	0.8
Inyo	0.0	0.0	0.0
Lassen	0.4	0.0	0.4
Mariposa	0.3	0.0	0.2
Modoc	0.0	0.0	0.0
Mono	0.2	0.0	0.1
Nevada	1.4	0.1	1.3
Plumas	0.1	0.0	0.1
Sierra	0.0	0.0	0.0
Siskiyou	0.1	0.1	0.0
Trinity	0.0	0.0	0.0
Tuolumne	0.7	0.0	0.6
Mountain Region	**4.5**	**0.3**	**4.2**
California	**125.5**	**241.9**	**-116.4**

Source: California Department of Finance

The region's school enrollment is more heavily represented by minority groups than is the overall population. Almost 75% of the 2002-2003 school enrollment is Hispanic, Asian and Black. Only in Ventura County do White Non Hispanic students account for close to 50% of total enrollment.

Los Angeles Basin
K-12 School Enrollment
2002-2003
(Thousands)

		Percent of Total			
	2002-2003 Enrollment	**Hispanic**	**White Non Hispanic**	**Black**	**Asian & Other**
Imperial	34.4	84.6%	10.7%	1.7%	3.0%
Los Angeles	1,736.2	60.7%	17.6%	10.8%	10.9%
Orange	512.1	43.6%	38.5%	1.9%	15.9%
Riverside	349.6	49.2%	37.0%	8.1%	5.7%
San Bernardino	407.2	49.5%	32.2%	11.9%	6.4%
Ventura	144.3	44.7%	45.8%	2.3%	7.2%
Los Angeles Basin	3,184.0	54.8%	26.2%	8.7%	10.3%

Source: California Department of Education

San Francisco Bay Area

The Bay Area will add nearly 600,000 residents between 2002 and 2010 to reach a total population of 7.5 million.

The Bay Area is projected to have the slowest regional population growth rate among the nine California regions. In part, the low population growth rate reflects the region's low job growth rate. In part, Bay Area population growth has been held back because some workers live in adjacent counties outside the nine-county region.

The Bay Area is projected to have an 11.8% gain in jobs between 2000 and 2010, reflecting the poor job performance since 2000. The Bay Area will grow at the national growth rate for the decade after outperforming the nation during the late 90s boom.

It is possible that recent trends will slightly reduce the tendency for workers to live outside the region. The job losses have made more housing available within the region and held down price increases while producing a decline in average rents. In addition, land previously designated for nonresidential uses is being converted to housing. And, finally after a long wait, housing permit levels are rising in response to decisions by developers and cities to address the region's longstanding housing shortages.

Ultimately, if the greater Bay Area cannot provide sufficient affordable housing, the region will lose a portion of its economic competitiveness and CCSCE's job projections will not be met.

Within the region, growth rates will be highest in the North and East Bay. Solano County will be the region's fastest growing county (+16.6% to 2010) providing lower cost housing for commuters. Contra Costa and Sonoma are also projected to post above average growth rates as the Bay Area growth pushes outward. Santa Clara County is projected to add the most residents (146,500) while growing by 8.5%

County by County Population Growth 1995 – 2010					
	Average Annual Growth				
	1995-2002	2002-2010	Growth in 2002-2010	Pop in 2010 (Thousands)	% Growth 2002-2010
Alameda	1.6%	1.0%	119.4	1,609.4	8.0%
Contra Costa	1.8%	1.2%	99.8	1,086.8	10.1%
Marin	0.6%	0.8%	16.8	265.9	6.7%
Napa	1.4%	1.1%	11.9	140.8	9.2%
San Francisco	0.9%	0.4%	26.1	815.9	3.3%
San Mateo	0.8%	0.7%	43.8	757.6	6.1%
Santa Clara	1.3%	1.0%	146.5	1,865.0	8.5%
Solano	1.5%	1.9%	68.0	476.7	16.6%
Sonoma	1.5%	1.4%	56.6	526.8	12.0%
San Francisco Bay Area	1.3%	1.0%	588.9	7,544.9	8.5%

Since 1990, about 35% of the region's growth came from migration as shown on Table 1C. San Francisco, Sonoma and Napa got above average shares from migration while Santa Clara and San Mateo received the highest share of growth from natural increase.

However, the 1997-2002 trends, shown below, are a better guide to the future. Population growth accelerated after 1997 and so did the contribution of migration to the region. Net migration accounted for 44% of the 88,000 annual population gain between 1997 and 2002.

Migration was the predominant source of growth in Contra Costa, Napa, San Francisco and Sonoma. Only in Santa Clara, San Mateo and Alameda was natural increase the largest component of growth.

Since 1990, foreign immigration into the region averaged 42,900 per year as shown on Table 1D. Most foreign immigrants went to the larger urban counties – Alameda, San Francisco, San Mateo and Santa Clara. Relatively few foreign immigrants located initially in other parts of the region.

Recent Population Growth Trends
1997-2002
(Thousands Per Year)

	Natural Increase	Net Migration	Foreign Immigration	Domestic Migration
Alameda	11.6	11.1	8.2	2.9
Contra Costa	6.1	10.9	3.6	7.3
Marin	0.9	1.1	0.7	0.4
Napa	0.2	1.5	0.7	0.8
San Francisco	1.7	6.4	7.0	-0.6
San Mateo	5.4	-0.7	5.3	-6.0
Santa Clara	18.0	0.5	12.5	-12.0
Solano	3.2	3.7	1.1	2.6
Sonoma	1.8	4.5	1.6	3.0
San Francisco Bay Area	48.9	39.0	40.7	-1.6

Source: California Department of Finance

Between 1997 and 2002 foreign immigration remained near the decade average and accounted for 100% of the region's net migration. Foreign immigration was higher than net migration in San Francisco, San Mateo and Santa Clara.

Domestic migration was negative (-15,300 per year) for the 1990-2002 period as shown on Table 1D. However, domestic migration was close to zero (-1,600 per year) during the 1997-2001 period and was concentrated in the North and East Bay subregions. Santa Clara had negative domestic migration of 12,000 per year.

All of the domestic migration numbers should be considered in relationship to the region's total population – 7 million – and recent annual growth of near 100,000 per year. The net migration numbers are relatively small in relationship to these larger regional trends.

High housing prices are becoming an increasingly important factor in the location of population growth for Bay Area workers. Lower housing prices on the fringes of the region and in adjacent counties have pushed growth to the edge of the region and beyond.

Even in the face of a severe regional recession, housing prices rose for the year ending in August 2003. Resale price gains were modest in both 2002 and 2003 compared to in other regions, but the existence of any price increases at all is a statement about the growing shortage in production of new housing in the nine-county region.

Median Home Price Detached Homes and Condos August 2003					
In Region		**vs 2002**	**Adjacent**		**vs 2002**
Contra Costa County	$388,000	+8.8%	Patterson	$270,000	+19.6%
San Francisco County	$565,000	+2.7%	Modesto	$225,000	+10.8%
Santa Clara County	$565,000	+2.7%	Salinas	$397,000	+23.5%
Solano County	$310,000	+12.9%	Stockton	$235,000	+18.1%
			Tracy	$347,000	+11.0%

Source: California Association of Realtors

A small, but increasing, portion of households that work in the Bay Area are finding residences in adjacent counties. The region's population would be even larger if these households could find housing within the region. However, as shown above, housing price gains in adjacent counties are closing the gap. Housing prices in most adjacent markets increased at double-digit rates during the past year.

The Bay Area's population growth is currently being led by gains in Asian and Hispanic population. Between 2000 and 2002, Asians and Hispanics accounted for 200% of the region's population gain (Table 1B) offset by a large loss in the non Hispanic white population. By 2002 Asians represented 21.2% of Bay Area population – the highest share in the United States outside of Hawaii. In San Francisco County one-third of the population was Asian in 2002.

The region had 1.4 million Hispanic residents in 2002 – 20% of the regional total. Santa Clara County had the largest Hispanic population and the highest Hispanic share (24.8%) among Bay Area counties.

The Bay Area already has a majority of minorities in K-12 enrollment. In the 2002-2003 school year 62.4% of the K-12 enrollment was Hispanic, Asian and Black. In San Francisco County, Asians accounted for just above 50% of the school population.

San Francisco Bay Area K-12 School Enrollment 2002-2003 (Thousands)					
		Percent of Total			
	2002-2003 Enrollment	Hispanic	White Non Hispanic	Black	Asian & Other
Alameda	218.0	25.6%	28.8%	18.6%	26.9%
Contra Costa	164.5	23.2%	49.5%	12.0%	15.3%
Marin	28.6	16.6%	70.3%	3.7%	9.4%
Napa	19.7	39.0%	52.4%	2.0%	6.6%
San Francisco	60.0	21.7%	10.2%	15.2%	52.9%
San Mateo	89.0	32.7%	37.1%	4.5%	25.8%
Santa Clara	250.4	34.2%	31.5%	3.5%	30.9%
Solano	72.8	22.6%	40.5%	20.1%	16.7%
Sonoma	73.0	25.8%	64.1%	2.3%	7.8%
San Francisco Bay Area	976.0	27.6%	37.6%	10.2%	24.4%

Source: California Department of Education

San Diego Region

The San Diego region is expected to add approximately 400,000 residents between 2002 and 2010 to reach a total population of just over 3.3 million.

CCSCE projects that total jobs in San Diego will increase by 24.6% compared to the 11.6% nationwide gain between 2000 and 2010. But projected gains are well below those expected a year ago as the nation's jobless recovery has extended. CCSCE's population projection for 2010 is slightly below last year's projected growth, but San Diego is still expected to grow faster than the state and nation. The projected job gains will put pressure on the county to expand the housing supply to accommodate the projected growth. Land availability is already tight and housing prices and rents are well above the state average.

The region has expanded to the north and east within San Diego County and commuting from the Temecula area in Riverside County is increasing.

Nearly 80% of San Diego Region's growth came from natural increase between 1990 and 2002. However, migration rebounded during the past five years (averaging 26,700 per year) based on strong job growth and is expected to be an important component of future population growth.

San Diego County received 15,900 foreign immigrants per year from 1990 through 2002. Foreign immigration was relatively constant during the decade and should continue near current levels to 2010.

San Diego has historically drawn residents from other states and regions of California. This pattern of domestic migration was interrupted with the early 90s recession. Between 1990 and 1997 domestic migration was negative – averaging -20,500 per year.

However, the 1997-2002 period is probably more typical of future trends. Domestic migration recently turned positive in response to strong job growth – averaging 10,500 per year for the past five years.

Recent Population Growth Trends
San Diego County
1990-2002
(Thousands)

	Natural Increase	Net Migration	Foreign Immigration	Domestic Migration
1990-97	29.9	-4.9	15.6	-20.5
1997-2002	24.3	26.7	16.2	10.5
1990-2002	27.6	8.3	15.9	-7.6

Source: California Department of Finance

Hispanic and Asian residents accounted for nearly 90% of San Diego's population growth between 2000 and 2002 (Table 1B). By 2002, San Diego had an Hispanic population of more than 800,000 (third largest in California) which represented 28.4% of the county total population.

San Diego County already has a majority of minorities in K-12 school enrollment. In the 2002-2003 school year K-12 enrollment was 60.2% Hispanic, Asian and Black students.

San Diego K-12 School Enrollment 1990-2002 (Thousands)				
	1990/91	**2002/03**	**Change**	**% in 2001**
Hispanic	110.7	199.0	88.3	39.8%
White Non Hispanic	206.0	199.0	-7.0	39.8%
Black	31.2	39.3	8.1	7.9%
Asian & Other	45.1	62.5	17.4	12.5%
Total	393.0	499.8	106.8	100.0%

Source: California Department of Education

Sacramento Region

The Sacramento region will add more than 360,000 residents to be California's fifth largest region with nearly 3 million residents in 2010.

Job growth will draw new residents to the region. Growth pressures are pushing housing prices and rents upward though they remain well below the state average. Land availability to accommodate the projected growth is less of a problem in the Sacramento region than in the Bay Area or San Diego.

Migration will be the major component of regional population growth. Migration accounted for approximately 60% of Sacramento regional population growth between 1990 and 2002 – the highest share among California's large regions (Table 1C). The migration share will remain high in the decade ahead as jobs and households are attracted to the lower cost and less crowded environment in the region.

Migration also accounted for more than 70% of the region's growth during the past five years – averaging 33,600 per year.

Recent Population Growth Trends 1997-2002 (Thousands Per Year)				
	Natural Increase	**Net Migration**	**Foreign Immigration**	**Domestic Migration**
El Dorado	0.5	2.5	0.3	2.3
Placer	1.1	7.8	0.3	7.5
Sacramento	9.1	20.6	4.3	16.3
Yolo	1.1	2.7	0.9	1.8
Sacramento Region	11.8	33.6	5.8	27.9

Source: California Department of Finance

Migration continues to be driven by the large differential in housing prices and the region's strong job growth.

The high cost of housing in the coastal markets combined with low levels of production is finally having a significant impact on housing prices in the inland markets. Between August of 2002 and 2003 prices in Sacramento, Riverside, San Bernardino and the Central Valley increased at double-digit rates for the third year in a row.

Foreign immigration is not a major contributor to population growth. In the 1990-2002 period 5,800 foreign immigrants per year located in the region mostly in Sacramento County (Table 1D). Foreign immigration remained near the decade average during the past five years. However, domestic migration increased substantially since 1997. Domestic migration averaged 27,900 between 1997 and 2002, triple the average for 1990-97.

County by County Population Growth
1995-2010

	Average Annual Rate of Growth				
	1995-2002	**2002-10**	**Growth in 2002-2010**	**Pop in 2010 (Thousands)**	**% Growth 2002-2010**
El Dorado	1.9%	2.6%	37.6	202.8	22.7%
Placer	3.6%	2.8%	67.6	338.3	25.0%
Sacramento	2.1%	2.0%	226.6	1,524.2	17.5%
Yolo	2.1%	2.1%	32.7	211.7	18.3%
Sacramento Region	2.3%	2.2%	364.5	2,277.0	19.1%

All counties in the region will grow faster than both the state and nation in the years ahead. Sacramento, like other regions, is experiencing faster growth on the fringes.

El Dorado and Placer are among the state's fastest growing counties in both the 1980s and 1990s and the first decade of the next century. However, more than 60% of the regional growth will occur in Sacramento County. The region will also account for some residential developments in nearby counties – Sutter, Nevada and Yuba.

The Sacramento region is affected by California's changing ethnic composition. The White Non Hispanic population represented about 64% of the regional total in 2000 (Table 1A), but 2/3 of the growth after 2000 has been from minority population groups.

The school enrollment data shows the same trends toward increasing minority population in the Sacramento region. In Sacramento and Yolo Counties the 2002-2003 enrollment was just under 50% for White Non Hispanic students.

Sacramento Region
K-12 School Enrollment
2002-2003
(Thousands)

		Ethnic Distribution			
	2002-2003 Enrollment	Hispanic	White Non Hispanic	Black	Asian & Other
El Dorado	29.1	11.3%	80.0%	0.9%	7.8%
Placer	60.7	11.0%	78.5%	2.2%	8.3%
Sacramento	232.6	20.6%	44.8%	15.6%	19.0%
Yolo	29.5	36.4%	49.5%	3.1%	11.1%
Sacramento Region	351.9	19.5%	54.0%	11.0%	15.6%

Source: California Department of Education

Population Growth in Other Regions

The 38 counties in CCSCE's Rest of State region had 6.2 million residents – about 17.6% of the state's population according to the 2002 DOF population estimates.

In contrast to the Los Angeles, San Francisco and Sacramento regions, the five regions in the Rest of State are not regions in the sense of commuting basins or regional economic units. They are groups of counties with adjacent geographical location in California and roughly similar economic bases. But the linkages among counties are usually limited to one or two nearby counties. For example, in the Sacramento Valley, Shasta's growth is not tied to Butte's activity; in the Coastal region, San Benito and Santa Barbara are totally independent; in the San Joaquin Valley, Kern and San Joaquin counties have different growth determinants.

In addition to the fact that most counties in the Rest of State region grow independently from their neighbors, most counties are relatively small. Of the 38 counties, 23 had populations under 100,000 in 2002 and four had populations between 100,000 and 200,000. Only eleven counties – all except Butte are located in the Coastal and San Joaquin Valley regions – had populations above 200,000.

The best methodology for developing population projections for these counties would be a county by county case study approach. Job trends would be analyzed as in CCSCE's regional projections. Commuting interrelationships would be examined. Information on specific proposed developments would be evaluated.

This approach was not followed in **California County Projections**. The required analysis, roughly 38 case studies, is well beyond the scope of the **California County Projections** project.

CCSCE's approach to projecting population for counties in the five Rest of State regions is as follows:

- The San Joaquin Valley regional population total was projected based on projected job growth.

- The Rest of State region (the remaining 30 counties combined) is projected as one of CCSCE's major economic regions. Job growth is the principal determinant of population growth.

- The four subregions – Sacramento Valley, Coastal, San Joaquin, North Coast and Mountain – are allocated shares of the total population growth based on

    – Recent growth trends
    – CCSCE's judgment

- Counties within each region are allocated shares of regional population growth based on

    – Recent county growth shares
    – Specific new developments like prisons
    – CCSCE's judgment
    – Department of Finance projections

San Joaquin Valley

The San Joaquin Valley is California's third largest region with nearly 3.5 million residents in 2002. The Valley is projected to be California's second fastest growing region in the period to 2010 with population increasing at 2.2% per year.

The Valley is now home to California's tenth largest county – Fresno – which will have nearly one million residents by 2010. Kern, Stanislaus and San Joaquin will each have populations over 500,000. **All counties in the region are projected to grow faster than both the state and nation.**

Merced, San Joaquin, Stanislaus, Madera, and Kern all rank among the ten fastest growing counties. The projected growth in San Joaquin and Stanislaus will be linked to job and housing growth in the Bay Area. The projections for Merced incorporate the impact of the proposed new University of California campus. Kern County will begin to be a commuting area for the Los Angeles Basin by 2010.

Foreign immigration added 18,400 residents per year since 1990 out of a total population gain of 60,700 annually. The largest number of foreign immigrants settled in Fresno County – 5,200 per year. Foreign immigration trends were similar during the past five years.

County by County Population Growth 1995-2010

	Average Annual Rate of Growth				
	1995-2002	**2002-2010**	**Growth in 2002-2010**	**Pop in 2010 (Thousands)**	**% Growth 2002-2010**
Fresno	1.4%	1.7%	122.6	958.0	14.7%
Kern	1.7%	2.4%	145.3	842.4	20.8%
Kings	2.2%	1.9%	22.3	157.0	16.6%
Madera	2.6%	2.4%	27.2	159.0	20.7%
Merced	1.6%	2.8%	54.4	277.1	24.4%
San Joaquin	2.1%	2.4%	128.7	734.4	21.3%
Stanislaus	1.8%	2.2%	88.7	558.9	18.9%
Tulare	1.2%	1.9%	61.0	443.0	16.0%
San Joaquin Valley	1.7%	2.2%	650.5	4,129.9	18.7%

Domestic migration turned positive (9,000 per year) in the San Joaquin Valley between 1997 and 2002, primarily the result of migration from the Bay Area into Stanislaus and San Joaquin.

Recent Population Growth Trends 1997-2002 (Thousands Per Year)				
	Natural Increase	**Net Migration**	**Foreign Immigration**	**Domestic Migration**
Fresno	8.8	3.4	5.6	-2.3
Kern	6.9	5.4	3.3	2.0
Kings	1.4	1.9	0.7	1.2
Madera	1.2	1.7	0.9	0.8
Merced	2.4	1.7	1.7	0.0
San Joaquin	4.9	8.9	3.2	5.7
Stanislaus	3.8	6.3	2.3	4.0
Tulare	4.4	0.5	2.9	-2.4
San Joaquin Valley	33.8	29.8	20.6	9.0

Source: California Department of Finance

The absence of large domestic migration into Fresno and Kern is somewhat surprising in view of the much lower housing prices in the Valley. These trends do confirm the importance of being near job growth centers for sustained population growth.

While there is no direct evidence, it is likely that movements into the Valley from the Bay Area and Southern California continued strong during the latter half of the 1990s. These movements must have been offset by reduced migration from other states and increased out migration of existing residents to be consistent with the overall migration trends reported by the California Department of Finance.

By the 2000 Census, the Valley had more than 1.3 million Hispanic residents representing 39.7% of the region's total population. All Valley counties except Stanislaus had a majority of minority groups as of April 1, 2000. Nearly 80% of the region's population growth between 2000 and 2002 was Hispanic.

Minority group students make up over 65% of the San Joaquin Valley's K-12 school enrollment in the 2002-2003 school year.

San Joaquin Valley
K-12 School Enrollment
2002-2003
(Thousands)

	2002-2003 Enrollment	Percent of Total Hispanic	White Non Hispanic	Black	Asian & Other
Fresno	187.7	52.3%	27.2%	7.1%	13.4%
Kern	154.9	49.8%	37.7%	7.4%	5.2%
Kings	26.4	54.0%	33.1%	6.9%	6.1%
Madera	26.4	58.3%	35.1%	2.7%	3.9%
Merced	53.8	55.8%	28.8%	4.7%	10.8%
San Joaquin	128.4	37.5%	34.3%	9.8%	18.5%
Stanislaus	104.0	42.9%	45.0%	3.9%	8.2%
Tulare	88.3	63.3%	29.1%	2.2%	5.4%
San Joaquin Valley	769.9	49.8%	33.7%	6.3%	10.2%

Source: California Department of Education

HOUSEHOLD GROWTH – THE OUTLOOK TO 2010

HOUSEHOLDS

Summary

California has recorded low household growth and low levels of annual housing construction since 1990. Household growth averaged 116,700 per year between 1990 and 2003, after averaging 175,000 per year in the 1980s.

The low level of housing production has become one of the state's most serious challenges — both in terms of providing enough housing to keep pace with job growth and in terms of housing price levels that are an impediment to residents and new businesses alike.

There is some good news to report in 2003. Residential permit levels should exceed 180,000 — the largest number since 1989. In addition, developers and communities are finding ways to convert existing land to housing from nonresidential uses. Market factors and the growing awareness of the need for more housing throughout California are leading many communities to approve innovative approaches for infill development.

CCSCE projects that household growth will average between 150,600 and 223,400 per year to 2010 and CCSCE has prepared a midrange projection of 186,300 additional households per year.

Future job growth and changes in California's age structure support the projection of a rising level of household growth. Job growth in California should reach 2.9 million between 2000 and 2010 — up from 2.1 million in the 1990s. The share of the population in household forming age groups will increase to 2010 in contrast to the rising share of children in the population in the 1990s. And the aging of the population will begin an era of falling household size and changing demand for housing in terms of home size and location.

Affordability remains a serious threat to household growth in California. Rapidly rising home prices have pushed affordability to the lowest levels since right before the early 90s housing market crash. For the first time, median resale home prices in California exceeded $400,000 in August 2003. This trend shows that homes are still in strong demand as price increases in many markets were above 20% during the past year.

But, at the same time, the percent of Californians able to afford the median-priced home fell to 23% compared to the 56% national average.

Housing Construction Surges

Housing permit levels have risen steadily since 1995 and should reach 180,000 in 2003 — the highest level since 1989. Permit levels are up strongly in most regional markets in California as shown in the following pages.

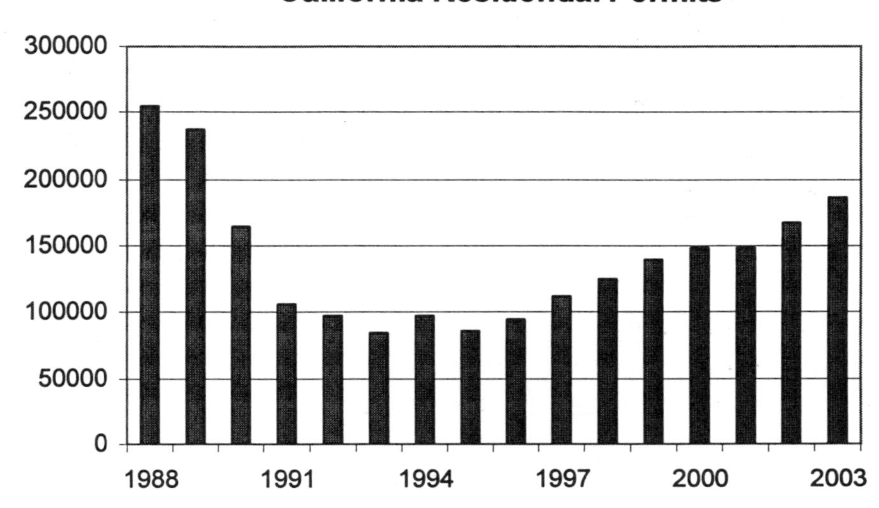

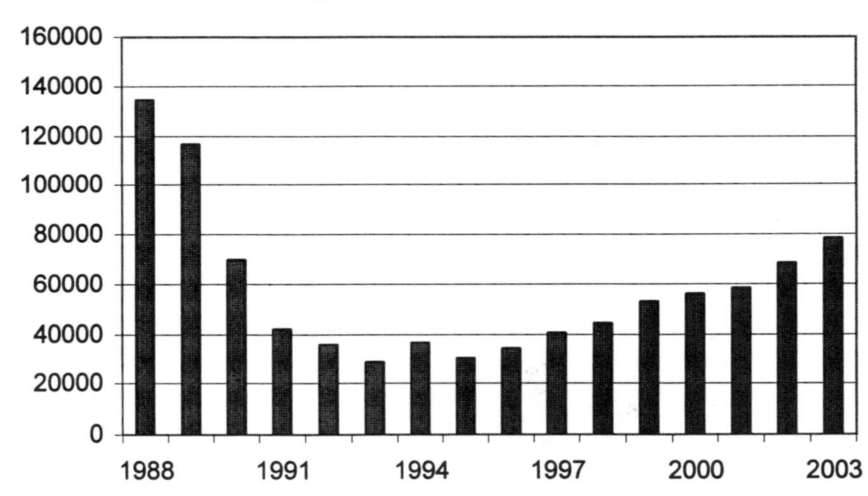

Strong demand is pushing both prices and construction levels higher. Last year brought double–digit price gains throughout California except in the recession-slowed Bay Area market. As a result, prices in Orange and San Diego are approaching Bay Area levels and prices throughout Southern California have reached record highs in each of the past several months.

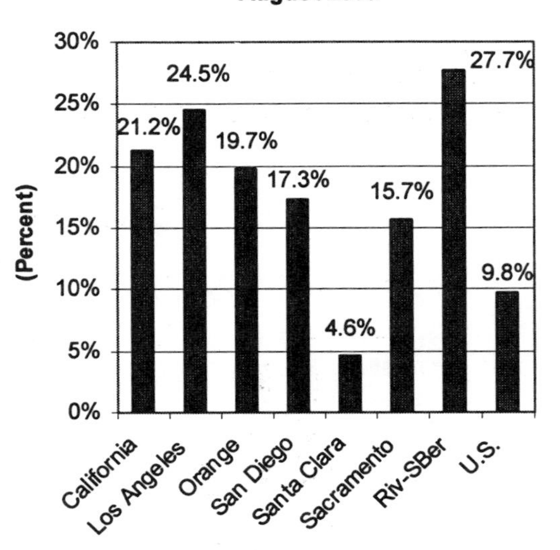

Yet, so far the increased levels of housing construction have not stopped the rapid increase in home prices. Only in the Bay Area, which has lost more than 300,000 jobs, have price increases slowed or stopped.

In most markets throughout California, prices and affordability compare unfavorably with the nation and the gap is growing. For example, prices and affordability in the Sacramento Region and Inland Empire are now significantly worse than the national average after being markets that compared favorably with other regions for many years.

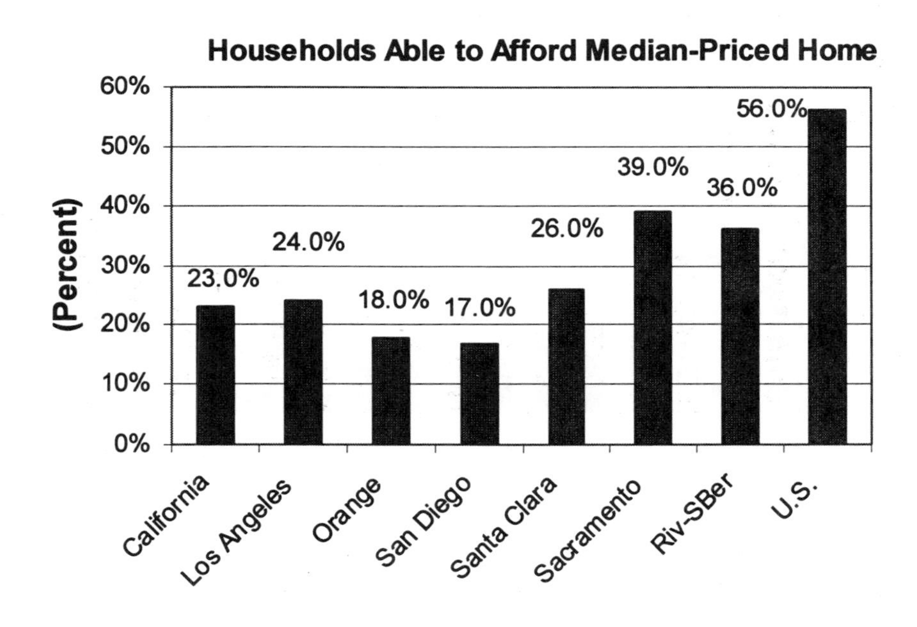

Some communities believe they do not have enough land for much additional housing. However, the "not enough land" argument often misses the point. While some of the state's new housing will be built on vacant land or in new communities, **much of the future housing need will be developed on land that is already in use.** For example, in the Los Angeles Basin, Dowell Myers of USC estimates that from 30% to 50% of the demand for new housing will be for smaller units in dense, walkable communities.

One of the newer developments in 2003 is the growing number of instances where existing land is being rezoned either to allow housing or to allow more housing. The collapse in office construction has led some landowners to convert nonresidential uses to housing.

Hotel space in Southern California is being converted to housing. Loft housing is replacing other uses in downtown Los Angeles. Downtown Los Angeles and Pasadena are in the midst of building booms and apartments are, once again, part of the mix of new housing.

High-rise housing developments are going up in San Francisco, San Diego and San Jose. A medical facility will be replaced with housing in Orange County. An empty industrial zone is being considered for housing in the San Fernando Valley.

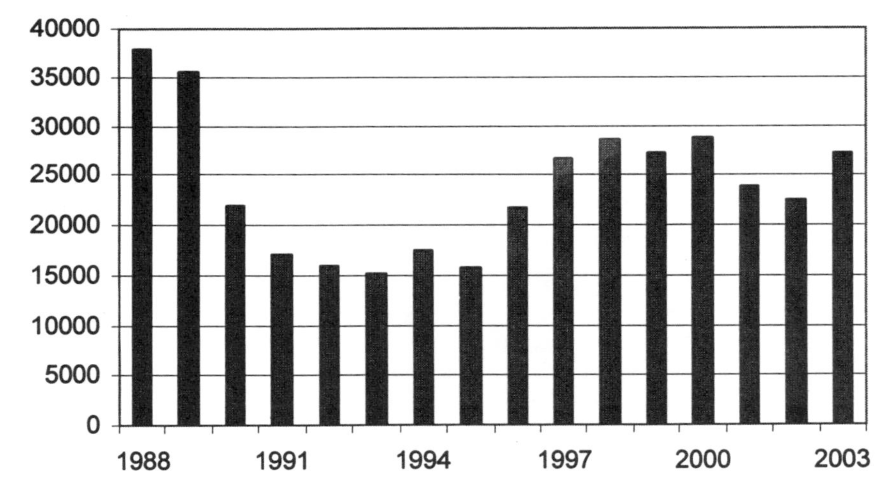

San Diego Residential Permits

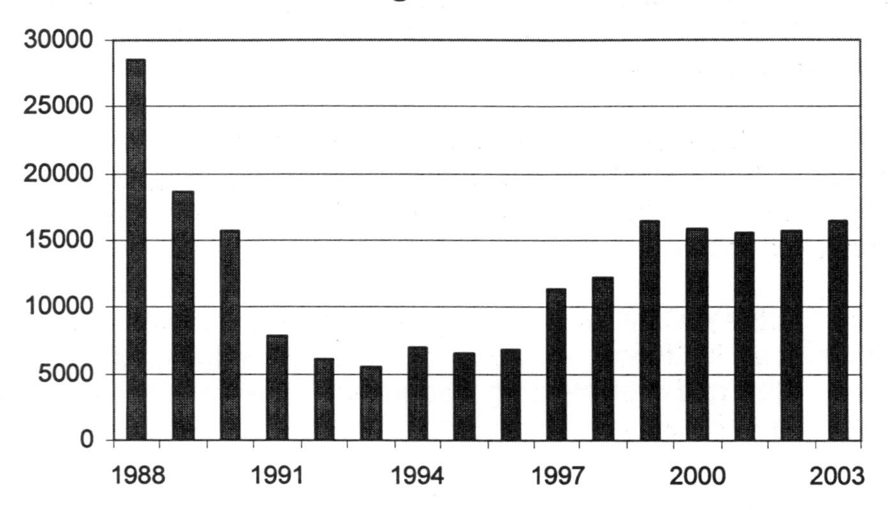

Housing permit levels for 2003 will be close to the levels needed to match CCSCE's midway projection series as shown on Table 2. If permit levels can be increased further, particularly for apartments and moderate-priced ownership housing, household growth might begin to edge up toward the level suggested by demographic trends. Success in raising housing production would be helpful for the state's "business climate" as well as providing some relief from the growing gap between housing prices in California and elsewhere.

Housing Permits and Household Growth
(Thousands)

Region	Estimated Permits 2003	Average Household Growth (Midway Projection) Jan. 1,2003-July 1,2010
Los Angeles Basin	78.5	75.4
San Francisco Bay Area	27.1	33.2
San Diego	17.3	17.2
Sacramento	24.1	16.9
San Joaquin Valley	28.2	25.2
California	**186.8**	**186.3**

Source: CCSCE

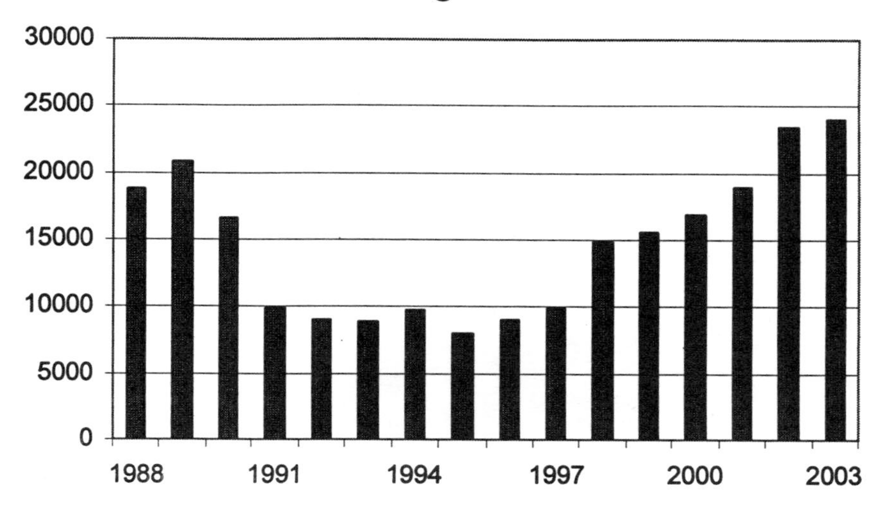
Sacramento Region Residential Permits
30000
25000
20000
15000
10000
5000
0
1988
1991
1994
1997
2000
2003

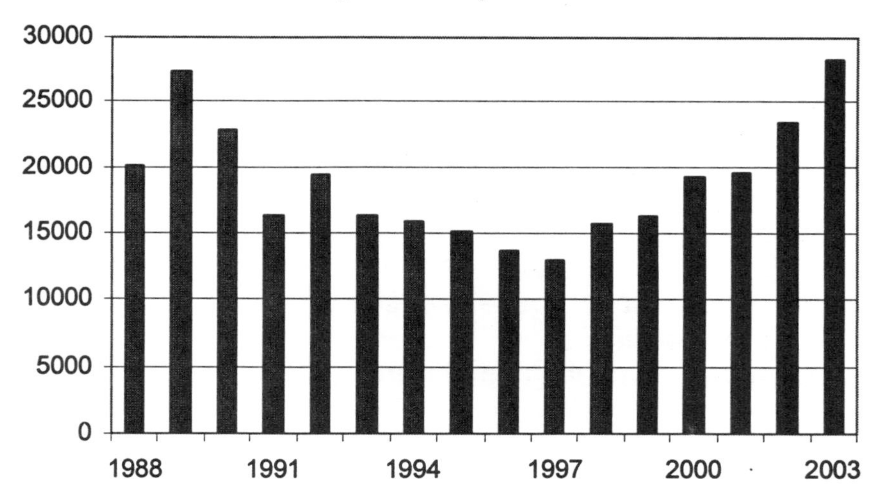
San Joaquin Valley Residential Permits
30000
25000
20000
15000
10000
5000
0
1988
1991
1994
1997
2000
2003

Housing Production and Population Growth in the 1990s

Household growth kept pace with population growth in many areas of the state between 1990 and 2003. The number of persons per household rose slightly from 2.79 in 1990 to 2.93 in 2003.

California and Economic Regions
Household and Population Growth
1990-2003
(Thousands)

	Households		HH	Pop in HH	Persons Per HH		
	1990	2003	Growth	Growth	1990	1990-2003	2003
Los Angeles Basin	4,933.6	5,521.1	587.5	2,759.0	2.91	4.70	3.10
San Francisco Bay Area	2,245.9	2,532.6	286.7	981.5	2.61	3.42	2.71
San Diego Region	887.4	1,029.2	141.8	466.5	2.69	3.29	2.78
Sacramento Region	556.5	714.1	157.6	446.1	2.60	2.83	2.65
Sacramento Valley Region	203.7	235.0	31.3	88.2	2.61	2.82	2.63
Coastal Region	418.0	470.8	52.8	184.1	2.75	3.49	2.83
San Joaquin Valley	896.6	1,082.6	186.0	732.0	2.98	3.94	3.14
North Coast Region	105.6	120.1	14.5	29.4	2.50	2.03	2.45
Mountain Region	133.6	161.1	27.5	53.5	2.48	1.95	2.39
CALIFORNIA	**10,380.9**	**11,866.8**	**1,485.7**	**5,740.2**	**2.79**	**3.86**	**2.93**

Source: 1990 and 2000 Census

The estimates of persons per household shown above and throughout this section are based on estimates of household population (excluding group quarters' population) divided by the number of households.

The persons per household trends in the 1990s are compatible with two other demographic trends: 1) the rising share of children in the population and 2) the increase in the percentage of Hispanic residents in California. The under 18 population increased by 19.3% compared to just 11.9% for the 18 and older population groups. As a result, a substantial proportion of the increase in persons per household was accounted for by children.

California
Persons Per Household
1990 and 2000

	1990	**2000**
Under 18	.74	.80
18 and older	2.05	2.07
Total Households	2.79	2.87
Hispanic	4.19	4.06
Non-Hispanic White	2.43	2.38
Black	2.88	2.71
Asian	3.58	3.70
Two or more Races		3.77

Source: 1990 and 2000 Census

Three-quarters of the statewide gain in persons per household between 1990 and 2000, was accounted for by the increase from .74 to .80 in the number of children per household. The number of adults per household remained nearly constant.

The regions with the highest number of new residents per household were the regions with the largest shares of Hispanic and Asian population growth. For example, the Los Angeles Basin added 1 household for every 4.70 added residents between 1990 and 2003. The average Hispanic household size statewide is 4.06 so the Basin household growth was low, but not extremely low, compared to the demographic trends.

Most regions had large increases in persons per household in the 90s. For example, the Bay Area added just 1 household per 3.42 residents, well below the 2003 average household size of 2.71. A similar trend occurred in the San Joaquin Valley.

However, as discussed on the following page, demographic factors suggest the possibility of a **decline** in average household size in the current decade.

Household Growth Should Increase Substantially To 2010

Four factors should push future household growth well above the 112,000 annual gains of the 1990s:

1) Job growth will be higher
2) Population growth will be higher
3) Age trends favor increased household formation
4) More communities are beginning to allow and plan for infill housing

Job and Population Growth

CCSCE projects job growth of 2.9 million between 2000 and 2010. The projected growth compares with the 2.1 million jobs gain of the 1990s.

CCSCE projects population growth of 5.7 million residents between 2000 and 2010 – 40% higher than the 4.1 million growth of the 1990s. The annual gains since 2000 are over 600,000 per year but will taper off slightly between 2003 and 2010.

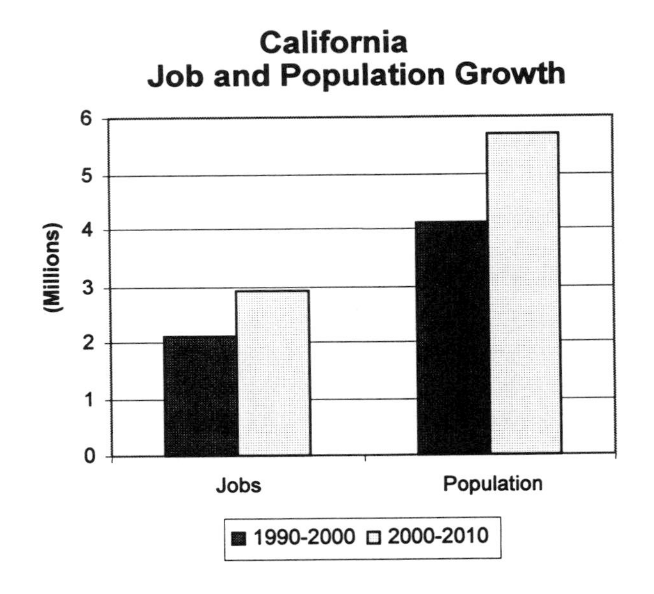

Age Trends

The number of residents under 20 rose as a share of California's population in the 1990s – from 29.1% in 1990 to 30.1% in 2000. As a result, the adult population, which is the household forming group, grew more slowly than average which was a negative factor for household formation.

Between 2000 and 2010 the 20 and older population will grow more rapidly than the 0-19 age group. By 2010 the 0-19 age group will account for 28.3% of California's population – down from 30.1% in 2000. The above average growth of the adult population will be a positive factor in pushing household growth higher.

There are significant changes in the age distribution of population growth for the adult population.

- There will be a gain of 930,000 in the 20-34 age group. Between 1990 and 2000 population in this age group, where people often get their first home or apartment, fell by more than 500,000.
- There will be almost no change in the 35-44 age group, reversing a gain of more than 700,000 between 1990 and 2000.
- There will be a substantial increase in growth of California's population ages 55-64 and 65+, with a gain of 2.5 million residents by 2010. This trend is important because these groups have the highest housing demand per 1,000 people – the result of divorces, separations and deaths. These age groups also have the lowest average household size because they have few children remaining in the household.

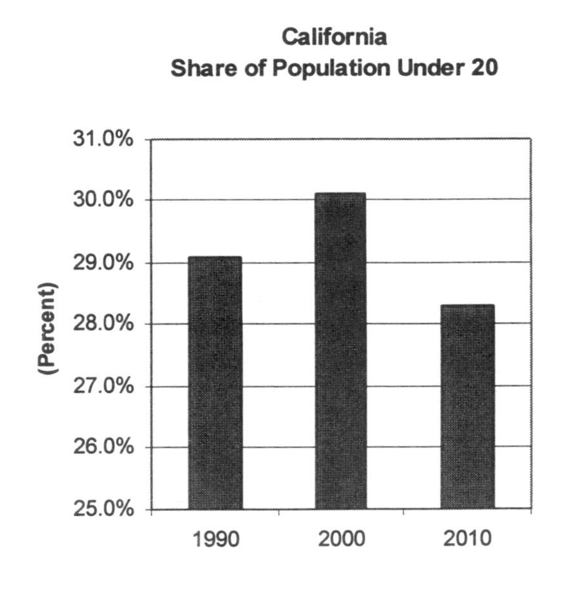

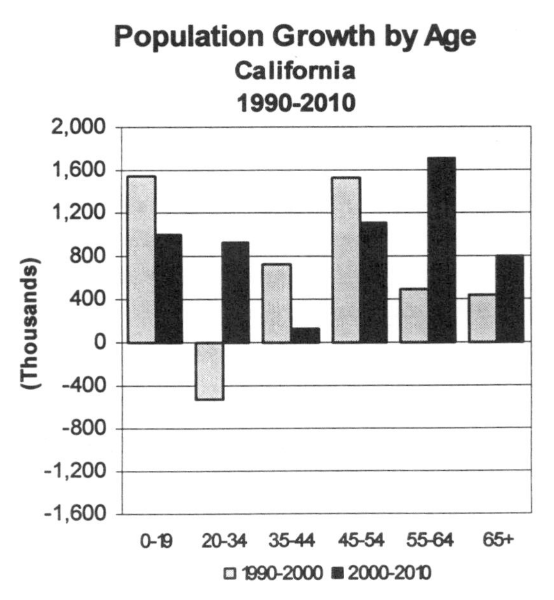

State Household Projections to 2010

CCSCE has prepared three sets of household projections based on different assumptions about household formation rates. The middle set, shown on Table 2, is used in projecting household income later in the report.

The demographic trend projections, shown on Table 2A, assume that the household formation rates by age and ethnic group reported in the 2000 Census remain constant to 2010. As a result, the major forces affecting household growth are the projected changes in total population and population by age and ethnic group.

The demographic trend projections result in the highest rate of household growth – 223,400 per year between 2003 and 2010. Meeting these projections will require a substantial increase in the level of annual housing construction from the 2003 production level of 185,000 units per year.

CCSCE has also prepared a lower set of household growth projections presented on Table 2A. In the current trend projections, CCSCE assumes that the decline in household formation rates in the early 1990s will be continued. This alternative is possible if 1) California's housing supply disincentives are not reduced, 2) income gains do not materialize as expected or 3) the cultural patterns of multi-family households for immigrants remain stronger for recent immigrants than for previous generations despite rapid gains in income.

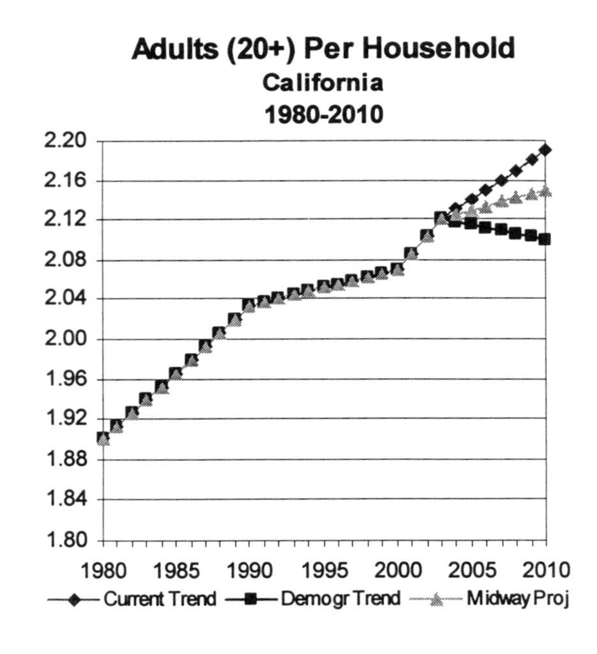

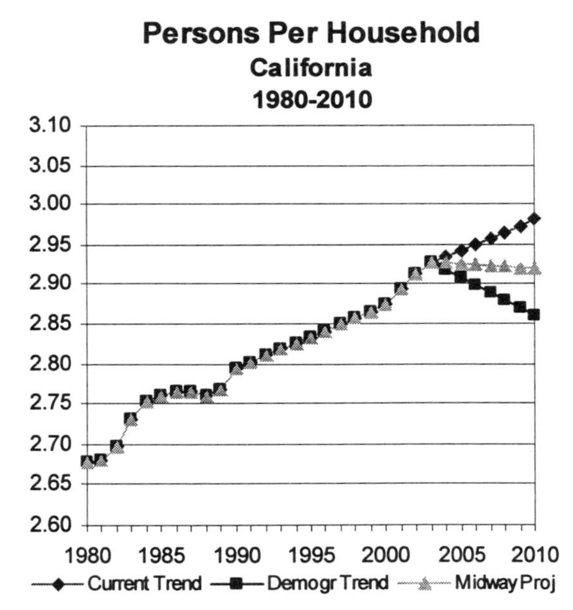

The current trend assumptions result in 545,400 fewer households being formed in California between 2003 and 2010 compared to the high alternative. Household growth will equal near 1 million or roughly 150,000 per year between 2003 and 2010.

Finally, CCSCE has a midway projection household growth alternative which is roughly midway between the demographic trends and current trends projections.

California
Alternative Household Projections
1990-2010
(Thousands)

				Average Annual Growth	
Households	1990 Census	2003 Census Jan 1	2010 July	1990-2003	2003-2010
Demographic Trend	10,380.9	11,866.8	13,542.0	116.5	223.4
Current Trend			12,996.6		150.6
Midway Projection			13,263.7		186.3

The midway projection alternative will result in 13.3 million households in 2010. Household growth would average over 185,000 per year between 2003 and 2010.

All three alternatives project a higher level of household formation than has been recorded since 1990. The housing permit levels in 2003 match the annual projected household growth in the midway alternative – the first year this has been true in more than a decade.

As mentioned earlier, the desire of some landowners to build housing on land previously considered for nonresidential uses plus the increasing desire of many cities to expand infill housing opportunities give hope that even higher levels of housing production may be seen by 2010.

Average household size would begin to turn down in the midway alternative as shown on the previous page. The number of children per household will decline slightly and the number of older (and smaller) households will increase. Household size only continues to increase under the alternative where household growth averages just 150,000 per year.

County Household Projections – 2003-2010

County by county household projections for CCSCE's midway alternative are presented on Table 2. The statewide rate of household growth is 1.5% a year for 2003-2010 – far higher than the 1.1% annual rate since 1990.

County by county projections for CCSCE's current trends and demographic trends alternative are shown on Table 2A. Annual household growth rates are 1.2% and 1.8% for the state as a whole.

The county household projections were developed based on the statewide projections described above and trends in relative household size (compared to the state average) for each county.

In general the household projection trends follow the same pattern as the population projections.

Placer County had the largest household growth since 1990 among the larger counties with a gain of 4.2% annually. Next came Riverside and El Dorado. All four counties in the Sacramento region were among the ten fastest growing larger counties.

Imperial, Riverside, Merced, Placer and El Dorado top the list of fastest growing largest counties to 2010.

Ten Fastest Growing Larger Counties 1990-2010

1990-2003	Average Annual Growth Rate	Midway Alt. 2003-2010	Average Annual Growth Rate
Placer	4.2%	Imperial	3.2%
Riverside	2.5%	Riverside	2.8%
El Dorado	2.3%	Merced	2.8%
Imperial	2.3%	Placer	2.8%
Yolo	1.7%	El Dorado	2.7%
Stanislaus	1.6%	Kern	2.4%
San Joaquin	1.6%	San Luis Obispo	2.4%
Sacramento	1.6%	San Joaquin	2.3%
Merced	1.5%	Stanislaus	2.2%
San Luis Obispo	1.5%	Solano	2.2%
CALIFORNIA	1.0%	**CALIFORNIA**	1.7%

San Benito was the fastest growing smaller county between 1990 and 2003 with average annual household growth of 3.1%. Next came Calaveras, Mono and Madera. San Benito, Calaveras and Madera are projected to be the fastest growing smaller counties to 2010 as shown below.

Ten Fastest Growing Smaller Counties 1990-2010

1990-2003	Average Annual Growth Rate	Midway Alt. 2003-2010	Average Annual Growth Rate
San Benito	3.1%	San Benito	4.2%
Calaveras	2.6%	Calaveras	2.5%
Mono	2.4%	Madera	2.5%
Madera	2.3%	Tehama	2.5%
Amador	1.9%	Lake	2.5%
Nevada	1.8%	Alpine	2.3%
Mariposa	1.8%	Colusa	2.3%
Kings	1.7%	Mariposa	2.2%
Sutter	1.6%	Nevada	2.2%
Tuolumne	1.4%	Lassen	2.2%
CALIFORNIA	1.0%	**CALIFORNIA**	1.7%

Table 2
California, Economic, Regions, and Counties
HOUSEHOLDS AND MIDWAY PROJECTIONS
1990 – 2010
(Thousands)

	1990	2003	2010	Average Annual Growth Rate	
				1990-2003	2003-2010
Imperial	32.8	41.3	52.2	1.8%	3.2%
Los Angeles	2,989.5	3,170.7	3,379.2	0.5%	0.9%
Orange	827.1	959.4	1,062.0	1.2%	1.4%
Riverside	402.1	549.3	677.4	2.5%	2.8%
San Bernardino	464.7	547.3	630.5	1.3%	1.9%
Ventura	217.3	253.1	285.1	1.2%	1.6%
Los Angeles Basin	4,933.6	5,521.1	6,086.3	0.9%	1.3%
Alameda	479.5	534.4	583.2	0.9%	1.2%
Contra Costa	300.3	355.7	389.7	1.3%	1.2%
Marin	95.0	102.0	109.2	0.6%	0.9%
Napa	41.3	47.2	51.0	1.1%	1.0%
San Francisco	305.6	338.9	361.2	0.8%	0.9%
San Mateo	241.9	257.8	280.5	0.5%	1.1%
Santa Clara	520.2	582.3	644.8	0.9%	1.4%
Solano	113.1	136.2	159.9	1.5%	2.2%
Sonoma	149.0	178.1	201.8	1.4%	1.7%
San Francisco Bay Area	2,245.9	2,532.6	2,781.3	0.9%	1.3%
San Diego	887.4	1,029.2	1,157.9	1.2%	1.6%
San Diego Region	887.4	1,029.2	1,157.9	1.2%	1.6%
El Dorado	46.8	62.4	76.2	2.3%	2.7%
Placer	64.1	108.2	132.8	4.2%	2.8%
Sacramento	394.5	480.5	558.2	1.6%	2.0%
Yolo	51.0	63.0	73.8	1.7%	2.1%
Sacramento Region	556.5	714.1	841.1	2.0%	2.2%
Butte	71.7	82.5	94.1	1.1%	1.8%
Colusa	5.6	6.2	7.4	0.8%	2.3%
Glenn	8.8	9.3	10.4	0.4%	1.5%
Shasta	56.0	66.1	73.0	1.3%	1.3%
Sutter	23.1	28.2	31.8	1.6%	1.6%
Tehama	18.7	21.7	26.0	1.2%	2.5%
Yuba	19.8	21.0	23.5	0.5%	1.5%
Sacramento Valley Region	203.7	235.0	266.3	1.1%	1.7%

	1990	2003	2010	Average Annual Growth Rate 1990-2003	2003-2010
Monterey	113.0	124.9	144.1	0.8%	1.9%
San Benito	11.4	16.8	23.0	3.1%	4.2%
San Luis Obispo	80.3	97.3	116.2	1.5%	2.4%
Santa Barbara	129.8	139.4	155.6	0.6%	1.5%
Santa Cruz	83.6	92.4	104.6	0.8%	1.7%
Coastal Region	418.0	470.8	543.5	0.9%	1.9%
Fresno	220.9	261.6	298.8	1.3%	1.8%
Kern	181.5	218.4	261.6	1.5%	2.4%
Kings	29.1	35.9	41.0	1.7%	1.8%
Madera	28.4	38.1	45.9	2.3%	2.5%
Merced	55.3	67.1	82.5	1.5%	2.8%
San Joaquin	158.2	193.5	229.9	1.6%	2.3%
Stanislaus	125.4	153.4	180.3	1.6%	2.2%
Tulare	97.9	114.6	131.7	1.2%	1.9%
San Joaquin Valley	896.6	1,082.6	1,271.6	1.5%	2.2%
Del Norte	8.0	9.3	10.0	1.2%	0.9%
Humboldt	46.4	52.3	54.6	0.9%	0.6%
Lake	20.8	24.3	29.2	1.2%	2.5%
Mendocino	30.4	34.1	37.7	0.9%	1.3%
North Coast Region	105.6	120.1	131.5	1.0%	1.2%
Alpine	0.5	0.5	0.6	1.0%	2.3%
Amador	10.5	13.4	14.5	1.9%	1.1%
Calaveras	12.6	17.6	21.3	2.6%	2.5%
Inyo	7.6	7.8	8.5	0.2%	1.2%
Lassen	8.5	9.9	11.6	1.1%	2.2%
Mariposa	5.6	7.0	8.3	1.8%	2.2%
Modoc	3.7	3.8	4.3	0.3%	1.4%
Mono	4.0	5.4	6.2	2.4%	1.9%
Nevada	30.8	38.6	45.5	1.8%	2.2%
Plumas	8.1	9.4	10.1	1.1%	1.0%
Sierra	1.3	1.5	1.6	1.1%	0.5%
Siskiyou	17.3	19.0	21.2	0.7%	1.5%
Trinity	5.2	5.7	6.0	0.7%	0.8%
Tuolumne	18.0	21.5	24.6	1.4%	1.8%
Mountain Region	133.6	161.1	184.2	1.5%	1.8%
California	10,380.9	11,866.8	13,263.7	1.1%	1.5%

Source: 1990 – Census Bureau; 2003 – DOF; 2010 - CCSCE

Table 2A
California, Economic Regions and Counties
CURRENT TREND AND DEMOGRAPHIC HOUSEHOLD PROJECTIONS
1990 – 2010
(Thousands)

		Current Trend	Demogr. Projection	Current Trend	Demogr. Projection
	2003	2010	2010	2003-2010	2003-2010
Imperial	41.3	51.1	53.3	2.9%	3.4%
Los Angeles	3,170.7	3,311.2	3,450.1	0.6%	1.1%
Orange	959.4	1,040.6	1,084.3	1.1%	1.6%
Riverside	549.3	663.7	691.6	2.6%	3.1%
San Bernardino	547.3	617.8	643.7	1.6%	2.2%
Ventura	253.1	279.3	291.1	1.3%	1.9%
Los Angeles Basin	5,521.1	5,963.8	6,214.0	1.0%	1.6%
Alameda	534.4	571.5	595.5	0.9%	1.5%
Contra Costa	355.7	381.8	397.9	1.0%	1.5%
Marin	102.0	107.0	111.5	0.6%	1.2%
Napa	47.2	50.0	52.1	0.8%	1.3%
San Francisco	338.9	353.9	368.7	0.6%	1.1%
San Mateo	257.8	274.8	286.3	0.9%	1.4%
Santa Clara	582.3	631.8	658.4	1.1%	1.7%
Solano	136.2	156.6	163.2	1.9%	2.4%
Sonoma	178.1	197.7	206.0	1.4%	2.0%
San Francisco Bay Area	2,532.6	2,725.3	2,839.6	1.0%	1.5%
San Diego	1,029.2	1,134.6	1,182.2	1.3%	1.9%
San Diego Region	1,029.2	1,134.6	1,182.2	1.3%	1.9%
El Dorado	62.4	74.7	77.8	2.4%	3.0%
Placer	108.2	130.2	135.6	2.5%	3.1%
Sacramento	480.5	547.0	569.9	1.7%	2.3%
Yolo	63.0	72.3	75.3	1.9%	2.4%
Sacramento Region	714.1	824.1	858.7	1.9%	2.5%
Butte	82.5	92.2	96.1	1.5%	2.1%
Colusa	6.2	7.2	7.5	2.0%	2.6%
Glenn	9.3	10.2	10.7	1.3%	1.8%
Shasta	66.1	71.6	74.6	1.1%	1.6%
Sutter	28.2	31.1	32.4	1.3%	1.9%
Tehama	21.7	25.5	26.6	2.2%	2.8%
Yuba	21.0	23.0	24.0	1.2%	1.8%
Sacramento Valley Region	235.0	260.9	271.9	1.4%	2.0%

		Current Trend	Demogr. Projection	Current Trend	Demogr. Projection
	2003	2010	2010	2003-2010	2003-2010
Monterey	124.9	141.2	147.1	1.6%	2.2%
San Benito	16.8	22.5	23.5	4.0%	4.5%
San Luis Obispo	97.3	113.9	118.7	2.1%	2.7%
Santa Barbara	139.4	152.5	158.9	1.2%	1.8%
Santa Cruz	92.4	102.5	106.8	1.4%	1.9%
Coastal Region	470.8	532.5	554.9	1.7%	2.2%
Fresno	261.6	292.8	305.0	1.5%	2.1%
Kern	218.4	256.4	267.1	2.2%	2.7%
Kings	35.9	40.2	41.9	1.5%	2.1%
Madera	38.1	44.9	46.8	2.2%	2.8%
Merced	67.1	80.8	84.2	2.5%	3.1%
San Joaquin	193.5	225.3	234.7	2.0%	2.6%
Stanislaus	153.4	176.7	184.1	1.9%	2.5%
Tulare	114.6	129.0	134.4	1.6%	2.1%
San Joaquin Valley	1,082.6	1,246.0	1,298.3	1.9%	2.5%
Del Norte	9.3	9.8	10.2	0.6%	1.2%
Humboldt	52.3	53.5	55.7	0.3%	0.9%
Lake	24.3	28.6	29.9	2.2%	2.8%
Mendocino	34.1	36.9	38.5	1.1%	1.6%
North Coast Region	120.1	128.8	134.2	0.9%	1.5%
Alpine	0.5	0.6	0.6	2.0%	2.6%
Amador	13.4	14.2	14.8	0.8%	1.3%
Calaveras	17.6	20.8	21.7	2.3%	2.8%
Inyo	7.8	8.3	8.7	0.9%	1.5%
Lassen	9.9	11.4	11.9	1.9%	2.5%
Mariposa	7.0	8.1	8.4	1.9%	2.5%
Modoc	3.8	4.2	4.4	1.1%	1.7%
Mono	5.4	6.1	6.3	1.6%	2.2%
Nevada	38.6	44.6	46.4	1.9%	2.5%
Plumas	9.4	9.9	10.3	0.7%	1.3%
Sierra	1.5	1.6	1.6	0.3%	0.8%
Siskiyou	19.0	20.7	21.6	1.2%	1.8%
Trinity	5.7	5.9	6.1	0.5%	1.0%
Tuolumne	21.5	24.1	25.1	1.5%	2.1%
Mountain Region	161.1	180.5	188.1	1.5%	2.1%
California	**11,866.8**	**12,996.6**	**13,542.0**	**1.2%**	**1.8%**

Source: 2003 – DOF; 2010 – CCSCE

WEALTH BY COUNTY – THE OUTLOOK TO 2010

PER CAPITA PERSONAL INCOME

Summary

California has a long history of above-average wage levels leading to per capita and average household income levels higher than the national average.

California's relative standing fell in the early 90s led by the loss of high wage aerospace and construction jobs. In the mid 90s, average wage and income levels surged led by the explosion of high tech jobs. Between 2000 and 2002, California's relative wage and income levels fell as shown below, but they remained well above the national average.

In the past few years, California has been two states with regard to wages and income levels as the Bay Area first outpaced other regions and then, after 2000, accounted for the entire slowdown in wage and income levels in California. California, outside the Bay Area, has kept pace with national wage and income growth during the past three years.

Bay Area counties still lead the state and nation as the highest-income region, but the gap has narrowed since 2000 and will narrow again in 2003.

High productivity growth rates will lead to strong gains in real wages and income beginning in 2004. California will participate in these real income gains.

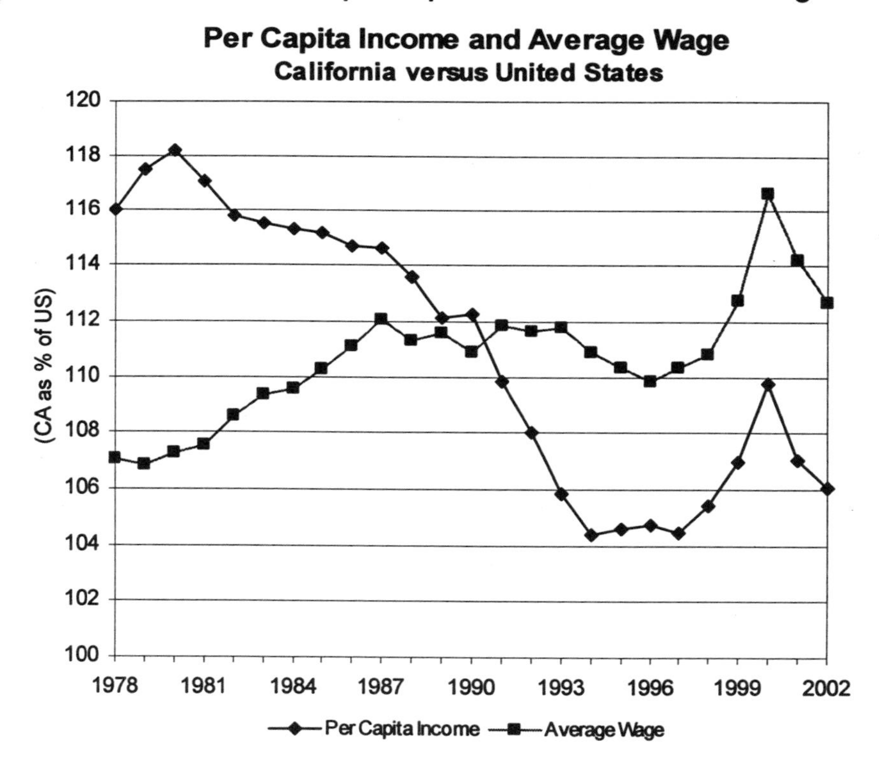

State Per Capita Income

California was 9th among states in per capita income in 1990 with income levels 12% above the national average. After the protracted early 90s recession, state per capita income fell to just 4% above the national average and California dropped to 16th among all states.

Wage levels surged in 1999 and 2000 and California per capita income rose to 10% above the national average as the state ranked 9th in per capita income-the same as in 1990. After 2000, wage levels dropped throughout the Bay Area, which kept state wage and income growth levels low. As a result, per capita income in California increased by just 2.2% between 2000 and 2002 compared to the 5.0% nationwide increase. In 2002, California ranked 11th among all states in per capita income.

Per Capita Income
Top Ten States in 2002

	1990	2000	2002	Percent Change 2000-2002
Connecticut	$26,736	$40,702	$42,706	4.9%
District of Columbia	26,627	38,838	42,120	8.4%
New Jersey	24,766	37,118	39,453	6.3%
Massachusetts	23,223	37,704	39,244	4.1%
Maryland	23,023	33,482	36,298	8.4%
New York	23,315	34,689	36,043	3.9%
New Hampshire	20,713	33,169	34,334	3.5%
Minnesota	20,000	31,935	34,071	6.7%
Illinois	20,756	31,856	33,404	4.9%
Colorado	19,703	32,434	33,276	2.6%
California	**21,978**	**32,111**	**32,831**	**2.2%**
United States	**$19,584**	**$29,469**	**$30,941**	**5.0%**

California Wages Remain High

Average wage levels in California remained 10% above the national average throughout the 1990s. California was the sixth highest ranking state measured by average wages in 2000 – up from 7th in 1990.

Average Annual Pay			
	2000	**2002**	**Percent Change 2000-2002**
District of Columbia	$52,965	$57,907	9.3%
Connecticut	$45,486	$46,881	3.1%
New York	$45,358	$46,132	1.7%
New Jersey	$43,676	$45,190	3.5%
Massachusetts	$44,168	$44,955	1.7%
California	**$41,207**	**$41,408**	**0.5%**
Illinois	$38,045	$39,675	4.3%
Delaware	$36,535	$39,669	8.6%
United States	**$35,320**	**$36,744**	**4.0%**

Wage growth stalled in California after 2000. Average wage levels increased by just 0.5% between 2000 and 2002 compared to the 4.0% nationwide gain. California retained the 6th highest wage levels among all states but lost ground to most states after 2000.

Wage levels dropped substantially in two counties — San Mateo and Santa Clara — as high-wage jobs were lost and stock option income levels plunged. Wage growth was slow in San Francisco and Sonoma as well as shown on Table 3B.

However, outside of these counties, wage growth in California kept pace with or outpaced nationwide wage gains. For example, between 2000 and 2002, wage gains were strong in many San Joaquin Valley counties. Since wage data is reported at the place of employment, these wage gains do **not** reflect commuting patterns.

Wage gains in Los Angeles Basin counties also outpaced nationwide wage growth, particularly in Riverside and San Bernardino.

CCSCE used the 2002 wage data to develop unofficial estimates of county per capita income for 2002 shown on Table 3.

Recent County Income Trends

The most recent U.S. Department of Commerce (www.bea.gov) estimates of personal income for counties were published in May 2003 including estimates through 2001. CCSCE's summary of 1995-2001 per capita income trends by county is presented in Table 3A. Per capita income is calculated by dividing total personal income for each year by the July 1 estimate of total population published by the California Department of Finance.

Bay Area Leads the Way

Bay Area counties have posted the largest gains in per capita income since 1995. The Bay Area had the highest regional per capita income in 1995 and the region's advantage has grown since then fueled by California's highest wage gains and, until 2001, large stock option income growth.

The Bay Area led the state in per capita income in 2001 ($45,890), per capita income growth between 1995 and 2001 (46.7%), and per capita income growth adjusted for inflation – (23.3%).

In 2001, and again in 2002, the Bay Area gave back some of the region's recent income gains. Between 2000 and 2001, Bay Area per capita income **fell** by 3.3% while per capita income in the rest of California **increased** by 2.4%. Still, Bay Area per capita income remains the highest in the state and nation.

For the 1995-2001 period as a whole, real per capita income rose by 23.3% in the Bay area, by 9.7% outside the Bay Area and by 13.4% for the state.

Per Capita Income by Economic Region
1995-2001

			Percent Change		
			1995-2001		2000-2001
	1995	2001	(in 01$)	(in Curr$)	(in Curr$)
San Francisco Bay Area	$31,279	$45,890	23.3%	46.7%	-3.3%
San Diego	23,929	33,742	19.5%	41.0%	2.7%
Mountain Region	18,757	24,844	12.2%	32.5%	3.5%
Coastal Region	24,153	31,590	10.8%	30.8%	0.5%
North Coast Region	18,336	23,811	10.1%	29.9%	2.4%
Sacramento Region	23,853	30,712	9.1%	28.8%	2.3%
Los Angeles Basin	23,438	30,158	9.0%	28.7%	2.7%
Sacramento Valley Region	18,110	22,743	6.4%	25.6%	1.4%
San Joaquin Valley	17,622	21,317	2.5%	21.0%	1.8%
California	24,328	32,563	13.4%	33.8%	0.7%
California Except Bay Area	$22,590	$29,244	9.7%	29.5%	2.4%

Source: U.S. Department of Commerce; CCSCE

San Mateo County had the highest growth in per capita income since 1995 as shown on Table 3A. Per capita income in 2001 was $57,405 or 58.3% above the 1995 level which represented a 34.1% increase adjusted for inflation. In contrast state per capita income grew by just 13.4% between 1995 and 2001 adjusted for inflation.

The Bay Area had the top seven counties in terms of per capita income in 2001, led by Marin at $63,322.

Table 3B
California and Selected Counties
AVERAGE WAGE LEVELS
2000 - 2002

	2000	2001	2002	% Change 2000-2002
Imperial	$24,410	$26,221	$27,440	12.4%
Los Angeles	$39,671	$40,891	$41,678	5.1%
Orange	$39,243	$40,252	$41,225	5.1%
Riverside	$29,137	$29,971	$30,955	6.2%
San Bernardino	$29,914	$30,995	$32,135	7.4%
Ventura	$37,090	$37,783	$38,179	2.9%
Los Angeles Basin				
Alameda	$45,113	$46,489	$47,324	4.9%
Contra Costa	$42,319	$44,744	$46,022	8.8%
Marin	$42,611	$43,547	$45,213	6.1%
Napa	$33,015	$34,684	$35,539	7.6%
San Francisco	$57,646	$61,068	$58,616	1.7%
San Mateo	$67,070	$62,288	$57,228	-14.7%
Santa Clara	$76,252	$65,931	$63,020	-17.4%
Solano	$31,670	$33,496	$34,018	7.4%
Sonoma	$35,742	$36,145	$36,492	2.1%
San Francisco Bay Area				
San Diego	$37,560	$38,418	$39,280	4.6%
San Diego Region				
El Dorado	$29,443	$31,243	$31,851	8.2%
Placer	$33,403	$34,773	$35,824	7.2%
Sacramento	$37,761	$39,173	$40,623	7.6%
Yolo	$33,451	$35,312	$35,568	6.3%
Sacramento Region				
Butte	$25,139	$26,499	$27,183	8.1%
Colusa	$23,362	$25,435	$26,493	13.4%
Glenn	$24,180	$25,496	$26,061	7.8%
Shasta	$26,966	$28,129	$28,951	7.4%
Sutter	$24,790	$26,206	$27,150	9.5%
Tehama	$25,055	$26,043	$26,905	7.4%
Yuba	$28,180	$30,091	$31,629	12.2%
Sacramento Valley Region				

	2000	2001	2002	% Change 2000-2002
Monterey	$29,962	$31,735	$32,443	8.3%
San Benito	$28,574	$29,595	$31,127	8.9%
San Luis Obispo	$28,096	$29,092	$29,961	6.6%
Santa Barbara	$32,566	$33,626	$34,387	5.6%
Santa Cruz	$35,819	$35,022	$35,654	-0.5%
Coastal Region				
Fresno	$26,164	$27,878	$28,920	10.5%
Kern	$28,585	$30,106	$31,205	9.2%
Kings	$25,736	$26,742	$27,798	8.0%
Madera	$23,846	$25,701	$26,706	12.0%
Merced	$24,842	$25,479	$26,773	7.8%
San Joaquin	$29,264	$30,818	$31,905	9.0%
Stanislaus	$28,221	$29,591	$30,751	9.0%
Tulare	$23,743	$24,732	$25,691	8.2%
San Joaquin Valley				
Del Norte	$24,862	$25,710	$26,234	5.5%
Humboldt	$25,282	$25,824	$26,695	5.6%
Lake	$22,502	$24,044	$26,251	16.7%
Mendocino	$24,401	$25,198	$26,049	6.8%
North Coast Region				
Alpine	$16,801	$21,106	$22,094	31.5%
Amador	$25,906	$27,390	$28,919	11.6%
Calaveras	$23,463	$25,077	$26,303	12.1%
Inyo	$25,023	$26,596	$27,042	8.1%
Lassen	$28,657	$28,866	$29,485	2.9%
Mariposa	$24,672	$25,251	$26,655	8.0%
Modoc	$21,506	$22,460	$23,900	11.1%
Mono	$22,881	$24,056	$25,662	12.2%
Nevada	$28,466	$29,640	$30,314	6.5%
Plumas	$25,725	$26,450	$27,065	5.2%
Sierra	$29,924	$30,095	$24,387	-18.5%
Siskiyou	$22,540	$23,611	$24,109	7.0%
Trinity	$22,749	$23,649	$24,705	8.6%
Tuolumne	$25,460	$26,469	$28,362	11.4%
Mountain Region				
California	**$41,207**	**$41,327**	**$41,408**	**0.5%**

Source: U.S. Bureau of Labor Statistics

How to Decide Which Income Series to Use

CCSCE expects national GDP growth of 3.4% per year between 2002 and 2010 with productivity growth of 2% annually and job growth of 1.4% per year.

CCSCE expects higher job growth for California between 2002 and 2010 – approximately 2% per year.

As a result, CCSCE's moderate growth projection for real personal income in California is 4.0% per year between 2002 and 2010. In this alternative per capita and average household income would grow at near the national growth rate. California's higher growth rate for total personal income would reflect higher growth rates for jobs and population.

The high growth alternative projects a real growth rate of 4.6% per year for total personal income in the state. This could happen if:

--U.S. GDP grew by 3.5% annually instead of 3.0% as a result of higher productivity gains.

--Wage gains in California outpace the national gains as a result of a resurgence in technology and stock option income.

--Job growth in the state outpaces CCSCE's projection.

The low growth alternative projects a real growth rate of 3.5% per year for total personal income in the state. This could happen if:

--Productivity and GDP growth are lower than 3% annually in the nation.

--Job growth in California fails to outpace the national average.

--Wage gains trail the national average.

San Diego Moves into Second Place

San Diego had the second highest growth rate in per capita income since 1995. As a result, per capita income was above the state average in 2001 – equaling $33,742 compared to $32,563 for the state. San Diego now ranks second in the state behind the Bay Area.

Per Capita Income by County 1995-2001					
			Percent Change		
			1995-2001		2000-2001
	1995	2001	(in 01$)	(in Curr$)	(in Curr$)
Fastest Growing Counties					
San Mateo	$32,627	$57,405	34.1%	58.3%	-5.8%
Santa Clara	32,627	51,014	32.5%	56.4%	-8.1%
San Francisco	36,307	54,950	28.3%	51.3%	0.1%
Nevada	21,067	31,087	25.1%	47.6%	5.4%
Marin	43,485	63,322	23.4%	45.6%	0.6%
Santa Cruz	25,914	36,579	19.6%	41.2%	-3.1%
Slowest Growing Counties					
Colusa	21,073	21,608	-13.1%	2.5%	-7.7%
Lassen	17,097	17,863	-11.5%	4.5%	-0.4%
Imperial	16,467	17,599	-9.4%	6.9%	2.7%
Kings	14,695	16,674	-3.8%	13.5%	4.4%

Source: U.S. Department of Commerce, CCSCE

Los Angeles Basin Incomes Finally Recovering

Between 1995 and 2001, per capita incomes grew by 28.7% in the Los Angeles Basin – just below the 33.8% average statewide gain. Between 2000 and 2001, regional per capita income grew by 2.7% compared to statewide growth of 0.7%. Orange County had the highest Basin per capita income gain and in 2001 had the ninth highest county per capita income ($36,568).

The Basin had the 3rd lowest regional per capita income performance since 1995 with a 9.0% gain in per capita income, adjusted for inflation.

Within the Basin, Orange, Riverside and Los Angeles counties had the largest income gains between 1995 and 2001.

Coastal and Mountain Regions Had Average Gains

Real per capita income in the Mountain region grew by 12.2% between 1995 and 2001 resulting in a 2001 per capita income of $24,844. Nevada County had the state's fourth highest gain in per capita income. The Coastal region posted a 10.8% gain in real per capita income. The region includes Santa Cruz, which has the sixth largest county growth rate. Santa Cruz has California's eighth highest per capita income, benefiting from proximity to Silicon Valley. Santa Barbara also had per capita income above the state average in 2001.

Table 3A
California, Economic Regions, and Counties
PER CAPITA PERSONAL INCOME
1995 – 2001
(Current$)

	1995	2001	% change 1995-2001 2001$	% change 1995-2001 Current $	2000-2001 Current $
Imperial	$16,467	$17,599	-9.4%	6.9%	2.7%
Los Angeles	23,728	30,439	8.7%	28.3%	2.9%
Orange	27,455	36,568	12.9%	33.2%	3.1%
Riverside	19,691	25,843	11.2%	31.2%	2.6%
San Bernardino	18,098	22,167	3.8%	22.5%	1.5%
Ventura	25,514	32,198	7.0%	26.2%	0.7%
Los Angeles Basin	**$23,438**	**$30,158**	**9.0%**	**28.7%**	**2.7%**
Alameda	$27,445	$38,514	18.9%	40.3%	0.0%
Contra Costa	31,039	42,165	15.1%	35.8%	-0.7%
Marin	43,485	63,322	23.4%	45.6%	0.6%
Napa	27,426	37,269	15.2%	35.9%	-0.9%
San Francisco	36,307	54,950	28.3%	51.3%	0.1%
San Mateo	36,266	57,405	34.1%	58.3%	-5.8%
Santa Clara	32,627	51,014	32.5%	56.4%	-8.1%
Solano	20,747	27,034	10.4%	30.3%	1.1%
Sonoma	25,448	34,639	15.4%	36.1%	-1.7%
San Francisco Bay Area	**$31,279**	**$45,890**	**24.3%**	**46.7%**	**-3.3%**
San Diego	$23,929	$33,742	19.5%	41.0%	2.7%
San Diego Region	**$23,929**	**$33,742**	**19.5%**	**41.0%**	**2.7%**
El Dorado	$23,813	$33,313	18.6%	39.9%	1.6%
Placer	26,080	36,377	18.2%	39.5%	2.8%
Sacramento	23,570	29,634	6.5%	25.7%	2.5%
Yolo	22,898	27,625	2.2%	20.6%	-0.1%
Sacramento Region	**$23,853**	**$30,712**	**9.1%**	**28.8%**	**2.3%**
Butte	$17,751	$22,841	9.0%	28.7%	2.7%
Colusa	21,073	21,608	-13.1%	2.5%	-7.7%
Glenn	15,480	17,857	-2.2%	15.4%	-5.3%
Shasta	19,994	25,139	6.6%	25.7%	2.7%
Sutter	20,386	23,989	-0.3%	17.7%	-2.2%
Tehama	15,136	19,982	11.9%	32.0%	3.6%
Yuba	14,554	19,247	12.1%	32.2%	2.0%
Sacramento Valley Region	**$18,110**	**$22,743**	**6.4%**	**25.6%**	**1.4%**

	1995	2001	% change 1995-2001		2000-2001
			2001$	Current $	Current $
Monterey	$24,494	$30,034	3.9%	22.6%	2.3%
San Benito	18,792	23,480	5.9%	24.9%	-4.8%
San Luis Obispo	20,520	27,864	15.1%	35.8%	1.9%
Santa Barbara	25,525	33,401	10.9%	30.9%	1.6%
Santa Cruz	25,914	36,579	19.6%	41.2%	-3.1%
Coastal Region	**$24,153**	**$31,590**	**10.8%**	**30.8%**	**0.5%**
Fresno	$18,404	$21,846	0.6%	18.7%	3.0%
Kern	17,747	20,914	-0.1%	17.8%	2.1%
Kings	14,695	16,674	-3.8%	13.5%	4.4%
Madera	15,168	17,986	0.5%	18.6%	0.3%
Merced	15,058	18,639	4.9%	23.8%	1.4%
San Joaquin	19,012	23,374	4.2%	22.9%	0.5%
Stanislaus	18,078	22,831	7.0%	26.3%	0.2%
Tulare	16,294	20,131	4.7%	23.5%	3.1%
San Joaquin Valley	**$17,622**	**$21,317**	**2.5%**	**21.0%**	**1.8%**
Del Norte	$14,482	$17,557	2.7%	21.2%	0.1%
Humboldt	18,632	23,813	8.3%	27.8%	2.4%
Lake	18,219	23,750	10.5%	30.4%	2.9%
Mendocino	19,253	25,828	13.7%	34.1%	2.4%
North Coast Region	**$18,336**	**$23,811**	**10.1%**	**29.9%**	**2.4%**
Alpine	$20,250	$25,134	5.2%	24.1%	1.5%
Amador	18,382	23,611	8.9%	28.4%	3.7%
Calaveras	17,452	23,693	15.1%	35.8%	3.1%
Inyo	20,673	25,699	5.3%	24.3%	3.4%
Lassen	17,097	17,863	-11.5%	4.5%	-0.4%
Mariposa	17,856	23,327	10.7%	30.6%	7.0%
Modoc	17,149	20,912	3.3%	21.9%	-2.2%
Mono	19,056	23,924	6.4%	25.5%	1.6%
Nevada	21,067	31,087	25.1%	47.6%	5.4%
Plumas	19,821	26,458	13.1%	33.5%	1.2%
Sierra	18,805	24,820	11.9%	32.0%	0.4%
Siskiyou	17,859	22,469	6.6%	25.8%	1.0%
Trinity	16,475	21,162	8.9%	28.4%	5.2%
Tuolumne	17,776	23,414	11.6%	31.7%	4.0%
Mountain Region	**$18,757**	**$24,844**	**12.2%**	**32.5%**	**3.5%**
California	**$24,328**	**$32,563**	**13.4%**	**33.8%**	**0.7%**

Source: U.S. Department of Commerce; 2001$ comparisons based on California Consumer Price Index

Sacramento Region Incomes Grow

The Sacramento region has the sixth highest per capita income gains since 1995 at 28.8% or 9.1% adjusted for inflation. The region had the tenth fastest growing county, Placer, where high tech job gains pushed real per capita incomes up by 18.2%. Placer County had one of the highest per capita incomes of any county outside the Bay Area in 2001 ($36,377).

San Joaquin Valley and Nonmetro Areas Fall Further Behind

The San Joaquin Valley had the smallest gains in per capita income since 1995. The state's economic surge has been mostly concentrated in the large, urban regions. The 21.0% gain in Valley per capita income between 1995 and 2001 is compared to the statewide average gain of 33.8%.

For the 2000-2001 period, per capita income in the Valley rose by 1.8%.

The San Joaquin Valley and nonmetropolitan counties continue to have low per capita incomes compared to most urban counties. Per capita incomes in most counties are 20% to 40% below the state average.

Per Capita Income Growth — A Range of Projections

CCSCE believes there is uncertainty about the rate at which real income will grow in the nation and state during the next decade. As a result, CCSCE's income and taxable sales projections for the year 2010, presented on Tables 3 through 7, show a range of possible growth trends.

Wage growth stalled in California after 2000. Average wage levels increased by just 0.5% between 2000 and 2002 compared to the 4.0% nationwide gain. California retained the 6th highest wage levels among all states but lost ground to most states after 2000.

Wage levels dropped substantially in two counties — San Mateo and Santa Clara — as high-wage jobs were lost and stock option income levels plunged. Wage growth was slow in San Francisco and Sonoma as well as shown on Table 3B.

However, outside of these counties, wage growth in California kept pace with or outpaced nationwide wage gains. For example, between 2000 and 2002, wage gains were strong in many San Joaquin Valley counties. Since wage data is reported at the place of employment, these wage gains do **not** reflect commuting patterns. Wage gains in Los Angeles Basin counties also outpaced nationwide wage growth , particularly in Riverside and San Bernardino.

CCSCE used the 2002 wage data to develop unofficial estimates of county per capita income for 2002 shown on Table 3.

The following discussion covers the period 2002 – 2010 and income is stated in 2002$. Estimates for county per capita income for 2002 are unofficial and were developed by CCSCE.

Per capita income in California (in 2002$) is projected to grow from $32,831 in 2002 to between $38,535 and $41,663 in 2010 as shown on Table 3. Per capita income (in 2002$) in California will reach $40,072 by 2010 in the moderate growth alternative.

The variations in per capita income growth depend on different assumptions about productivity growth and the growth of real wages. Lower productivity growth will lead to slower growth in real per capita income, other things being equal.

CCSCE projects that productivity growth in California will range from 1.4% per year (low) – to 2.5% per year (high). Productivity is projected to grow by 2.0% per year in the moderate growth alternative.

Real (i.e., inflation adjusted) per capita income will grow by between 2.0% per year and 3.0% per year in California between 2002 and 2010. In the 1980s real per capita income increased at 1.1% annually while in the 1995-2002 period real growth rose to 1.6% annually.

Part of the reason for the high growth rates for 2002 – 2010 is that the projections assume some rebound from the recession – depressed levels of 2002 as well as long-term growth.

California
Components of Real Income Growth
Average Annual Growth

			2002-2010		
	1980-1990	**1995-2002**	**Low Growth**	**Moderate Growth**	**High Growth**
Total Personal Income	3.4%	3.2%	3.5%	4.0%	4.6%
Per Capita Income	1.1%	1.6%	2.0%	2.5%	3.0%
Population	2.3%	1.5%	1.5%	1.5%	1.5%

County Per Capita Income Projections 2002-2010

Projections of per capita income by county for 2010 are shown on Table 3 along with estimates for 1995 and 2002. All incomes are in 2002 prices. CCSCE prepared a range of income projections for each county based on alternative rates of growth in productivity and real wages. CCSCE also projected different relative per capita income growth rates by county after examining recent trends and considering the key industries in selected counties.

High Incomes Are Concentrated In A Few Counties

For 2002 CCSCE estimates that only 15 California counties have per capita incomes above the state average. In fact, only 17 counties have per capita incomes in excess of the national average. Thus, while the average per capita income in California is similar to that in the nation, nearly three-quarters of the state's county markets have per capita incomes below the national average.

The high income counties are located primarily in the major metropolitan regions. Three – Orange, Ventura and Los Angeles – are in the Los Angeles Basin. Eight high income counties – Alameda, Contra Costa, Marin, Napa, San Francisco, San Mateo, Santa Clara, and Sonoma – are in the San Francisco Bay Area. The other six counties with per capita income above the national average are El Dorado, Nevada, Placer, San Diego, Santa Barbara, and Santa Cruz.

The geographical pattern of the state's high income counties did not change much in the 1980s and 1990s and is not projected to vary much in the decade ahead. Marin, San Mateo, San Francisco, Contra Costa and Santa Clara are the top 5 counties in 1995, 2002 and 2010.

Ten Counties With Largest Per Capita Income
1995-2010

1995	**(2002$)**	**2002**	**(2002$)**	**2010 Moderate**	**(2002$)**
Marin	$52,520	Marin	$61,897	Marin	$76,692
San Francisco	43,851	San Mateo	54,160	San Francisco	67,387
San Mateo	43,802	Santa Clara	50,137	San Mateo	66,949
Santa Clara	39,407	San Francisco	53,851	Santa Clara	61,478
Contra Costa	37,489	Contra Costa	41,781	Contra Costa	51,292
Orange	33,159	Alameda	38,376	Orange	46,620
Alameda	33,148	Napa	37,603	Napa	46,519
Napa	33,125	Orange	37,376	Santa Cruz	46,248
Placer	31,500	Santa Cruz	37,351	Alameda	45,771
Santa Cruz	31,299	Placer	37,064	Placer	45,116
CALIFORNIA	$29,581	**CALIFORNIA**	$32,831	**CALIFORNIA**	$40,072

Marin led all counties in 2002 with an estimated per capita income of $61,897 or double the national average. San Mateo, San Francisco and Santa Clara Counties all had per capita incomes over $50,000 in 2002.

The top ten counties are projected to remain nearly the same throughout the next decade. By 2010 Marin will still have the highest per capita income – $76,692 in 2002$ – and seven of the top ten counties will still be located in the San Francisco Bay Area.

The Impact of Inflation

The per capita personal income estimates and projections on Table 3 are measured in 2002 prices. The changes are, therefore, changes in real income, i.e., excluding the impact of inflation. CCSCE projects that inflation will average around 2.5% in the period to 2010. This compares with the 4.9% average inflation rate experienced in the 1980s and the 2.6% growth between 1990 and 2000.

To convert the per capita income projected for 2010 to current dollars (i.e., including 2.5% yearly inflation) multiply by 1.2184. Thus per capita income in California in 2010 is projected to be $48,824 measured in 2010 prices.

Growth in Economic Regions

- The San Francisco Bay Area is California's wealthiest region. The region's 2002 per capita income of $44,876 is approximately 45% above the national average. Bay Area income levels in 2010 – $55,031 in 2002$ – will be 37% above the state average (the same as in 2002) compared to 46% above in 2000. The main reason is that the 2000 "regional advantage" was inflated by high stock option income.

- Real per capita incomes grew slightly (+8.7%) between 1995 and 2002 in the Los Angeles Basin. The Los Angeles region – home to half of California's population – fell to fifth place among the nine regions with a per capita income of $30,778 – 9.4% below the state average. However, Basin incomes will keep pace with statewide growth in the decade ahead and reach $37,853 in 2010 – up 23.0% from 2002.

- The San Diego region had the second highest per capita income in 2002 ($34,407) and was the only region besides the Bay Area to top the state average. Per capita incomes will grow to $42,145 in 2010 and San Diego will remain second behind the Bay Area.

Table 3
California, Economic Regions, and Counties
PER CAPITA PERSONAL INCOME
1995 – 2002
(2002$)

	1995	2002	2010 Low	2010 Moderate	2010 High
Imperial	$19,431	$18,128	$23,038	$23,957	$24,908
Los Angeles	27,999	31,010	36,265	37,712	39,209
Orange	32,396	37,376	44,832	46,620	48,471
Riverside	23,235	26,471	32,279	33,567	34,899
San Bernardino	21,356	22,759	28,241	29,367	30,532
Ventura	30,106	32,880	39,160	40,722	42,338
Los Angeles Basin	**$27,657**	**$30,778**	**$36,401**	**$37,853**	**$39,355**
Alameda	$32,385	38,376	44,015	45,771	47,587
Contra Costa	36,626	41,781	49,325	51,292	53,328
Marin	51,312	61,897	73,750	76,692	79,736
Napa	32,363	37,603	44,735	46,519	48,365
San Francisco	42,842	53,851	64,803	67,387	70,062
San Mateo	42,794	54,160	64,381	66,949	69,606
Santa Clara	38,500	50,137	59,120	61,478	63,918
Solano	24,482	27,235	32,835	34,145	35,500
Sonoma	30,029	34,663	40,562	42,180	43,854
San Francisco Bay Area	**$36,909**	**$44,876**	**$52,921**	**$55,031**	**$57,215**
San Diego	$28,237	$34,407	$40,528	$42,145	$43,818
San Diego Region	**$28,237**	**$34,407**	**$40,528**	**$42,145**	**$43,818**
El Dorado	$28,099	33,999	40,316	$41,924	$43,588
Placer	30,775	37,064	43,386	45,116	46,907
Sacramento	27,813	30,244	35,866	37,296	38,777
Yolo	27,019	28,235	33,863	35,213	36,611
Sacramento Region	**$28,147**	**$31,214**	**$37,193**	**$38,677**	**$40,212**
Butte	$20,946	$23,274	$27,252	$28,339	$29,463
Colusa	24,866	22,367	29,425	30,599	31,813
Glenn	18,266	18,215	21,509	22,367	23,254
Shasta	23,593	25,581	29,646	30,828	32,052
Sutter	24,056	24,582	30,072	31,272	32,513
Tehama	17,860	20,278	22,975	23,892	24,840
Yuba	17,174	19,630	23,158	24,082	25,038
Sacramento Valley Region	**$21,369**	**$23,132**	**$27,296**	**$28,385**	**$29,511**

	1995	2002	2010		
			Low	Moderate	High
Monterey	$28,903	$30,647	$36,291	$37,739	$39,236
San Benito	22,175	24,162	30,486	31,702	32,960
San Luis Obispo	24,214	28,355	32,860	34,171	35,527
Santa Barbara	30,120	33,989	39,389	40,960	42,586
Santa Cruz	30,578	37,351	44,474	46,248	48,083
Coastal Region	**$28,501**	**$32,207**	**$37,715**	**$39,219**	**$40,775**
Fresno	$21,717	$22,107	$24,474	$25,450	$26,460
Kern	20,942	21,169	23,481	24,418	25,387
Kings	17,340	16,968	19,664	20,448	21,260
Madera	17,899	18,436	22,595	23,496	24,429
Merced	17,769	19,216	24,578	25,559	26,573
San Joaquin	22,434	23,964	29,424	30,598	31,812
Stanislaus	21,332	23,403	28,696	29,840	31,025
Tulare	19,227	20,556	24,480	25,456	26,466
San Joaquin Valley	**$20,793**	**$21,630**	**$25,475**	**$26,492**	**$27,543**
Del Norte	$17,089	$17,939	$21,458	$22,314	$23,200
Humboldt	21,985	24,276	28,536	29,674	30,852
Lake	21,498	24,180	28,130	29,252	30,413
Mendocino	22,719	26,268	30,305	31,514	32,765
North Coast Region	**$21,636**	**$24,252**	**$28,327**	**$29,457**	**$30,626**
Alpine	$23,894	$25,706	$30,987	$32,223	$33,502
Amador	21,691	24,027	27,845	28,955	30,104
Calaveras	20,593	24,041	27,212	28,298	29,421
Inyo	24,394	26,061	29,362	30,533	31,745
Lassen	20,175	18,168	20,967	21,803	22,669
Mariposa	21,070	23,685	26,956	28,031	29,143
Modoc	20,236	21,475	26,684	27,748	28,850
Mono	22,487	24,377	28,543	29,682	30,860
Nevada	24,859	31,635	36,661	38,123	39,636
Plumas	23,388	26,948	31,452	32,707	34,005
Sierra	22,190	25,270	29,403	30,575	31,789
Siskiyou	21,073	22,858	26,422	27,476	28,566
Trinity	19,441	21,523	24,842	25,833	26,858
Tuolumne	20,976	23,945	28,840	29,990	31,180
Mountain Region	**$22,133**	**$25,236**	**$29,388**	**$30,560**	**$31,773**
California	**$28,707**	**$32,831**	**$38,535**	**$40,072**	**$41,663**

Source: 1995 – U.S. Department of Commerce (adjusted to 2002$); 2002 and 2010 - CCSCE

- The Sacramento region, led by per capita income gains related to high tech job growth, moved up to fourth place among regions in 2002 with a per capita income of $31,214. The Sacramento region is projected to stay in fourth place in 2010 with a per capita income of $38,677 – just below the state average.

- The Coastal region moved up to third place in per capita income in 2002 ($32,207) and will grow at near the state average to 2010.

- The San Joaquin Valley is expected to have the lowest per capita income in 2010 – $26,492 or 34% below the state average.

- The other regions will continue to have per capita income levels below the state **and** below the national average.

Per Capita Income by Economic Region
1995-2010
(2002$)

Region	1995	2002	2010 Moderate
San Francisco Bay Area	$37,778	$44,876	$55,031
San Diego	28,902	34,407	42,145
Coastal Region	29,172	32,207	39,129
Sacramento Region	28,810	31,214	38,677
Los Angeles Basin	28,309	30,778	37,853
Mountain Region	22,654	25,236	30,560
North Coast Region	22,146	24,252	29,457
Sacramento Valley Region	21,873	23,132	28,385
San Joaquin Valley	21,283	21,630	26,492
CALIFORNIA	$29,383	$32,831	$40,072

AVERAGE HOUSEHOLD INCOME

Different Ways to Measure Household Income

The first part of this section describes the different ways that household income can be measured.

CCSCE uses estimates of total **personal** income to derive estimates of household income. The Census Bureau uses a total **money** income definition, which is lower. In addition, median household income figures based on the **money** income definition are often quoted in the media. Median household income using a **money** income definition is much lower than average household income using a total **personal** income definition.

The 2000 Census reported that average household income in 1999 (The Census asks about income for the previous year) was $65,978. Average personal income per household in 1999 (total personal income divided by the number of households as of January 1 of the following year) was $86,704. In addition, the Census reported median household income in1999 was $47,493.

Household Income in 1999	
Average Personal Income per Household (CCSCE)	$86,704
Average Money Income per Household (Census)	$65,978
Median Money Income per Household (Census)	$47,493

Money Income (Census) Versus Personal Income (DOF/CCSCE) Estimates of Per Capita and Average Household Income

CCSCE prepared Table 4B to help readers compare income estimates published from the 2000 Census with the income estimates and projections in **California County Projections**.

CCSCE's estimates and projections are based on the estimates of total personal income published for each county by the United States Department of Commerce. These personal income estimates include money income **plus** fringe benefits, the computed rental value of owner-occupied homes and payments to medical providers by government (e.g., Medicare payments). As a result, estimates of personal income are generally much higher than estimates of money income.

The estimates of per capita income on Table 3A in the previous section correspond to total personal income per capita and are similar to the measures of per capita income reported by the California Department of Finance. In 1999:

- DOF reported state per capita income = $29,846
- The Census estimate (money income) = $22,711

The Census estimate was 24% below the corresponding personal income per capita estimate.

Similarly, as reported above, the average household income estimate from the Census for 1999 ($65,978 calculated by CCSCE) was 24% below the average household income ($86,704) reported on Table 4A.

Another major reason for the large difference between the money income and personal income estimates is the **existence of substantial underreporting of money income by respondents to the Census Bureau surveys**. Money income is underreported by 10 – 15% each year.

Finally, Table 4B shows estimates of median household income (half of all households have more than the median, half have less) from the 2000 Census. Readers should be aware that median income is lower than average household income and that the gap has been growing as high income households received above average income gains in the 1990s.

Median money income per household in 1999 ($47,493) was 28% below average money income. In 1989, median income was just 24% below average income.

Most of the county income estimates shown on Table 4B follow the statewide pattern of relationships between money income and personal income. The Census income estimates for a few smaller counties – San Benito, Kings, Tulare, Alpine, Amador, Calaveras and Mono – look suspiciously high.

It is important to read the material in Appendix B which explains the various household income measures and definitions.

Average Household Income in California

Real (i.e., inflation adjusted) average household income declined between 1990 and 1994 and then rebounded sharply to reach $101,818 (in 2002$) in 2000. Real income fell in 2001 and 2002 to reach $98,793 and will probably decline again in 2003. CCSCE projects that average household income in California will rise to $118,449 (in 2002$) by 2010.

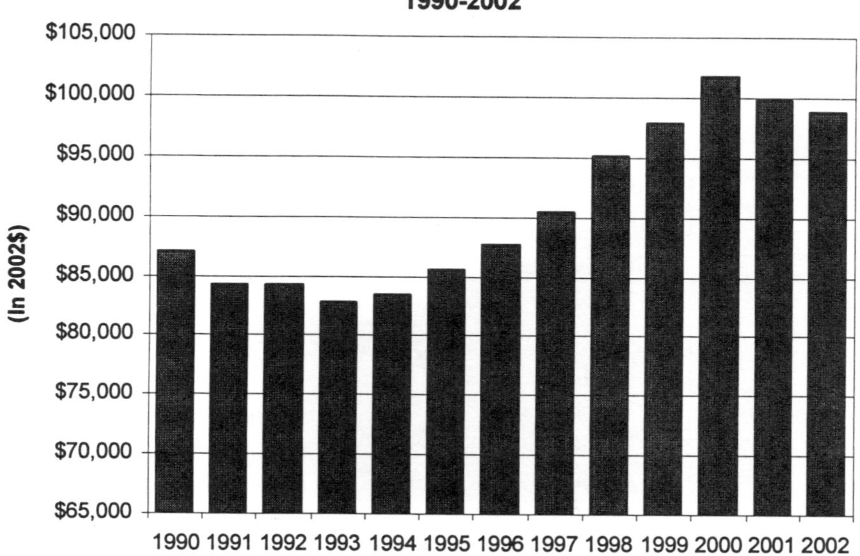

Short Term Trends in Average Household Income

The most recent estimates of personal income for counties were published in May 2003 including estimates through 2001. CCSCE's summary of 1995 - 2001 average household income trends by county is presented in Table 4A.

CCSCE has developed unofficial estimates of average household income for 2002 and these are shown on Table 4.

It is likely that average household income fell in many counties in 2001 and 2002 (particularly in the Bay Area) and rose slowly in other counties. Adjusted for inflation, average household income fell widely throughout the state in 2001 and 2002, with a recovery expected beginning in 2004.

Neither the U.S. Department of Commerce nor the California Department of Finance publish estimates of average household income. CCSCE's household income estimates for a specific year are based on total personal income in that year divided by the number of households on January 1 of the following year – the same procedure used by the Census Bureau.

Bay Area Leads Household Income Growth

Bay Area counties posted the largest gains in average household income since 1995. The Bay Area had the highest regional average household income in 1995 and the region's advantage has grown, fueled by California's largest wage gains and the surge in stock option income in 1999 and 2000.

Table 4B
California, Economic Regions, and Counties
COMPARISON OF INCOME MEASURES
1999
(Current$)

	Per Capita Income		Average HH Income		Median
	Money Census	Personal DOF	Money Census	Personal CCSCE	HH Income Census
Imperial	$13,329	$18,438	$47,652	$65,915	$31,870
Los Angeles	20,683	28,240	62,001	84,655	42,189
Orange	25,826	33,118	77,392	99,244	58,820
Riverside	18,689	23,679	55,919	70,850	42,887
San Bernardino	16,856	20,996	53,674	66,858	42,066
Ventura	24,600	29,805	75,135	91,034	59,666
Los Angeles Basin	**$21,102**	**$27,893**	**$63,773**	**$84,295**	**$45,844**
Alameda	$26,680	$34,248	$72,552	$93,131	$55,946
Contra Costa	30,615	38,343	83,384	104,432	63,575
Marin	44,962	56,992	109,455	138,741	71,306
Napa	26,395	34,266	71,394	92,685	51,738
San Francisco	34,556	48,267	80,337	112,214	55,221
San Mateo	36,045	49,983	99,411	137,853	70,819
Santa Clara	32,795	46,091	96,525	135,658	74,335
Solano	21,731	24,525	64,710	73,031	54,099
Sonoma	25,724	31,315	67,667	82,375	53,076
San Francisco Bay Area	**$30,941**	**$41,081**	**$84,101**	**$111,664**	**$62,917**
San Diego	$22,926	$30,434	$63,989	$84,944	$47,067
San Diego Region	**$22,926**	**$30,434**	**$63,989**	**$84,944**	**$47,067**
El Dorado	$25,560	$30,602	$67,046	$80,272	$51,484
Placer	27,963	33,609	72,842	87,548	57,535
Sacramento	21,142	27,201	56,146	72,235	43,816
Yolo	19,365	26,260	53,889	73,077	40,769
Sacramento Region	**$22,301**	**$28,292**	**$59,253**	**$75,172**	**$46,149**
Butte	$17,517	$21,229	$44,365	$53,765	$31,924
Colusa	14,730	23,720	44,937	72,363	35,052
Glenn	14,069	18,308	40,342	52,497	32,107
Shasta	17,738	23,308	45,380	59,631	34,335
Sutter	17,428	24,268	50,286	70,022	38,375
Tehama	15,793	18,321	41,713	48,389	31,206
Yuba	14,124	18,106	41,406	53,080	30,460
Sacramento Valley Region	**$16,830**	**$21,552**	**$44,693**	**$57,230**	**$33,259**

	Per Capita Income		Average HH Income		Median
	Money Census	Personal DOF	Money Census	Personal CCSCE	HH Income Census
Monterey	$23,422	$28,199	$76,257	$91,810	$48,305
San Benito	20,932	22,536	68,785	74,057	57,469
San Luis Obispo	21,864	25,569	57,478	67,218	42,428
Santa Barbara	23,059	30,697	66,662	88,742	46,677
Santa Cruz	26,396	33,168	73,364	92,186	53,998
Coastal Region	**$23,497**	**$29,176**	**$68,751**	**$85,369**	**$48,080**
Fresno	$15,495	$20,654	$48,384	$64,495	$34,725
Kern	15,760	19,775	49,342	61,911	35,446
Kings	15,848	15,418	58,662	57,072	35,749
Madera	14,682	17,680	49,421	59,510	36,286
Merced	14,257	18,033	46,369	58,650	35,543
San Joaquin	17,365	22,169	53,042	67,716	41,282
Stanislaus	16,913	21,887	51,392	66,506	40,101
Tulare	21,015	19,139	69,346	63,154	38,725
San Joaquin Valley	**$16,580**	**$20,251**	**$52,313**	**$63,896**	**$37,345**
Del Norte	$14,573	$17,033	$43,703	$51,080	$29,642
Humboldt	17,203	22,065	42,470	54,473	31,226
Lake	16,825	21,899	40,424	52,615	29,627
Mendocino	19,443	23,569	50,148	60,789	35,996
North Coast Region	**$17,533**	**$22,001**	**$44,321**	**$55,616**	**$32,126**
Alpine	$24,431	$25,214	$59,181	$61,077	$41,875
Amador	22,412	20,938	61,041	57,026	42,280
Calaveras	21,420	20,945	52,415	51,254	41,022
Inyo	19,639	24,277	46,019	56,887	35,006
Lassen	14,749	17,224	51,564	60,218	36,310
Mariposa	18,190	20,625	46,623	52,866	34,626
Modoc	17,285	21,920	43,053	54,598	27,522
Mono	23,422	21,714	57,449	53,261	44,992
Nevada	24,007	27,251	59,149	67,141	45,864
Plumas	19,391	24,573	44,707	56,656	36,351
Sierra	18,815	21,614	46,790	53,750	35,827
Siskiyou	17,570	21,168	41,899	50,480	29,530
Trinity	16,868	19,080	39,400	44,568	27,711
Tuolumne	14,006	20,835	36,075	53,666	33,982
Mountain Region	**$19,481**	**$22,428**	**$49,443**	**$56,921**	**$37,959**
California	**$22,711**	**$29,846**	**$65,978**	**$86,704**	**$47,493**

Average Household Income by Economic Region 1995-2001					
			Percent Change		
			1995-2001		2000-2001
	1995	2001	(in 01$)	(in Curr$)	(in Curr$)
San Francisco Bay Area	$84,796	$126,401	26.3%	49.1%	-2.8%
San Diego Region	66,759	95,747	21.5%	43.4%	3.3%
Los Angeles Basin	70,449	93,409	12.4%	32.6%	3.9%
Coastal Region	70,333	93,183	12.3%	32.5%	0.6%
Mountain Region	48,394	62,908	10.2%	30.0%	3.2%
Sacramento Region	63,517	82,269	9.8%	29.5%	2.6%
Sacramento Valley Region	47,044	60,646	9.2%	28.9%	1.4%
North Coast Region	46,909	60,395	9.1%	28.7%	2.5%
San Joaquin Valley	54,661	68,197	5.7%	24.8%	2.5%
California	70,341	96,327	16.1%	36.9%	1.5%
California Except Bay Area	$66,420	$88,132	12.4%	32.7%	3.3%

Source: U.S. Department of Commerce; CCSCE

The Bay Area led the state in average household income in 2001 ($126,401), household income growth between 1995 and 2001 (49.1%), and household income growth adjusted for inflation (26.3%).

Between 2000 and 2001, real average household income in the Bay Area **fell** by 2.8% compared to a 3.3% inflation-adjusted gain for the rest of California. Declines were heaviest in Santa Clara and San Mateo counties.

San Mateo County had the largest growth in average household income between 1995 and 2001 as shown on Table 4A. Average household income in 2001 was $160,008 or 61.4% above the 1995 level which represented a 36.8% increase in six years adjusted for inflation. In contrast, state average household income grew by just 16.1%, adjusted for inflation, during the same period.

Despite the income losses in 2001, which continued in 2002, Bay Area counties led the state in average household income **and** income growth between 1995 and 2001. Santa Clara County matched the San Mateo gains and San Francisco, Marin and Alameda were also among the six fastest growing counties measured by average household income as shown on Table 4A.

California Except the Bay Area

Income gains throughout the rest of California were much smaller than in the Bay Area. The explanation is that tech wage and stock option gains were concentrated in Bay Area counties. As a result, real household income grew by

26.3% in the Bay Area versus 12.4% outside the region between 1995 and 2001 resulting in an overall statewide gain of 16.1%.

In contrast, between 2000 and 2001, average household income outside the Bay Area rose by 3.3% compared to the 2.8% drop in the Bay Area.

San Diego and Coastal Regions Post Strong Gains

San Diego had the second fastest regional growth in average household income between 1995 and 2001. In 2001, San Diego had the 2nd highest average household income ($95,747), a real growth of 21.5% since 1995 and a strong 3.3% gain in household income in 2001.

The Coastal region had the 4th highest average household income and the 4th highest growth rate since 1995. Monterey, Santa Barbara and Santa Cruz are among the small number of counties with average household incomes above the state average in 2001.

Sacramento Region

The region had one of the state's strongest income gains in the early 1990s, followed by an average performance since 1995. Placer and El Dorado have the highest regional incomes. The region has the highest average household income of the non-coastal regions.

Average household income increased by 2.6% in 2001 and probably had another modest gain in 2002.

Average Household Income by County 1995-2001					
			Percent Change		
			1995-2001		2000-2001
	1995	2001	(in 01$)	(in Curr$)	(in Curr$)
Fastest Growing Counties					
San Mateo	$99,138	$160,008	36.8%	61.4%	-5.8%
Santa Clara	94,825	151,688	35.6%	60.0%	-7.8%
San Francisco	86,678	128,218	25.4%	47.9%	0.2%
Nevada	53,149	77,100	22.9%	45.1%	5.8%
Marin	107,047	154,701	22.5%	44.5%	0.3%
Alameda	74,338	107,377	22.4%	44.4%	1.3%
Slowest Growing Counties					
Imperial	59,311	64,579	-7.7%	8.9%	2.5%
Colusa	60,995	67,077	-6.8%	10.0%	-7.0%
Mono	51,370	59,269	-2.2%	15.4%	2.0%
Del Norte	44,714	52,207	-1.1%	16.8%	-0.7%

Source: U.S. Department of Commerce; CCSCE

San Joaquin Valley and Nonmetro Counties Lag in Household Income Growth

The San Joaquin Valley had the smallest inflation adjusted gain in average household income between 1995 and 2001 – just 5.7%. However, the Valley kept pace with the state outside the Bay Area in 2001 and wage gains continued into 2002.

Stanislaus did better than other Valley counties aided by the movement of households from Silicon Valley. The two biggest Valley counties, Fresno and Kern, posted real household income growth of 4% for the period since 1995 — below the state and Valley average.

Average household income growth in the Sacramento Valley, North Coast and Mountain regions was also well below the state average. All regions were below average during the 1995-2001 growth surge in California. Nevada County was an exception posting the 4th highest growth rate. Only a few other counties in these four regions managed to post gains near the state average in the 1990s.

Moreover, counties in these four regions have the lowest average household incomes in California. Of these four regions, the San Joaquin Valley had the highest regional average in 2001 – $68,197 or 29% below the state average. Average household income was near $60,000 in the other three regions.

Los Angeles Basin Incomes Begin to Recover

Real average household incomes fell in the Basin between 1990 and 1994 as a result of the deep regional recession. However, the region had the third highest household income growth between 1995 and 2001. By 2001, real average household income in the region was 12.4% above 1995 levels.

Orange County had the highest rate of household income growth in the region. In 2001, Orange County average household income was $111,679 – the highest of any non Bay Area county in California.

Los Angeles County had an average household income of $93,884 in 2001 – 3% below the state average. After having one of the state's smallest gains between 1990 and 1994, Los Angeles County was near average in household income growth between 1995 and 2001.

A Range of Income Growth Projections 2002 - 2010

As explained above in this section, CCSCE believes there is considerable uncertainty about the rate at which real income will grow in the nation and state during the next ten years. As a result, CCSCE's income and taxable sales projections for the year 2010 show a range of possible growth trends.

Average household income in California (in 2002$) is projected to grow from $97,640 in 2002 to between $113,905 and $123,149 in 2010 as shown on Table 4. Average household income in California will reach $118,449 in 2010 under the moderate growth alternative. Real average household income is projected to grow by 2.4% per year to 2010 in the moderate growth projections.

Average Annual Growth in Average Household Income California

1980-1990	1.5%	2002-2010 Low	1.9%
1990-2000	1.6%	Moderate	2.4%
1995-2000	3.4%	High	2.9%
2000-2002	-1.7%		

Table 4
California, Economic Regions, and Counties
AVERAGE HOUSEHOLD INCOME
1995 – 2002
(2002$)

	1995	2002	2010 Low	2010 Moderate	2010 High
Imperial	$69,987	$66,674	$82,576	$85,869	$89,277
Los Angeles	83,265	96,851	114,597	119,168	123,897
Orange	96,468	115,100	136,706	142,158	147,800
Riverside	70,644	80,821	97,756	101,655	105,690
San Bernardino	67,117	75,338	93,411	97,137	100,992
Ventura	92,406	102,068	119,403	124,165	129,093
Los Angeles Basin	**$83,129**	**$96,308**	**$114,290**	**$118,848**	**$123,565**
Alameda	$87,719	$107,000	$120,462	$125,267	$130,238
Contra Costa	99,134	115,934	136,086	141,514	147,130
Marin	126,315	151,163	178,482	185,601	192,967
Napa	85,716	102,690	122,379	127,260	132,310
San Francisco	102,280	125,498	145,817	151,633	157,651
San Mateo	116,977	149,960	172,650	179,536	186,661
Santa Clara	111,894	147,965	169,344	176,099	183,088
Solano	73,121	81,725	96,443	100,290	104,270
Sonoma	78,545	91,512	104,766	108,945	113,269
San Francisco Bay Area	**$100,060**	**$123,772**	**$142,307**	**$147,983**	**$153,856**
San Diego	$78,775	$98,122	$114,911	$119,494	$124,236
San Diego Region	**$78,775**	**$98,122**	**$114,911**	**$119,494**	**$124,236**
El Dorado	$77,124	$90,010	$104,507	108,676	$112,989
Placer	84,446	92,729	107,676	111,971	116,415
Sacramento	72,931	81,675	96,232	100,070	104,041
Yolo	75,234	80,223	95,404	99,209	103,146
Sacramento Region	**$74,950**	**$83,950**	**$98,733**	**$102,671**	**$106,745**
Butte	$52,097	$58,904	$68,075	$70,790	$73,600
Colusa	71,974	70,166	90,459	94,067	97,801
Glenn	51,084	52,431	61,475	63,927	66,464
Shasta	59,226	66,217	76,268	79,310	82,457
Sutter	66,156	71,927	87,450	90,938	94,547
Tehama	46,024	53,633	56,887	59,156	61,504
Yuba	50,264	58,268	67,734	70,436	73,231
Sacramento Valley Region	**$55,512**	**$62,022**	**$71,870**	**$74,737**	**$77,703**

	1995	2002	2010		
			Low	Moderate	High
Monterey	$91,810	$101,093	$118,554	$123,283	$128,175
San Benito	73,310	80,357	100,171	104,167	108,301
San Luis Obispo	65,117	74,166	82,831	86,134	89,553
Santa Barbara	86,493	99,431	113,054	117,563	122,229
Santa Cruz	85,212	104,696	120,520	125,327	130,301
Coastal Region	**$82,993**	**$95,002**	**$108,910**	**$113,253**	**$117,748**
Fresno	$66,700	$70,598	$77,266	$80,348	$83,536
Kern	63,818	67,568	73,977	76,928	79,981
Kings	62,329	63,666	73,787	76,730	79,775
Madera	57,585	63,843	76,331	79,375	82,525
Merced	57,514	63,777	80,877	84,103	87,441
San Joaquin	68,365	74,988	92,044	95,716	99,514
Stanislaus	63,971	71,734	87,107	90,581	94,176
Tulare	62,144	68,521	80,861	84,086	87,423
San Joaquin Valley	**$64,501**	**$69,822**	**$81,120**	**$84,356**	**$87,703**
Del Norte	$52,763	$53,547	$63,437	$65,967	$68,585
Humboldt	54,989	59,181	69,264	72,026	74,885
Lake	53,336	60,715	68,735	71,476	74,313
Mendocino	58,021	67,676	77,055	80,129	83,309
North Coast Region	**$55,353**	**$61,468**	**$70,936**	**$73,766**	**$76,693**
Alpine	$59,105	$61,515	$69,836	$72,621	$75,504
Amador	61,117	65,081	73,613	76,549	79,587
Calaveras	54,282	57,711	62,570	65,065	67,648
Inyo	56,999	61,250	66,746	69,409	72,163
Lassen	62,809	62,868	72,333	75,218	78,203
Mariposa	54,318	58,883	64,156	66,715	69,363
Modoc	50,186	51,955	62,224	64,706	67,274
Mono	60,616	60,478	67,911	70,620	73,423
Nevada	62,716	78,356	86,745	90,205	93,785
Plumas	53,542	60,137	67,188	69,867	72,640
Sierra	56,791	57,611	64,462	67,033	69,694
Siskiyou	51,309	53,390	59,358	61,726	64,175
Trinity	48,156	49,758	57,470	59,762	62,134
Tuolumne	55,393	62,514	74,477	77,447	80,521
Mountain Region	**$57,105**	**$63,774**	**$71,833**	**$74,698**	**$77,662**
California	**$83,003**	**$97,640**	**$113,905**	**$118,449**	**$123,149**

Source: 1995 - U.S. Department of Commerce (adjusted to 2002$); 2002 and 2010 - CCSCE

Table 4A
California, Economic Regions, and Counties
AVERAGE HOUSEHOLD INCOME
1995 – 2001
(Current$)

			% Change 1995-2001		2000-2001
	1995	**2001**	**2001$**	**Current $**	**Current $**
Imperial	$59,311	$64,579	-7.7%	8.9%	2.5%
Los Angeles	70,563	93,884	12.8%	33.0%	4.4%
Orange	81,752	111,679	15.8%	36.6%	3.9%
Riverside	59,867	78,480	11.1%	31.1%	3.4%
San Bernardino	56,879	72,551	8.1%	27.6%	3.0%
Ventura	78,310	99,273	7.4%	26.8%	0.9%
Los Angeles Basin	**$70,449**	**$93,409**	**12.4%**	**32.6%**	**3.9%**
Alameda	$74,338	$107,377	22.4%	44.4%	1.3%
Contra Costa	84,012	116,990	18.0%	39.3%	0.1%
Marin	107,047	154,704	22.5%	44.5%	0.3%
Napa	72,641	102,002	19.0%	40.4%	-0.7%
San Francisco	86,678	128,218	25.4%	47.9%	0.2%
San Mateo	99,133	160,008	36.8%	61.4%	-5.8%
Santa Clara	94,825	151,688	35.6%	60.0%	-7.8%
Solano	61,967	81,153	11.0%	31.0%	1.1%
Sonoma	66,564	91,839	16.9%	38.0%	-1.4%
San Francisco Bay Area	**$84,796**	**$126,401**	**26.3%**	**49.1%**	**-2.8%**
San Diego	$66,759	$95,747	21.5%	43.4%	3.3%
San Diego Region	**$66,759**	**$95,747**	**21.5%**	**43.4%**	**3.3%**
El Dorado	$65,359	$88,376	14.6%	35.2%	1.8%
Placer	71,564	92,760	9.8%	29.6%	1.7%
Sacramento	61,806	79,817	9.4%	29.1%	3.2%
Yolo	63,757	77,500	3.0%	21.6%	0.2%
Sacramento Region	**$63,517**	**$82,269**	**9.8%**	**29.5%**	**2.6%**
Butte	$44,150	$57,763	10.9%	30.8%	2.3%
Colusa	60,995	67,077	-6.8%	10.0%	-7.0%
Glenn	43,291	51,310	0.4%	18.5%	-5.7%
Shasta	50,192	64,850	9.5%	29.2%	2.9%
Sutter	56,064	69,971	5.8%	24.8%	-2.2%
Tehama	39,004	52,796	14.7%	35.4%	3.4%
Yuba	42,596	56,717	12.8%	33.2%	3.0%
Sacramento Valley Region	**$47,044**	**$60,646**	**9.2%**	**28.9%**	**1.4%**

	1995	2001	% Change 1995-2001		2000-2001
			2001$	Current $	Current $
Monterey	$77,805	$98,682	7.5%	26.8%	2.5%
San Benito	62,127	77,956	6.3%	25.5%	-5.5%
San Luis Obispo	55,184	73,326	12.6%	32.9%	1.7%
Santa Barbara	73,300	97,616	12.9%	33.2%	1.8%
Santa Cruz	72,213	102,499	20.3%	41.9%	-3.1%
Coastal Region	**$70,333**	**$93,183**	**12.3%**	**32.5%**	**0.6%**
Fresno	$56,526	$69,284	3.9%	22.6%	3.6%
Kern	54,083	66,442	4.1%	22.9%	2.8%
Kings	52,821	62,897	0.9%	19.1%	4.7%
Madera	48,801	62,296	8.2%	27.7%	0.3%
Merced	48,740	61,136	6.3%	25.4%	2.4%
San Joaquin	57,936	72,572	6.2%	25.3%	1.6%
Stanislaus	54,213	70,152	9.7%	29.4%	0.7%
Tulare	52,664	66,804	7.5%	26.8%	3.3%
San Joaquin Valley	**$54,661**	**$68,197**	**5.7%**	**24.8%**	**2.5%**
Del Norte	44,714	52,207	-1.1%	16.8%	-0.7%
Humboldt	46,601	58,385	6.2%	25.3%	2.2%
Lake	45,200	58,919	10.5%	30.4%	4.9%
Mendocino	49,170	66,791	15.1%	35.8%	2.2%
North Coast Region	**$46,909**	**$60,395**	**9.1%**	**28.7%**	**2.5%**
Alpine	$50,089	$60,424	2.2%	20.6%	-0.5%
Amador	51,794	64,171	5.0%	23.9%	3.0%
Calaveras	46,002	57,152	5.3%	24.2%	2.0%
Inyo	48,304	60,508	6.2%	25.3%	3.9%
Lassen	53,228	62,635	-0.3%	17.7%	-0.7%
Mariposa	46,032	57,836	6.5%	25.6%	3.9%
Modoc	42,531	51,692	3.0%	21.5%	-2.1%
Mono	51,370	59,269	-2.2%	15.4%	2.0%
Nevada	53,149	77,100	22.9%	45.1%	5.8%
Plumas	45,374	60,198	12.4%	32.7%	0.3%
Sierra	48,128	57,191	0.7%	18.8%	-1.9%
Siskiyou	43,482	53,104	3.5%	22.1%	0.1%
Trinity	40,810	48,837	1.4%	19.7%	4.6%
Tuolumne	46,943	60,958	10.0%	29.9%	4.4%
Mountain Region	**$48,394**	**$62,908**	**10.2%**	**30.0%**	**3.2%**
California	**$70,341**	**$96,327**	**16.1%**	**36.9%**	**1.5%**

Source: U.S. Department of Commerce and CCSCE

High Income County Markets

The geographical pattern of average household income among California counties is nearly identical to the pattern of per capita income. The high income counties are concentrated in the San Francisco Bay Area, the Los Angeles Basin, and the Coastal Region. High incomes are concentrated in the counties with high housing prices. Since the highest housing costs are expected to remain in the same counties in the next ten years, the geographical pattern of average household income in 2010 will look very much like today's pattern.

Ten Counties With Largest Average Household Income 1995-2010

1995	(2002$)	2002	(2002$)	2010 Moderate	(2002$)
Marin	$126,315	Marin	151,163	Marin	185,601
San Mateo	116,977	San Mateo	149,960	San Mateo	179,536
Santa Clara	111,894	Santa Clara	147,975	Santa Clara	176,099
San Francisco	102,280	San Francisco	125,498	San Francisco	151,633
Contra Costa	99,134	Contra Costa	115,934	Orange	142,158
Orange	96,488	Orange	115,100	Contra Costa	141,514
Ventura	92,406	Alameda	107,000	Napa	127,260
Monterey	91,810	Santa Cruz	104,696	Santa Cruz	125,327
Alameda	87,719	Napa	102,690	Alameda	125,267
Santa Barbara	86,493	Ventura	102,068	Ventura	124,165
CALIFORNIA	$83,003	**CALIFORNIA**	$97,640	**CALIFORNIA**	$118,449

Growth in Economic Regions

- The Bay Area has the highest regional average household income in California. In 2002 the Bay Area average was $123,772 – 26.8% above the state average.
- The Los Angeles Basin, San Diego and Coastal Region have household incomes near the state average.
- The next highest incomes are found in the Sacramento region – 14% below the state average.
- The other four regions – San Joaquin Valley, Mountain, North Coast and Sacramento Valley – all have much lower average household incomes.

Average Household Income by Economic Region 1995-2010 (2002$)			
	1995	**2002**	**2010**
San Francisco Bay Area	$100,060	$123,772	$147,983
San Diego Region	78,775	98,122	119,494
Los Angeles Basin	83,129	96,308	118,848
Coastal Region	82,993	95,002	113,253
Sacramento Region	74,950	83,950	102,671
San Joaquin Valley	64,501	69,822	84,356
Sacramento Valley Region	55,512	62,022	74,737
Mountain Region	57,105	63,774	74,698
North Coast Region	55,353	61,468	73,766
CALIFORNIA	$83,003	$97,640	$118,449

The Impact of Inflation

The average household income estimates and projections on Table 4 are measured in 2002 prices. The changes are, therefore, changes in real income, i.e., excluding the impact of inflation. CCSCE projects that inflation will average 2.5% in the years to 2010. This compares with the 4.9% average inflation rate experienced in the 1980s and 2.6% annual inflation between 1990 and 2000.

To convert the household income projected for 2010 to current dollars (i.e., including 2.5% yearly inflation) multiply by 1.2184 Thus average household income in California in 2010 is projected to be $144,318 in the moderate growth alternative, measured in 2010 prices.

MARKET GROWTH – THE OUTLOOK TO 2010

TOTAL PERSONAL INCOME

California is the World's Sixth Largest Market

California is one of the world's largest economies as measured by the total value of goods and services produced. According to estimates from the Los Angeles Economic Development Corporation, California would rank as the sixth largest economy – close behind France and the United Kingdom.

During the past three years, California has been either fifth or sixth in the rankings, changing places with France depending on foreign exchange rates. However, it is likely that China will pass both France and California by the end of the decade and become the world's fifth largest economy for a while before moving even higher in the rankings.

Gross Product in 2002 ($Billions)

Unites States	$10,446
Japan	3,996
Germany	1,995
United Kingdom	1,560
France	1,423
California	1,356
Mainland China	1,237
Italy	1,188
Canada	727
Spain	655

Source: LAEDC

California is the Largest U.S. Market

Total personal income is a measure of total market size. Total personal income in California exceeded $1.1 trillion in 2002 making California the largest state market in terms of buying power. California accounted for 13.0% of total personal income in the U.S., far outpacing other states.

Total Personal Income Largest State Markets in 2002 ($Billions)			
California	$1,158.7	Florida	$494.6
New York	690.5	Illinois	420.9
Texas	621.8	Pennsylvania	391.4

Source: U.S. Dept. of Commerce

Short Term Income Trends

Between 1995 and 2000, real personal income in California increased by 26% (4.7% per year above the rate of inflation) compared to a 20% (3.7% per year) nationwide gain. California did particularly well in 1999 and 2000 when stock option income shot up.

Since 2000, real personal income **fell** by 1.1% in California while rising by 1.7% nationwide. The poor performance in California reflects the loss of stock option income as the tech bubble burst in late 2000.

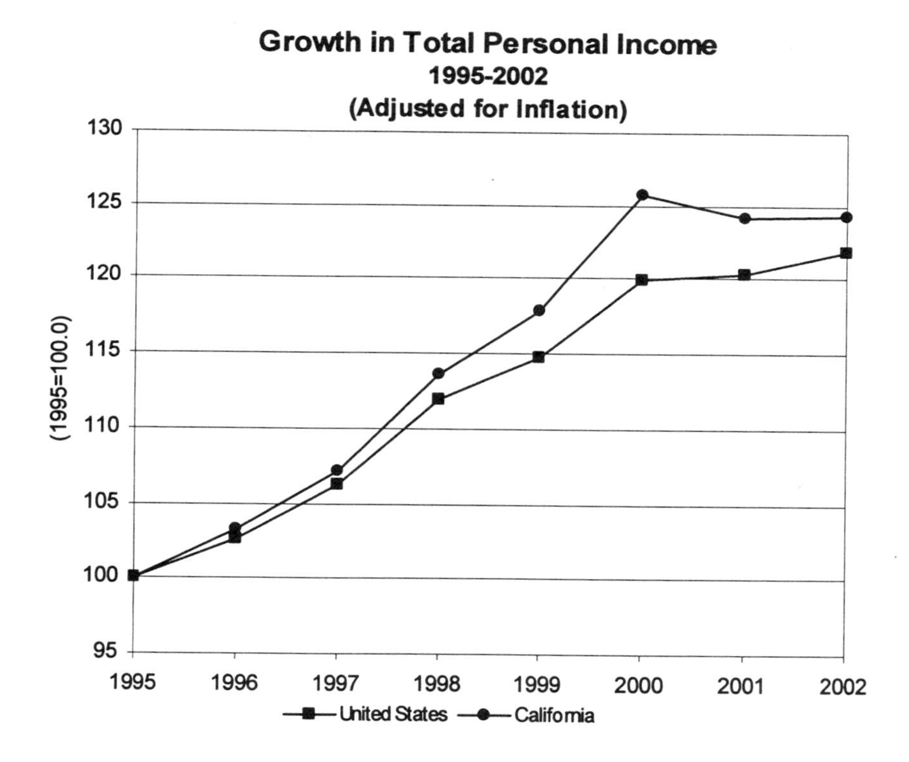

Short Term County Income Trends

The most recent estimates of personal income for counties were published in May 2003 including estimates through 2001. CCSCE's summary of county personal income trends for 1995 - 2001 is presented in Table 5A. CCSCE has prepared unofficial estimates of total personal income by county for 2002 which appear on Table 5.

Santa Clara County had the highest rate of county personal income growth in California since 1995 driven by large gains in tech earnings including stock options. Total personal income increased by 70.4% between 1995 and 2001 or 44.4% (6.3% per year) adjusted for inflation. San Mateo ranked 2nd with a six-year gain of 41.9% (60% per year). Placer County had the third highest income growth – 38.0% or 5.6% per year adjusted for inflation. All three counties are leading high tech centers.

Total Personal Income by County
1995-2001
($Millions)

			Percent Change		
			1995-2001		2000-2001
	1995	2001	(in 01$)	(in Curr$)	(in Curr$)
Fastest Growing Counties					
Santa Clara	$51,388.9	$87,478.6	44.4%	70.4%	-6.9%
San Mateo	24,512.2	41,038.8	41.9%	67.4%	-5.2%
Placer	5,518.6	8,986.9	38.0%	62.8%	1.8%
San Francisco	26,863.6	43,311.9	36.6%	61.2%	1.0%
Nevada	1,834.9	2,931.5	35.4%	59.8%	7.6%
San Benito	833.4	1,296.1	31.8%	55.5%	-2.3%
Slowest Growing Counties					
Colusa	376.2	413.8	-6.8%	10.0%	-6.5%
Modoc	171.1	197.1	-2.4%	15.2%	-2.0%
Glenn	408.7	475.9	-1.3%	16.5%	-4.9%
Imperial	2,242.8	2,615.2	-1.2%	16.6%	4.5%
California	771,470.2	1,129,868.2	24.1%	46.5%	2.7%

Source: U.S. Department of Commerce, CCSCE

Income growth was far stronger in the San Francisco Bay Area than elsewhere in California. Income growth in California outside the Bay Area just matched the national average since 1995.

Total Personal Income by County 1995-2001 ($Billions)					
			Percent Change		
			1995-2001		2000-2001
	1995	2001	(in 01$)	(in Curr$)	(in Curr$)
San Francisco Bay Area	$198,453.4	$317,397.6	35.5%	59.9%	-1.9%
California except SFBA	573,016.8	812,470.6	20.2%	41.8%	4.6%
California	771,470.2	1,129,868.2	24.1%	46.5%	2.7%
United States	6,200,900.0	8,667,490.0	20.3%	34.8%	3.2%

The Bay Area had a real (i.e. inflation adjusted) income gain of 35.5% since 1995 – nearly double the 20.3% national income growth. The rest of California had real income growth of 20.2% for the period and the state increase was 24.1%.

Counties in the Los Angeles Basin generally lagged the Bay Area for income growth but kept pace since 1995 with income gains outside the Bay Area. Real income increased by 19.1% in the Basin and by 16.3% in Los Angeles County between 1995 and 2001 compared to the 24.1% state average and the 20.2% gains for regions outside the Bay Area.

However, Southern California counties have outpaced the national economic recovery since 1995 as shown on Table 5A. Orange, Riverside and San Diego surpassed the national growth rate for personal income and other Southern California counties, Los Angeles, San Bernardino and Ventura, were close to the U. S. growth rate.

All Bay Area counties posted above average income gains since 1995. Other fast growing counties – Placer, El Dorado, San Benito and Nevada – were close to high tech job centers.

Despite large population gains, the San Joaquin Valley ranked 8th among the state's nine regions in total real income growth since 1995 – 13.0% versus the 24.1% state average. The Valley's growth was restrained by below average gains in the two large agricultural counties – Fresno (9.0%) and Kern (9.8%). Growth in the counties experiencing in-migration from the Bay Area – Stanislaus (19.3%) and San Joaquin (17.4%) – was closer to the national average.

Table 5A
California, Economic Regions, and Counties
TOTAL PERSONAL INCOME
1995 – 2001
(Current$)

	1995	2001	% Change 1995-2001 2001$	% Change 1995-2001 Current $	2000-2001 Current $
Imperial	$2,242.8	$2,615.2	-1.2%	16.6%	4.5%
Los Angeles	215,948.8	296,232.8	16.3%	37.2%	4.8%
Orange	71,505.5	106,284.5	26.0%	48.6%	4.9%
Riverside	27,149.4	41,708.1	30.2%	53.6%	6.5%
San Bernardino	28,602.2	39,133.9	16.0%	36.8%	4.3%
Ventura	17,989.6	24,828.2	17.0%	38.0%	2.6%
Los Angeles Basin	**$363,438.3**	**$510,802.7**	**19.1%**	**40.5%**	**4.8%**
Alameda	$36,641.9	$56,974.0	31.8%	55.5%	1.9%
Contra Costa	27,090.8	41,098.5	28.6%	51.7%	1.5%
Marin	10,366.7	15,697.4	28.3%	51.4%	0.7%
Napa	3,217.1	4,744.3	25.0%	47.5%	0.8%
San Francisco	26,863.6	43,311.9	36.6%	61.2%	1.0%
San Mateo	24,512.2	41,038.8	41.9%	67.4%	-5.2%
Santa Clara	51,338.9	87,478.6	44.4%	70.4%	-6.9%
Solano	7,624.6	10,881.2	20.9%	42.7%	2.9%
Sonoma	10,797.6	16,172.9	26.9%	49.8%	-0.4%
San Francisco Bay Area	**$198,453.4**	**$317,397.6**	**35.5%**	**59.9%**	**-1.9%**
San Diego	$62,580.0	$97,240.7	31.7%	55.4%	4.6%
San Diego Region	**$62,580.0**	**$97,240.7**	**31.7%**	**55.4%**	**4.6%**
El Dorado	$3,450.5	$5,040.0	23.8%	46.1%	-2.9%
Placer	5,518.6	8,986.9	38.0%	62.8%	1.8%
Sacramento	26,414.9	35,540.6	14.0%	34.5%	0.0%
Yolo	3,540.0	4,589.3	9.9%	29.6%	-1.9%
Sacramento Region	**$38,924.0**	**$54,156.8**	**17.9%**	**39.1%**	**-0.2%**
Butte	$3,505.8	$4,700.7	13.6%	34.1%	3.6%
Colusa	376.2	413.8	-6.8%	10.0%	-6.5%
Glenn	408.7	475.9	-1.3%	16.5%	-4.9%
Shasta	3,193.0	4,210.7	11.8%	31.9%	4.5%
Sutter	1,512.7	1,935.9	8.5%	28.0%	-0.6%
Tehama	826.4	1,129.0	15.8%	36.6%	4.5%
Yuba	900.9	1,177.9	10.8%	30.7%	3.3%
Sacramento Valley Region	**$10,723.6**	**$14,043.9**	**11.0%**	**31.0%**	**2.7%**

	1995	2001	% Change 1995-2001		2000-2001
			2001$	Current $	Current $
Monterey	$8,827.6	$12,229.9	17.4%	38.5%	3.6%
San Benito	833.4	1,296.1	31.8%	55.5%	-2.3%
San Luis Obispo	4,723.7	7,010.6	25.8%	48.4%	3.5%
Santa Barbara	9,794.0	13,510.6	16.9%	37.9%	2.5%
Santa Cruz	6,250.4	9,426.3	27.8%	50.8%	-2.6%
Coastal Region	**$30,429.2**	**$43,473.5**	**21.1%**	**42.9%**	**1.7%**
Fresno	$13,913.4	$17,898.4	9.0%	28.6%	4.9%
Kern	10,985.5	14,236.1	9.8%	29.6%	4.4%
Kings	1,703.1	2,207.7	9.9%	29.6%	6.1%
Madera	1,667.0	2,320.2	18.0%	39.2%	2.2%
Merced	2,996.6	4,033.4	14.1%	34.6%	4.3%
San Joaquin	9,926.0	13,753.3	17.4%	38.6%	4.3%
Stanislaus	7,507.7	10,568.3	19.3%	40.8%	3.1%
Tulare	5,716.0	7,549.0	11.9%	32.1%	4.7%
San Joaquin Valley	**$54,415.4**	**$72,566.4**	**13.0%**	**33.4%**	**4.3%**
Del Norte	$403.3	$483.7	1.6%	19.9%	-0.1%
Humboldt	2,329.0	3,026.6	10.1%	30.0%	2.9%
Lake	1,031.2	1,422.6	16.9%	38.0%	5.2%
Mendocino	1,613.4	2,252.2	18.3%	39.6%	3.0%
North Coast Region	**$5,376.9**	**$7,185.1**	**13.2%**	**33.6%**	**3.2%**
Alpine	$23.7	$29.9	7.0%	26.2%	0.7%
Amador	614.0	844.1	16.5%	37.5%	5.0%
Calaveras	669.3	980.9	24.2%	46.6%	4.9%
Inyo	378.3	469.0	5.1%	24.0%	4.3%
Lassen	494.1	612.7	5.1%	24.0%	0.1%
Mariposa	293.7	391.9	13.1%	33.4%	5.5%
Modoc	171.1	197.1	-2.4%	15.2%	-2.0%
Mono	217.2	314.6	22.7%	44.8%	3.6%
Nevada	1,834.9	2,931.5	35.4%	59.8%	7.6%
Plumas	412.3	554.3	13.9%	34.5%	1.9%
Sierra	66.9	87.6	10.9%	30.9%	-1.5%
Siskiyou	803.6	996.5	5.1%	24.0%	0.7%
Trinity	222.4	275.1	4.8%	23.7%	5.2%
Tuolumne	927.9	1,299.5	18.7%	40.0%	5.4%
Mountain Region	**$7,129.5**	**$9,984.7**	**18.7%**	**40.0%**	**4.6%**
California	**$771,470.2**	**$1,129,868.2**	**24.1%**	**46.5%**	**2.7%**

Source: U.S. Department of Commerce

A Range of County Income Growth Projections 2002-2010

As explained in Section 5, CCSCE believes there is uncertainty about the rate at which real income will grow in the nation and state during the next decade. As a result, CCSCE's income and taxable sales projections for the year 2010, presented on Tables 3 through 7, show a range of possible growth trends.

The projections on Tables 3 through 7 use 2002 as the base year. CCSCE has developed unofficial income estimates for 2002 based on published average wage data.

Total personal income (in 2002$) is projected to grow from $1,158.7 billion in 2002 to between $1,530.2 billion and $1,654.4 billion in 2010 as shown on Table 5. Total personal income will reach $1,591.3 billion in 2010 in the moderate growth alternative.

Growth in total personal income depends on two factors: 1) per capita income growth and 2) population growth. Variations in the rate of per capita income growth depend primarily on different assumptions about the outlook of productivity growth. CCSCE's assumptions about productivity and per capita income growth are discussed earlier in the section on per capita income.

Driven largely by rapid population growth, personal income in California rose by 3.4% per year in the 1980s. Annual gains in real per capita income were modest – averaging slightly above 1% annually.

Real income grew by 3.2% per year between 1995 and 2002, split between population growth and gains in per capita income. CCSCE expects a surge in real per capita income to 2010 based on continuing productivity gains and a rebound from the recession-depressed income levels of 2002. As a result, total personal income, adjusted for inflation, will increase by 4.0% per year in the moderate growth alternative – slightly above the 1980s growth rate despite much lower rates of population growth.

California
Components of Real Income Growth
Average Annual Growth

			2002-2010		
	1980-1990	1995-2002	Low Growth	Moderate Growth	High Growth
Total Personal Income	3.4%	3.2%	3.5%	4.0%	4.6%
Per Capita Income	1.1%	1.6%	2.0%	2.5%	3.0%
Population	2.3%	1.5%	1.5%	1.5%	1.5%

Largest County Markets

The Los Angeles Basin was a $532 billion market in 2002, larger than all states but New York and Texas. Los Angeles County, with total income of $307.1 billion in 2002, had more buying power than all but eight states.

California had eleven individual county markets of $30 billion or more in 2002. Eleven additional county markets had over $10 billion in total personal income. By the year 2010 these numbers will grow. In CCSCE's moderate growth alternative there will be twelve $30 billion+ markets and thirteen other $10 billion+ markets measured in 2002$.

The same ten counties are California's largest income markets in 1990, 2002 and 2010. All of the ten markets are in the Los Angeles Basin, Bay Area, San Diego and Sacramento regions. The largest county market outside these regions is Fresno County which will be less than half as large as 10th ranked San Francisco in terms of total personal income in 2010.

Ten Counties With Largest Total Personal Income
1995-2010
(Billions of 2002$)

1995		2002		2010 Moderate	
Los Angeles	$260.8	Los Angeles	$307.1	Los Angeles	$406.2
Orange	86.4	Orange	110.4	Orange	152.5
San Diego	75.6	San Diego	101.1	San Diego	140.2
Santa Clara	62.0	Santa Clara	86.2	Santa Clara	114.7
Alameda	44.3	Alameda	57.2	Alameda	73.7
San Bernardino	34.5	Riverside	44.4	Riverside	70.5
Riverside	32.8	San Francisco	42.5	San Bernardino	62.4
Contra Costa	32.7	Contra Costa	41.2	Sacramento	56.8
San Francisco	32.4	San Bernardino	41.2	Contra Costa	55.7
Sacramento	31.9	Sacramento	39.2	San Francisco	55.0
CALIFORNIA	$931.8	**CALIFORNIA**	$1,158.7	**CALIFORNIA**	$1,591.4

California Has Fast Growing Markets

Between 1995 and 2002 real total personal income in California increased by 24.4%. The California market grew by an inflation adjusted 3.2% annually over the seven year period including two years of recession.

Table 5
California, Economic Regions, and Counties
TOTAL PERSONAL INCOME
1995 – 2010
(2002$)

			2010		
	1995	**2002**	**Low**	**Moderate**	**High**
Imperial	$2,708.8	$2,753.6	$4,420.7	$4,597.0	$4,779.5
Los Angeles	260,821.2	307,085.8	390,629.3	406,209.5	422,330.7
Orange	86,363.8	110,426.7	146,697.8	152,548.8	158,603.0
Riverside	32,790.9	44,394.7	67,843.2	70,549.1	73,348.9
San Bernardino	34,545.5	41,232.3	59,966.4	62,358.2	64,833.0
Ventura	21,727.7	25,833.4	34,391.0	35,762.7	37,182.0
Los Angeles Basin	**$438,957.9**	**$531,726.5**	**$703,948.4**	**$732,025.3**	**$761,077.1**
Alameda	$44,255.8	$57,180.9	$70,838.8	$73,664.2	$76,587.7
Contra Costa	32,720.0	41,237.6	53,605.8	55,743.9	57,956.2
Marin	12,520.9	15,418.7	19,609.6	20,391.7	21,201.0
Napa	3,885.6	4,847.0	6,296.4	6,547.6	6,807.4
San Francisco	32,445.6	42,531.3	52,875.6	54,984.5	57,166.7
San Mateo	29,605.7	38,659.6	48,774.6	50,719.9	52,732.8
Santa Clara	62,006.7	86,160.3	110,259.9	114,657.6	119,208.0
Solano	9,208.9	11,130.9	15,653.4	16,277.7	16,923.7
Sonoma	13,041.3	16,298.3	21,367.0	22,219.2	23,101.0
San Francisco Bay Area	**$239,690.4**	**$313,464.6**	**$399,281.0**	**$415,206.3**	**$431,684.6**
San Diego	$75,583.6	$100,987.6	$134,785.4	$140,161.3	$145,723.9
San Diego Region	**$75,583.6**	**$100,987.6**	**$134,785.4**	**$140,161.3**	**$145,723.9**
El Dorado	$4,167.5	$5,616.6	$8,175.3	$8,501.3	$8,838.7
Placer	6,665.3	10,033.3	14,677.8	15,263.2	15,868.9
Sacramento	31,903.7	39,244.7	54,666.1	56,846.5	59,102.5
Yolo	4,275.6	5,054.0	7,169.7	7,455.7	7,751.6
Sacramento Region	**$47,012.1**	**$59,948.7**	**$84,688.9**	**$88,066.7**	**$91,561.8**
Butte	$4,234.2	$4,859.5	$6,516.4	$6,776.3	$7,045.2
Colusa	454.3	437.3	682.0	709.2	737.4
Glenn	493.6	489.1	652.2	678.2	705.2
Shasta	3,856.5	4,377.0	5,646.4	5,871.6	6,104.6
Sutter	1,827.0	2,028.0	2,824.0	2,936.7	3,053.2
Tehama	998.1	1,161.9	1,506.7	1,566.8	1,629.0
Yuba	1,088.1	1,224.9	1,612.8	1,677.2	1,743.7
Sacramento Valley Region	**$12,951.9**	**$14,577.7**	**$19,440.6**	**$20,215.9**	**$21,018.2**

	1995	2002	2010		
			Low	Moderate	High
Monterey	4$10,661.9	$12,626.5	$17,348.6	$18,040.6	$18,756.6
San Benito	1,006.6	1,353.1	2,383.9	2,479.0	2,577.4
San Luis Obispo	5,705.3	7,216.3	9,789.7	10,180.2	10,584.2
Santa Barbara	11,829.1	13,860.8	17,781.1	18,490.3	19,224.1
Santa Cruz	7,549.2	9,673.9	12,738.1	13,246.1	13,771.8
Coastal Region	**$36,752.1**	**$44,730.5**	**$60,041.5**	**$62,436.2**	**$64,914.1**
Fresno	$16,804.5	$18,468.3	$23,445.9	$24,381.1	$25,348.7
Kern	13,268.2	14,756.9	19,781.8	20,570.8	21,387.2
Kings	2,057.0	2,285.6	3,087.2	3,210.3	3,337.7
Madera	2,013.4	2,429.8	3,593.4	3,736.7	3,885.0
Merced	3,619.3	4,279.4	6,809.8	7,081.4	7,362.5
San Joaquin	11,988.6	14,510.2	21,609.4	22,471.3	23,363.1
Stanislaus	9,067.8	11,003.9	16,038.9	16,678.6	17,340.6
Tulare	6,903.8	7,852.5	10,844.7	11,277.2	11,724.8
San Joaquin Valley	**$65,722.5**	**$75,586.7**	**$105,211.2**	**$109,407.5**	**$113,749.6**
Del Norte	$487.1	$499.6	$641.5	$667.1	$693.6
Humboldt	2,812.9	3,095.2	3,800.6	3,952.2	4,109.0
Lake	1,245.5	1,477.4	2,050.5	2,132.3	2,216.9
Mendocino	1,948.7	2,309.0	2,938.0	3,055.1	3,176.4
North Coast Region	**$6,494.2**	**$7,381.1**	**$9,430.5**	**$9,806.7**	**$10,195.9**
Alpine	$28.6	$31.6	$43.2	$44.9	$46.7
Amador	741.5	873.4	1,077.8	1,120.8	1,165.3
Calaveras	808.3	1,015.7	1,356.4	1,410.5	1,466.4
Inyo	456.9	475.6	569.8	592.5	616.0
Lassen	596.8	620.4	858.3	892.5	928.0
Mariposa	354.8	412.1	539.0	560.5	582.7
Modoc	206.6	199.7	268.1	278.8	289.9
Mono	262.4	325.4	426.6	443.6	461.2
Nevada	2,216.2	3,027.4	4,014.0	4,174.1	4,339.7
Plumas	497.9	564.6	682.0	709.2	737.4
Sierra	80.9	89.0	103.8	107.9	112.2
Siskiyou	970.6	1,012.6	1,268.0	1,318.6	1,370.9
Trinity	268.6	282.0	347.5	361.3	375.7
Tuolumne	1,120.7	1,345.7	1,866.3	1,940.7	2,017.7
Mountain Region	**$8,611.0**	**$10,275.2**	**$13,420.6**	**$13,955.9**	**$14,509.8**
California	**$931,775.6**	**$1,158,678.6**	**$1,530,248.1**	**$1,591,281.8**	**$1,654,434.9**

Source: 1995 – U. S. Department of Commerce adjusted to 2002$; 2002, 2010 - CCSCE

The addition of unofficial estimates for 2002 makes a significant difference in county rankings compared to the 1995 – 2001 rankings on Table 5A.

Placer County was California's fastest growing market in terms of buying power with a 50.5% gain in real personal income. Santa Clara had the second fastest growth – 39.0% – after suffering income losses in 2001 and 2002. Both counties are locations for recent high tech job growth.

San Benito is expected to be the fastest growing county market in California between 2002 and 2010 in CCSCE's moderate growth alternative. Four San Joaquin Valley counties – Merced, San Joaquin, Madera and Stanislaus – are in the top 10 counties ranked by growth rate. Eleven county markets will have real income growth of 5.0% or higher between 2002 and 2010 and nine additional counties will have growth exceeding 4.5% per year.

Ten Fastest Growing Counties
1995-2010
(2002$)

1995-2002	Percent Growth in Total Income	2002-2010	Percent Growth in Total Income
Placer	50.5%	San Benito	83.2%
Santa Clara	39.0%	Imperial	66.9%
Nevada	36.6%	Merced	65.5%
Riverside	35.4%	Colusa	62.2%
El Dorado	34.8%	Riverside	58.9%
San Benito	34.4%	San Joaquin	54.9%
San Diego	33.6%	Madera	53.8%
San Francisco	31.1%	Placer	52.1%
San Mateo	30.6%	Stanislaus	51.6%
Alameda	29.2%	El Dorado	51.4%
CALIFORNIA	24.4%	**CALIFORNIA**	37.3%

The Impact of Inflation

The total personal income estimates and projections on Table 5 are measured in 2002 prices. The changes are, therefore, changes in real income, i.e., excluding the impact of inflation. CCSCE projects that inflation will average around 2.5% in the period to 2010. This compares with the 4.9% average inflation rate experienced in the 1980s, and 2.6% between 1990 and 2000.

To convert income for 2010 in 2002$ to current dollars (i.e., including 2.5% yearly inflation), multiply by 1.2182. Total personal income in California in 2010 for the moderate growth alternative is projected to be $1,938.5 billion in 2010 prices.

Between 2002 and 2010 total income will increase from $1,158.7 billion to $1,938.5 billion in current dollars. This represents a 6.6% annual gain including the impact of expected inflation.

Income Growth in Economic Regions

The San Diego and Bay Area regions led the state in income growth in the 1995-2002 period. The Bay Area had real income growth of 30.8% (3.9% per year). The Los Angeles Basin had the fifth largest increase (21.1%) in real personal income in California and had the largest dollar gain ($92.7 billion).

The Sacramento region is expected to lead the state in income growth (46.9%) to 2010 driven by high rates of population growth. The San Joaquin Valley will have the 2nd fastest gains.

The largest dollar growth will occur in the Los Angeles Basin (+$200.3 billion) and San Francisco Bay Area (+$101.7 billion) but Bay Area income gains will be the state's lowest because the tech-led job losses will take time to reverse.

Income Growth In Economic Regions
1995-2010
(Billions of 2002$)

	1995-2002		2002-2010 Moderate	
Regions	**Growth**	**% Change**	**Growth**	**% Change**
Sacramento Region	12.9	27.5%	28.1	46.9%
San Joaquin Valley	$9.9	15.0%	$33.8	44.7%
Coastal Region	8.0	21.7%	17.7	39.6%
San Diego Region	25.4	33.6%	39.2	38.8%
Sacramento Valley Region	1.6	12.6%	5.6	38.7%
Los Angeles Basin	92.7	21.1%	200.3	37.7%
Mountain Region	1.7	19.3%	3.7	35.8%
North Coast Region	-0.9	13.7%	2.4	32.9%
San Francisco Bay Area	73.8	30.8%	101.7	32.5%
CALIFORNIA	$226.9	24.4%	$432.6	37.3%

TAXABLE SALES

Taxable sales are another measure of total market size. In 2002 total taxable sales in California were approximately $438 billion representing about $1 in every $8 spent in the U.S.

Taxable sales, as measured in California, include items subject to sales tax under California law. Taxable sales include taxable sales sold by retail stores ("taxable retail sales") and taxable sales sold by other business establishments.

Approximately 40% of personal income is spent on taxable items in California. The major purchases not included in taxable sales are food and drugs, services, and housing. Internet transactions are often untaxed and the rapid growth of Internet commerce could reduce the rate of growth of **taxable** sales in future years.

Spending Surged in 1999 and 2000, Fell in 2001 and 2002

Taxable sales fell by 0.9% (-7.1% after adjusting for inflation) between 2000 and 2002 to reach $437.9 billion.

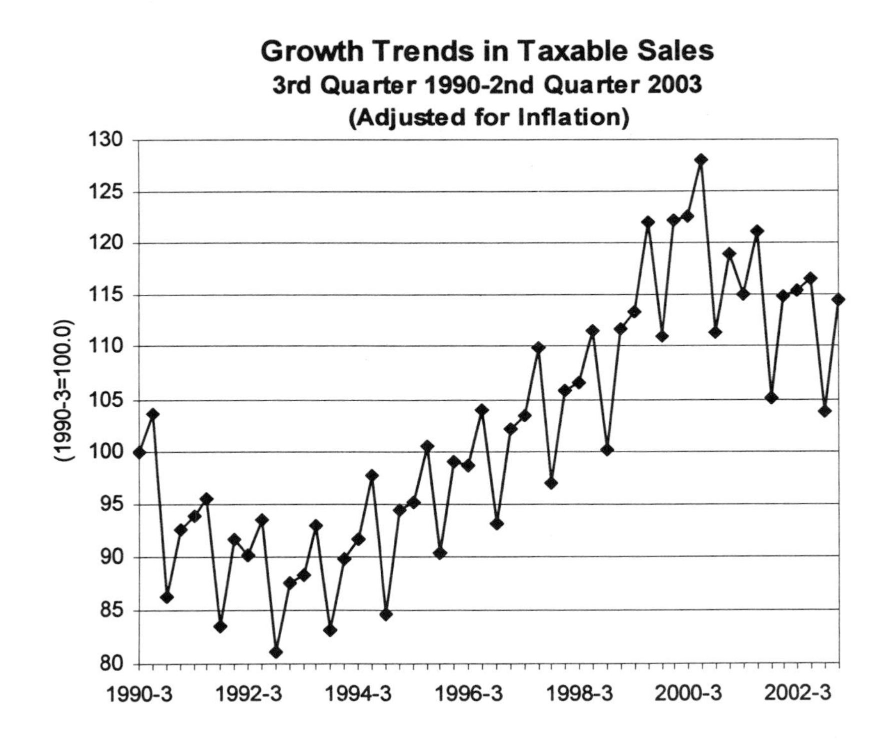

Taxable sales rose by 1.6% year over year in the 2nd quarter of 2003 compared to a 1.9% increase in consumer prices. The sharp downturn in taxable sales after 2000 has finally ended in California.

Short Term County Trends

County by county estimates for 2002 are shown on Table 6A. These estimates are based on actual data for the first three quarters of 2002.

Taxable sales plummeted in the Bay Area in 2001 and 2002. The region's taxable sales fell by 15.4% in just two years led by a 28.1% decline in Santa Clara. Business to business sales are a large component of taxable sales in the region's high tech economy and they fell sharply as high tech job and sales levels fell.

Average Taxable Sales by Economic Region
1995-2002

	1995	2002	2002$	1995-2002 (in Curr$)	2000-2002 (in Curr$)
San Diego Region	$23,452.0	$38,631.8	36.4%	64.7%	6.6%
Sacramento Region	16,452.6	26,885.4	35.3%	63.4%	7.2%
Coastal Region	10,537.2	16,300.5	28.1%	54.7%	1.6%
San Joaquin Valley	24,159.2	36,701.6	25.8%	51.9%	8.2%
Los Angeles Basin	139,043.6	203,730.5	21.3%	46.5%	3.2%
Sacramento Valley Region	4,691.1	6,870.7	21.3%	46.5%	6.9%
Mountain Region	2,681.2	3,856.3	19.1%	43.8%	5.8%
North Coast Region	2,166.0	2,987.4	14.2%	37.9%	4.4%
San Francisco Bay Area	75,633.6	100,447.1	10.0%	32.8%	-15.4%
California	300,914.3	437,907.0	20.5%	45.5%	-0.9%
California exc. Bay Area	$225,280.7	$337,459.9	24.0%	49.8%	4.4%

Taxable sales growth kept pace with inflation outside the Bay Area. Taxable sales in the other eight regions increased by 4.4% between 2000 and 2002.

San Diego and Sacramento had the highest regional growth rates for taxable sales since 1995. The San Diego region had a gain of 64.7% (36.4% after adjusting for inflation) and posted a 6.6% increase since 2000. The Sacramento region had a 7.2% gain since 2000 and a 63.4% increase (35.3% after inflation) between 1995 and 2002.

The San Joaquin Valley had the largest sales growth since 2000 (8.2%) and the fourth largest regional gain since 1995. The Coastal region ranked third since 1995 but growth slowed to 1.6% since 2000.

The Los Angeles Basin saw real taxable sales growth of 21.3% between 1995 and 2002, keeping pace with the 20.5% statewide gain. Growth slowed to 3.2% between 2000 and 2002.

Placer and Riverside headed the list of fastest-growing counties and each county had large taxable sales gains continuing after 2000. Placer had an inflation-adjusted gain of 82.4% in taxable sales since 1995 helped by population growth and high tech business to business sales. Placer had an increase of 16.8% between 2000 and 2002 while Riverside had a gain of 14.3% for the same period.

San Joaquin County ranked fifth with a real taxable sales gain of 44% between 1995 and 2002 driven by large population growth. Sales growth continued after 2000 with a 10.4% gain to 2002.

Average Taxable Sales by County
1995-2002

			Percent Change		
				1995-2002	**2000-2002**
	1995	**2002**	**(in 2002$)**	**(in Curr$)**	**(in Curr$)**
Fastest Growing Counties					
Placer	$2,512.9	$5,536.7	82.4%	120.3%	16.8%
Riverside	10,320.6	19,414.3	55.7%	88.1%	14.3%
Napa	1,111.9	1993.6	48.4%	79.3%	4.5%
Solano	2,883.6	5,149.1	47.8%	78.6%	16.4%
San Joaquin	4,176.0	7,263.8	44.0%	73.9%	10.4%
San Benito	282.6	487.2	42.7%	72.4%	2.4%
Slowest Growing Counties					
Modoc	79.7	72.0	-25.0%	-9.4%	-4.9%
Mariposa	116.5	130.8	-7.0%	12.3%	2.7%
Lassen	204.5	241.0	-2.4%	17.8%	9.0%
San Francisco	9,554.9	11,328.7	-1.8%	18.6%	-19.6%
Santa Clara	22,585.9	26,820.1	-1.7%	18.7%	-28.1%

A Range of County Taxable Sales Growth Projections to 2010

CCSCE's income and taxable sales projections for the year 2010 show a range of possible growth trends as discussed in Section 5 Taxable sales (in 2002$) are projected to grow from $437.9 billion in 2002 to between $556.9 billion and $636.5 billion in 2010.

Taxable sales will grow to $604.7 billion in 2010 in the moderate growth alterative. County by county projections of taxable sales are shown on Table 6.

Taxable sales grew more slowly than personal income during the 1980s and again during the 1990s period. Taxable sales in California are expected to keep pace with income in the rest of the decade.

However, the 2002 – 2010 grow rates for taxable sales are higher than normal because they begin from recession-depressed levels in 2002.

California
Components of Real Taxable Sales Growth
Average Annual Growth

			2002-2010		
	1980-1990	1995-2002	Low Growth	Moderate Growth	High Growth
Taxable Sales	2.0%	2.7%	3.1%	4.1%	4.8%
Total Personal Income	3.4%	3.2%	3.5%	4.0%	4.6%

Large County Markets

In 2002 there were eleven counties with taxable sales of more than $10 billion. Los Angeles, Orange, San Diego and Santa Clara are the top four county markets in California in 1995, 2002 and 2010. Los Angeles County will be a $139 billion taxable sales market by 2010, in 2002$.

By the year 2010 California will have fourteen county markets of $10+ billion and another seven county markets of $5 billion+ in the moderate growth alternative as shown on Table 6.

Table 6
California, Economic Regions and Counties
TAXABLE SALES
1995 - 2010
(Millions of 2002$)

	1995	2002	2010		
			Low	Moderate	High
Imperial	$1,183.8	$1,446.0	$1,938.0	$2,104.1	$2,214.8
Los Angeles	95,497.9	108,119.5	128,046.3	139,021.7	146,338.6
Orange	36,169.2	44,384.8	55,897.0	60,688.2	63,882.3
Riverside	12,465.2	19,414.3	29,036.7	31,525.5	33,184.8
San Bernardino	15,076.0	20,595.1	29,765.6	32,316.9	34,017.8
Ventura	7,543.7	9,770.8	12,642.1	13,725.7	14,448.1
Los Angeles Basin	**$167,935.8**	**$203,730.5**	**$257,325.6**	**$279,382.1**	**$294,086.4**
Alameda	$18,692.2	$21,095.7	$26,687.5	$28,975.0	$30,500.0
Contra Costa	10,072.7	12,160.0	14,675.4	15,933.3	16,771.9
Marin	3,244.2	3,814.4	4,540.4	4,929.6	5,189.1
Napa	1,343.0	1,993.6	2,553.7	2,772.6	2,918.5
San Francisco	11,540.4	11,328.7	14,749.5	16,013.8	16,856.6
San Mateo	10,595.4	11,397.1	14,283.0	15,507.3	16,323.5
Santa Clara	27,279.1	26,820.1	38,950.9	42,289.5	44,515.3
Solano	3,482.7	5,149.1	6,749.2	7,327.7	7,713.4
Sonoma	5,099.9	6,688.4	8,419.7	9,141.4	9,622.5
San Francisco Bay Area	**$91,349.7**	**$100,447.1**	**$131,609.4**	**$142,890.2**	**$150,410.8**
San Diego	$28,325.2	$38,631.8	$48,937.7	$53,132.4	$55,928.8
San Diego Region	**$28,325.2**	**$38,631.8**	**$48,937.7**	**$53,132.4**	**$55,928.8**
El Dorado	$1,116.9	$1,446.2	$1,872.0	$2,032.5	$2,139.5
Placer	3,035.0	5,536.7	8,244.4	8,951.1	9,422.2
Sacramento	13,809.1	17,546.6	23,113.3	25,094.5	26,415.2
Yolo	1,910.3	2,355.9	3,164.5	3,435.7	3,616.6
Sacramento Region	**$19,871.4**	**$26,885.4**	**$36,394.2**	**$39,513.7**	**$41,593.4**
Butte	$1,818.9	$2,219.1	$2,580.5	$2,801.6	$2,949.1
Colusa	208.3	205.8	294.6	319.9	336.7
Glenn	211.5	225.5	271.2	294.4	309.9
Shasta	1,826.0	2,247.5	2,546.2	2,764.4	2,909.9
Sutter	778.9	1,061.0	1,194.1	1,296.4	1,364.7
Tehama	436.0	514.5	589.5	640.1	673.8
Yuba	386.3	397.3	489.4	531.4	559.3
Sacramento Valley Region	**$5,665.9**	**$6,870.7**	**$7,965.5**	**$8,648.2**	**$9,103.4**

	1995	2002	2010		
			Low	Moderate	High
Monterey	$3,818.0	$4,788.0	$6,342.3	$6,885.9	$7,248.3
San Benito	341.3	487.2	787.0	854.5	899.5
San Luis Obispo	2,229.6	3,150.8	3,624.2	3,934.9	4,142.0
Santa Barbara	4,008.3	5,081.5	5,853.3	6,355.0	6,689.5
Santa Cruz	2,329.5	2,793.0	3,515.1	3,816.4	4,017.3
Coastal Region	**$12,726.8**	**$16,300.5**	**$20,121.9**	**$21,846.7**	**$22,996.5**
Fresno	$7,670.8	$9,024.0	$9,949.3	$10,802.1	$11,370.6
Kern	6,127.7	7,413.2	8,641.8	9,382.5	9,876.3
Kings	862.4	997.2	1,145.3	1,243.5	1,309.0
Madera	803.3	917.5	1,248.4	1,355.4	1,426.7
Merced	1,428.9	1,884.5	2,795.1	3,034.7	3,194.4
San Joaquin	5,043.8	7,263.8	9,429.7	10,238.0	10,776.8
Stanislaus	4,294.5	5,840.9	7,280.7	7,904.8	8,320.8
Tulare	2,948.0	3,360.5	4,222.7	4,584.6	4,825.9
San Joaquin Valley	**$29,179.3**	**$36,701.6**	**$44,713.0**	**$48,545.5**	**$51,100.5**
Del Norte	$171.4	$182.9	$204.8	$222.4	$234.1
Humboldt	1,243.3	1,337.0	1,487.8	1,615.3	1,700.3
Lake	363.4	444.1	544.7	591.4	622.5
Mendocino	837.9	1,023.4	1,167.8	1,267.8	1,334.6
North Coast Region	**$2,616.1**	**$2,987.4**	**$3,405.1**	**$3,696.9**	**$3,891.5**
Alpine	$19.1	$22.4	$32.7	$35.5	$37.4
Amador	289.2	385.9	475.4	516.1	543.3
Calaveras	191.4	252.6	303.3	329.3	346.6
Inyo	234.2	257.7	279.7	303.6	319.6
Lassen	247.0	241.0	286.6	311.2	327.6
Mariposa	140.7	130.8	167.2	181.6	191.1
Modoc	96.3	72.2	88.0	95.6	100.6
Mono	157.4	220.1	248.8	270.1	284.3
Nevada	801.3	1,034.1	1,288.9	1,399.4	1,473.1
Plumas	166.5	198.1	206.5	224.2	236.0
Sierra	18.7	26.9	23.0	25.0	26.3
Siskiyou	379.5	402.2	437.2	474.7	499.7
Trinity	63.7	65.9	74.0	80.4	84.6
Tuolumne	433.4	546.4	662.5	719.2	757.1
Mountain Region	**$3,238.4**	**$3,856.3**	**$4,573.9**	**$4,965.9**	**$5,227.3**
California	**$363,442.0**	**$437,907.0**	**$556,948.6**	**$604,687.1**	**$636,512.7**

Source: 1995 - Board of Equalization adjusted to 2002$; 2002, 2010 - CCSCE

Table 6A
California, Economic Regions and Counties
TOTAL TAXABLE SALES
1995 - 2002
(Current$)

			% Change 1995-2002		2000-2002
	1995	2002	2002$	Current$	Current$
Imperial	$980.2	$1,446.0	22.1%	47.5%	3.0%
Los Angeles	79,068.2	108,119.5	13.2%	36.7%	1.4%
Orange	29,946.5	44,384.8	22.7%	48.2%	-0.2%
Riverside	10,320.6	19,414.3	55.7%	88.1%	14.3%
San Bernardino	12,482.3	20,595.1	36.6%	65.0%	9.1%
Ventura	6,245.8	9,770.8	29.5%	56.4%	7.4%
Los Angeles Basin	**$139,043.6**	**$203,730.5**	**21.3%**	**46.5%**	**3.2%**
Alameda	$15,476.4	$21,095.7	12.9%	36.3%	-11.2%
Contra Costa	8,339.8	12,160.0	20.7%	45.8%	-1.4%
Marin	2,686.0	3,814.4	17.6%	42.0%	-6.0%
Napa	1,111.9	1,993.6	48.4%	79.3%	4.5%
San Francisco	9,554.9	11,328.7	-1.8%	18.6%	-19.6%
San Mateo	8,772.6	11,397.1	7.6%	29.9%	-18.8%
Santa Clara	22,585.9	26,820.1	-1.7%	18.7%	-28.1%
Solano	2,883.6	5,149.1	47.8%	78.6%	16.4%
Sonoma	4,222.5	6,688.4	31.1%	58.4%	-2.0%
San Francisco Bay Area	**$75,633.6**	**$100,447.1**	**10.0%**	**32.8%**	**-15.4%**
San Diego	$23,452.0	$38,631.8	36.4%	64.7%	6.6%
San Diego Region	**$23,452.0**	**$38,631.8**	**36.4%**	**64.7%**	**6.6%**
El Dorado	$924.8	$1,446.2	29.5%	56.4%	9.2%
Placer	2,512.9	5,536.7	82.4%	120.3%	16.8%
Sacramento	11,433.3	17,546.6	27.1%	53.5%	5.7%
Yolo	1,581.7	2,355.9	23.3%	49.0%	-2.5%
Sacramento Region	**$16,452.6**	**$26,885.4**	**35.3%**	**63.4%**	**7.2%**
Butte	$1,506.0	$2,219.1	22.0%	47.4%	8.8%
Colusa	172.4	205.8	-1.2%	19.4%	-7.5%
Glenn	175.1	225.5	6.6%	28.8%	-2.2%
Shasta	1,511.9	2,247.5	23.1%	48.7%	9.4%
Sutter	644.9	1,061.0	36.2%	64.5%	4.0%
Tehama	361.0	514.5	18.0%	42.5%	9.5%
Yuba	319.8	397.3	2.9%	24.2%	1.4%
Sacramento Valley Region	**$4,691.1**	**$6,870.7**	**21.3%**	**46.5%**	**6.9%**

	1995	2002	% Change 1995-2002		2000-2002
			2002$	Current$	Current$
Monterey	$3,161.2	$4,788.0	25.4%	51.5%	-2.2%
San Benito	282.6	487.2	42.7%	72.4%	2.4%
San Luis Obispo	1,846.0	3,150.8	41.3%	70.7%	7.7%
Santa Barbara	3,318.7	5,081.5	26.8%	53.1%	5.4%
Santa Cruz	1,928.7	2,793.0	19.9%	44.8%	-4.4%
Coastal Region	**$10,537.2**	**$16,300.5**	**28.1%**	**54.7%**	**1.6%**
Fresno	$6,351.1	$9,024.0	17.6%	42.1%	6.5%
Kern	5,073.5	7,413.2	21.0%	46.1%	6.8%
Kings	714.1	997.2	15.6%	39.7%	12.3%
Madera	665.1	917.5	14.2%	38.0%	4.1%
Merced	1,183.1	1,884.5	31.9%	59.3%	8.3%
San Joaquin	4,176.0	7,263.8	44.0%	73.9%	10.4%
Stanislaus	3,555.6	5,840.9	36.0%	64.3%	12.4%
Tulare	2,440.8	3,360.5	14.0%	37.7%	4.3%
San Joaquin Valley	**$24,159.2**	**$36,701.6**	**25.8%**	**51.9%**	**8.2%**
Del Norte	$141.9	$182.9	6.7%	28.9%	3.9%
Humboldt	1,029.4	1,337.0	7.5%	29.9%	3.4%
Lake	300.9	444.1	22.2%	47.6%	8.5%
Mendocino	693.8	1,023.4	22.1%	47.5%	4.2%
North Coast Region	**$2,166.0**	**$2,987.4**	**14.2%**	**37.9%**	**4.4%**
Alpine	$15.8	$22.4	17.3%	41.7%	-3.9%
Amador	239.5	385.9	33.4%	61.2%	5.6%
Calaveras	158.5	252.6	32.0%	59.4%	9.3%
Inyo	193.9	257.7	10.0%	32.9%	-0.4%
Lassen	204.5	241.0	-2.4%	17.8%	9.0%
Mariposa	116.5	130.8	-7.0%	12.3%	2.7%
Modoc	79.7	72.2	-25.0%	-9.4%	-4.9%
Mono	130.4	220.1	39.8%	68.8%	12.4%
Nevada	663.5	1,034.1	29.0%	55.9%	3.7%
Plumas	137.8	198.1	19.0%	43.7%	5.7%
Sierra	15.4	26.9	44.2%	74.1%	34.5%
Siskiyou	314.2	402.2	6.0%	28.0%	5.5%
Trinity	52.7	65.9	3.5%	25.0%	8.6%
Tuolumne	358.8	546.4	26.1%	52.3%	9.1%
Mountain Region	**$2,681.2**	**$3,856.3**	**19.1%**	**43.8%**	**5.8%**
California	**$300,914.3**	**$437,907.0**	**20.5%**	**45.5%**	**-0.9%**

Source: 1995 - Board of Equilization; 2002 - CCSCE based on first three quarters of data

Ten Counties With the Largest Taxable Sales
1995-2010
(Billions of 2002$)

1995	**(2002$)**	**2002**	**(2002$)**	**2010 Moderate**	**(2002$)**
Los Angeles	$95.5	Los Angeles	$108.1	Los Angeles	$139.0
Orange	36.2	Orange	44.4	Orange	60.7
San Diego	28.3	San Diego	38.6	San Diego	53.1
Santa Clara	27.3	Santa Clara	26.8	Santa Clara	42.3
Alameda	18.7	Alameda	21.1	San Bernardino	32.3
San Bernardino	15.1	San Bernardino	20.6	Riverside	31.5
Sacramento	13.8	Riverside	19.4	Alameda	29.0
Riverside	12.5	Sacramento	17.5	Sacramento	25.1
San Francisco	11.5	Contra Costa	12.2	San Francisco	16.0
San Mateo	10.6	San Mateo	11.4	Contra Costa	15.9
CALIFORNIA	$363.4	**CALIFORNIA**	$437.9	**CALIFORNIA**	$604.7

California's Fastest Growing County Markets

Generally, growth rates will be much higher in the decade ahead than in the years since 1980. Between 1980 and 2002 taxable sales, adjusted for inflation, rose by just under 2% annually. Between 2002 and 2010 taxable sales are projected to grow by 38.1% statewide – a 4.1% annual real increase.

San Benito is projected to lead all counties with a 75.4% (7.3% per year) real (i.e., inflation adjusted) gain. Riverside County ranks second with a projected real annual growth rate of 6.2%. Placer and San Bernardino rank in the top ten, along with Santa Clara County, which will rebound from the very depressed 2002 sales levels. All of the top ten counties have projected real taxable sales growth rates of at least 4.8% per year.

Placer, San Benito, Riverside and San Bernardino are in the top 10 counties for sales growth in both the 1995-2002 and 2002-2010 periods.

Ten Fastest Growing Counties
1995-2010
(2002$)

1995-2002	Percent Growth in Taxable Sales	Moderate 2002-2010	Percent Growth in Taxable Sales
Placer	82.4%	San Benito	75.4%
Riverside	55.7%	Riverside	62.4%
Napa	48.4%	Placer	61.7%
Solano	47.8%	Merced	61.0%
Sierra	44.2%	Alpine	58.6%
San Joaquin	44.0%	Santa Clara	57.7%
San Benito	42.7%	San Bernardino	56.9%
San Luis Obispo	41.3%	Colusa	55.4%
Mono	39.8%	Madera	47.7%
San Bernardino	36.6%	Yolo	45.8%
CALIFORNIA	20.5%	**CALIFORNIA**	38.1%

Key Assumptions

The key assumptions in projecting taxable sales are 1) projections of total personal income and 2) projections of the ratio of taxable sales to personal income. The share of income spent on taxable items has declined since 1980.

Taxable sales did not keep pace with personal income during the 1980s. In California total personal income increased by 3.4% per year while taxable sales grew by only 2.0% per year. The share of income spent on taxable items dropped from over 50% in 1980 to near 45% in 1990.

Taxable sales have fluctuated between 38% and 40% of personal income in the 1990s. The gains between 1994 and 2000 are attributable to the strong rise in non-retail (e.g., business to business) sales.

Taxation of Internet transactions will be an increasingly important factor in assessing the growth of taxable sales in California. If Internet transactions are mostly untaxed (as currently), taxable sales growth will fall further behind the growth in income.

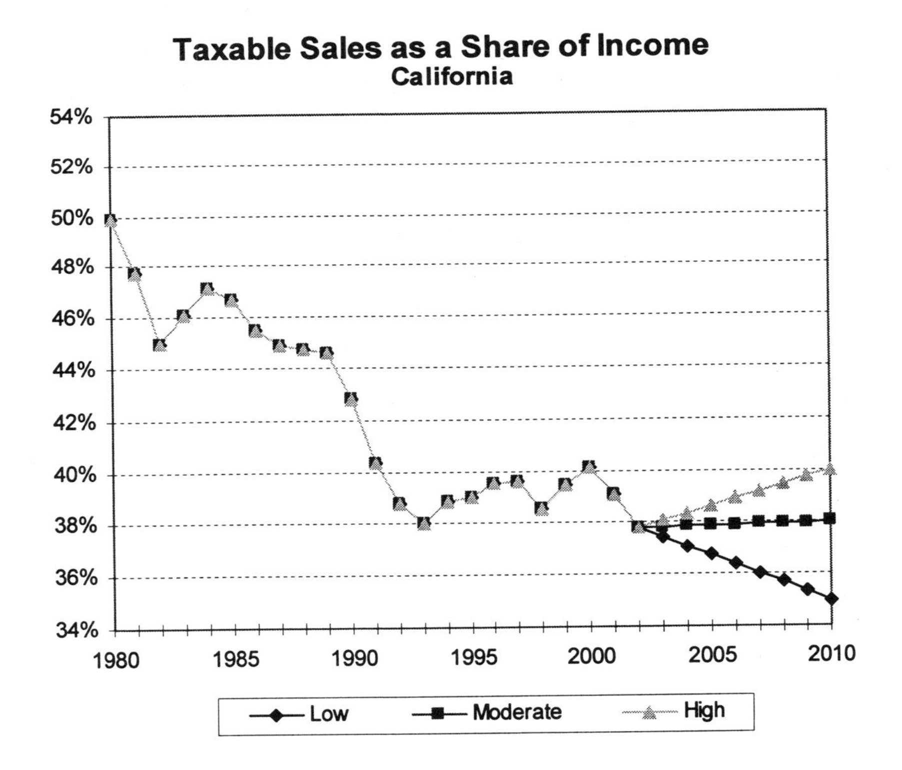

The share of income spent on taxable sales dropped from near 40% in 2000 to 38% in 2002.

CCSCE projects the ratio of taxable sales to income will remain at 38% to 2010. CCSCE anticipates a rebound in the ratio in 2004 and 2005 followed by gradual erosion of the taxable sales base unless e-commerce is significantly included in future years. A high and low set of projections were prepared based on a taxable sales to income ratio of .40 (high) and .35 (low).

County taxable sales were projected on the basis of 1) county total personal income and 2) the projected ratio of taxable sales to income. The county by county ratio of taxable sales to income was projected using the trend for the 1995-2002 period.

Situations in which taxable sales grow significantly faster or slower than income are difficult to project given the statewide perspective from which CCSCE operates. Local factors can often operate to create new markets or cause existing market niches to lose market share to neighboring areas. In Santa Clara and Placer high tech related business sales fluctuate up and down rapidly and independent of trends in local income. The CCSCE projections are a guide to the general trends to be expected in spending growth given the projected gains in population and income.

The Impact of Inflation

The taxable sales estimates and projections discussed above are measured in 2002 prices. The changes are, therefore, changes in real taxable sales, i.e., excluding the impact of inflation. CCSCE projects that inflation will average around 2.5% in the period to 2010. This compares with the 4.9% average inflation rate experienced in the 1980s and 2.6% between 1990 and 2000.

To convert the taxable sales projected for 2010 to current dollars (i.e., including 2.5% yearly inflation), multiply by 1.2182. Total taxable sales in California in 2010 for the moderate growth alternative are projected to be $736.6 billion measured in 2010 prices.

Measured in current dollars taxable sales in California increased from $142.8 billion in 1980 to $437.9 billion in 2002. This represents an average annual growth rate of 5.2% in current dollars.

Between 2002 and 2010, taxable sales will increase from $437.9 billion to $736.6 billion. This represents a 6.7% annual gain including inflationary gains.

Taxable Sales Projections and Transit District Financing

Many California counties now have transit districts financed by sales tax revenues. The ability of these districts to undertake new projects depends on the expected growth in taxable sales. The CCSCE projections of taxable sales presented in **California County Projections – 2003 Edition** should **not** be used for forecasting future district revenues. They are a good guide to the approximate increase in revenues to be expected in a particular county.

However, the CCSCE projections should be augmented by additional analysis. Some of the necessary refinements include:

1. Analysis of year by year trends in income. Specific business cycle assumptions should be incorporated.

2. Analysis of specific trends in inflation. Since transit district revenue accrues in current dollars, the assumption about inflation becomes much more important.

3. Analysis of alternatives. A range of projections including alternative assumptions about growth in population, income, and taxable sales should be examined.

4. Analysis of specific markets. If a particular economic sector (e.g., electronics) is important in a county, then analysis of job and production prospects in that industry may be appropriate for developing projections of sales tax revenues.

TAXABLE SALES IN RETAIL STORES

About two-thirds of taxable sales in California takes place in retail stores. In 2002 taxable retail sales reached $302 billion. Taxable retail sales exclude food for home consumption and prescription drugs.

A Range of Taxable Retail Sales Projections to 2010

Projections for taxable retail sales by county are shown on Table 7. All data shown on Table 7 are in 2002 dollars.

CCSCE's income and taxable sales projections for the year 2010 show a range of possible growth trends. Taxable retail sales (in 2002$) are projected to grow from $301.9 billion in 2002 to between $359.2 billion and $410.6 billion in 2010 as shown on Table 7. Taxable retail sales reach $390.0 billion in 2010 in the moderate growth alternative.

The variations in projected retail sales growth depend on CCSCE's range of personal income projections for each county, the projections of total taxable sales, and projections of the share of sales spent in retail stores.

Retail Spending Slows in 2001 and 2002

CCSCE estimates that retail spending (adjusted for inflation) fell by 1.1% between 2000 and 2002 following an 8.9% real gain in 2000. Even including the downturn in 2001 and 2002, real retail spending increased by 28.6% or 3.7% per year between 1995 and 2002.

County by county estimates for 2002 and a summary of 1995-2002 retail sales trends are shown on Table 7A. The 2002 estimates are based on data for the first three quarters of 2002 from the California Board of Equalization.

Placer County had the largest taxable retail sales growth since 1995 with a gain of 139.7% or 98.5% adjusted for inflation. Riverside ranked second among larger counties with a gain of 59.2% adjusted for inflation compared to the 28.6% state average. San Benito, Napa and San Luis Obispo led the smaller counties. San Joaquin County ranked fourth statewide with a 50.8% inflation adjusted gain.

The Sacramento region had the highest regional growth rate for taxable retail sales between 1995 and 2002 with an inflation-adjusted gain of 42.8% or 5.8% per year. Growth was strong after 2000 with a gain of 12.5% between 2000 and 2002.

The San Diego and Coastal regions ranked 2nd and 3rd in retail sales growth.

The Bay Area fell from 3rd place last year to 8th as a second year of spending declines occurred in 2002. Retail spending fell by 7.1% after 2000 led by sharp declines in San Francisco, San Mateo and Santa Clara counties.

The San Joaquin Valley ranked 4th in growth between 1995 and 2002 and 1st for the 2000-2002 period with a two-year gain of 13.4%. The Los Angeles Basin ranked 5th overall, slightly ahead of the statewide average growth. The Basin also outpaced the state in retail spending growth between 2000 and 2002.

Average Taxable Retail Sales by Economic Region
1995-2002

	1995	2002	2002$	1995-2002 (in Curr$)	2002-2002 (in Curr$)
Sacramento Region	$10,903.7	$18,803.2	42.8%	72.4%	12.5%
San Diego Region	16,181.3	27,460.0	40.5%	69.7%	10.0%
Coastal Region	7,473.7	12,036.8	33.4%	61.1%	6.9%
San Joaquin Valley	16,527.6	25,930.6	29.9%	56.9%	13.4%
Los Angeles Basin	90,306.4	140,905.6	29.2%	56.0%	8.2%
Sacramento Valley Region	3,382.6	5,067.6	24.0%	49.8%	12.8%
Mountain Region	1,702.7	2,555.5	20.0%	45.0%	8.7%
San Francisco Bay Area	46,016.4	66,505.9	19.7%	44.5%	-7.1%
North Coast Region	1,523.5	2,191.1	19.1%	43.8%	7.2%
California	$194,378.1	$301,873.9	28.6%	55.3%	5.2%

Average Taxable Retail Sales by County
1995-2002

			Percent Change		
	1995	2002	(in 2002$)	1995-2002 (in Curr$)	2000-2002 (in Curr$)
Fastest Growing Counties					
Placer	$1757.7	$4,213.4	98.5%	139.7%	24.5%
Riverside	7,435.4	14,298.4	59.2%	92.3%	17.3%
San Benito	161.4	297.3	52.5%	84.3%	5.1%
San Joaquin	2,817.4	5,131.0	50.8%	82.1%	17.0%
Napa	669.6	1,205.7	49.1%	80.1%	5.2%
San Luis Obispo	1,321.8	2,370.1	48.5%	79.3%	13.9%
Slowest Growing Counties					
Yuba	221.6	259.3	-3.0%	17.1%	-3.5%
Mariposa	37.1	43.6	-2.8%	17.4%	5.3%
Trinity	33.0	38.8	-2.6%	17.7%	3.2%
Lassen	122.9	147.2	-0.8%	19.8%	4.5%
San Francisco	6,150.8	7,565.6	1.8%	23.0%	-13.5%

Fast Growing County Markets

Taxable sales in retail stores are projected to increase by 29.2% in California between 2002 and 2010 in the moderate rate growth alternative – an annual gain of 3.3% adjusted for inflation. This growth is slightly lower than the 3.7% annual growth in the period from 1995 through 2002.

The focus of growth in the coming years will move to the San Joaquin Valley, Inland Empire, Sacramento Region and smaller non-metropolitan counties. Alpine, San Benito and Riverside head the list of projected fast growing counties to 2010. Placer, Riverside, San Benito and San Bernardino rank in the top 10 for both the 1995-2002 and 2002-2010 periods.

Ten Fastest Growing Counties
1995-2010
(2002$)

1995-2002	Percent Growth in Retail Sales	Moderate 2002-2010	Percent Growth in Retail Sales
Placer	98.5%	Alpine	67.3%
Riverside	59.2%	San Benito	63.9%
San Benito	52.5%	Riverside	56.5%
San Joaquin	50.8%	Merced	55.3%
Napa	49.1%	San Bernardino	51.8%
San Luis Obispo	48.5%	Placer	48.7%
San Diego	40.5%	Solano	45.6%
Sutter	40.2%	Madera	44.1%
Stanislaus	39.8%	Yolo	42.3%
San Bernardino	39.4%	Santa Clara	41.5%
CALIFORNIA	28.6%	**CALIFORNIA**	29.2%

Key Assumptions

Retail sales have accounted for between 63% and 69% of total taxable sales since 1990. The long-tem trend is down except that non-retail (e.g., business to business) sales fall sharply during economic downturns as in the early 90s and today. CCSCE projects that the statewide retail spending share will decline to 64.5% of total taxable sales in 2010 from the recession-induced high of 69% in 2002.

County projections were developed based on 1995-2002 trends for the ratio of taxable retail sales to total taxable sales.

Table 7
California, Economic Regions and Counties
TAXABLE RETAIL SALES
1995 - 2010
(Millions of 2002$)

			2010		
	1995	2002	Low	Moderate	High
Imperial	$796.1	$1,039.9	$1,306.8	$1,419.3	$1,493.9
Los Angeles	61,631.9	74,559.1	82,867.5	90,009.0	94,746.3
Orange	22,043.6	29,537.0	34,280.4	37,137.4	39,092.0
Riverside	8,980.4	14,298.4	20,539.5	22,382.3	23,560.3
San Bernardino	10,248.0	14,288.1	19,895.2	21,689.5	22,831.1
Ventura	5,371.3	7,183.1	8,868.9	9,655.9	10,164.1
Los Angeles Basin	**$109,071.3**	**$140,905.6**	**$167,758.3**	**$182,293.4**	**$191,887.8**
Alameda	$10,770.2	$13,418.5	$15,376.4	$16,615.7	$17,490.3
Contra Costa	6,774.2	9,133.2	10,271.8	11,145.8	11,732.4
Marin	2,342.3	2,871.0	3,246.9	3,532.9	3,718.8
Napa	808.7	1,205.7	1,529.8	1,674.0	1,762.1
San Francisco	7,428.9	7,565.6	9,267.2	10,069.4	10,599.4
San Mateo	6,566.4	7,707.4	8,810.9	9,530.9	10,032.6
Santa Clara	14,705.2	16,218.3	21,276.5	22,982.1	24,191.7
Solano	2,578.5	3,593.4	4,767.4	5,232.0	5,507.3
Sonoma	3,603.9	4,792.8	5,756.1	6,266.7	6,596.6
San Francisco Bay Area	**$55,578.3**	**$66,505.9**	**$80,303.0**	**$87,049.6**	**$91,631.1**
San Diego	$19,543.6	$27,460.0	$33,148.5	$36,083.0	$37,982.1
San Diego Region	**$19,543.6**	**$27,460.0**	**$33,148.5**	**$36,083.0**	**$37,982.1**
El Dorado	$789.9	$996.0	$1,262.9	$1,380.0	$1,452.6
Placer	2,122.9	4,213.4	5,784.6	6,267.1	6,597.0
Sacramento	9,160.8	12,232.9	15,264.5	16,602.0	17,475.8
Yolo	1,095.8	1,360.9	1,774.3	1,936.3	2,038.2
Sacramento Region	**$13,169.4**	**$18,803.2**	**$24,086.3**	**$26,185.3**	**$27,563.5**
Butte	$1,385.7	$1,680.5	$1,898.3	$2,071.8	$2,180.8
Colusa	120.1	134.9	172.3	185.8	195.5
Glenn	131.4	147.5	157.6	169.8	178.7
Shasta	1,265.2	1,614.4	1,750.6	1,906.7	2,007.1
Sutter	600.7	842.2	903.7	983.8	1,035.6
Tehama	314.7	388.6	419.6	456.0	480.0
Yuba	267.6	259.5	326.7	358.9	377.8
Sacramento Valley Region	**$4,085.5**	**$5,067.6**	**$5,628.7**	**$6,132.8**	**$6,455.6**

	1995	2002	2010		
			Low	Moderate	High
Monterey	$2,672.6	$3,486.2	$4,351.4	$4,729.1	$4,978.0
San Benito	195.0	297.3	448.9	487.3	512.9
San Luis Obispo	1,596.5	2,370.1	2,574.7	2,799.0	2,946.4
Santa Barbara	2,880.0	3,773.9	4,133.6	4,498.2	4,735.0
Santa Cruz	1,682.2	2,109.3	2,533.7	2,758.7	2,903.9
Coastal Region	**$9,026.2**	**$12,036.8**	**$14,042.3**	**$15,272.3**	**$16,076.1**
Fresno	$5,346.5	$6,540.3	$6,851.8	$7,455.4	$7,847.8
Kern	3,992.2	5,041.3	5,504.6	5,977.3	6,291.9
Kings	622.9	702.2	792.9	866.8	912.4
Madera	540.0	619.3	817.6	892.2	939.2
Merced	1,025.2	1,347.8	1,920.8	2,093.2	2,203.4
San Joaquin	3,402.9	5,131.0	6,277.6	6,822.7	7,181.8
Stanislaus	2,982.6	4,169.3	4,961.0	5,401.4	5,685.7
Tulare	2,049.6	2,379.4	2,840.1	3,090.2	3,252.8
San Joaquin Valley	**$19,961.9**	**$25,930.6**	**$29,966.4**	**$32,599.3**	**$34,315.1**
Del Norte	$114.5	$123.0	$135.8	$148.5	$156.3
Humboldt	869.9	986.8	1,054.2	1,148.7	1,209.1
Lake	268.4	327.0	390.6	426.5	448.9
Mendocino	587.3	754.3	824.8	898.6	945.9
North Coast Region	**$1,840.1**	**$2,191.1**	**$2,405.4**	**$2,622.2**	**$2,760.3**
Alpine	$3.6	$3.9	$6.0	$6.6	$6.9
Amador	216.1	297.3	347.5	378.1	398.0
Calaveras	126.6	168.8	195.5	213.2	224.4
Inyo	157.1	174.1	179.7	195.5	205.8
Lassen	148.4	147.2	176.9	194.1	204.3
Mariposa	44.9	43.6	53.5	58.3	61.4
Modoc	43.4	47.2	49.7	53.3	56.1
Mono	100.9	133.2	152.8	167.7	176.5
Nevada	566.5	703.7	868.9	950.9	1,000.9
Plumas	104.5	115.9	122.0	133.8	140.8
Sierra	8.7	10.2	9.1	10.0	10.6
Siskiyou	253.4	260.5	275.8	301.2	317.0
Trinity	39.8	38.8	43.6	47.8	50.3
Tuolumne	315.1	411.1	478.4	521.3	548.7
Mountain Region	**$2,129.0**	**$2,555.5**	**$2,959.4**	**$3,231.7**	**$3,401.8**
California	**$234,768.4**	**$301,873.9**	**$359,231.9**	**$390,023.2**	**$410,550.7**

Source: 1995 - Board of Equalization adjusted to 2002$; 2002 and 2010 - CCSCE

Table 7A
California, Economic Regions and Counties
TAXABLE RETAIL SALES
1995 - 2002
(Current$)

			% Change 1995-2002		2000-2002
	1995	2002	2002$	Current$	Current$
Imperial	$659.1	$1,039.9	30.6%	57.8%	10.6%
Los Angeles	51,028.5	74,559.1	21.0%	46.1%	6.0%
Orange	18,251.2	29,537.0	34.0%	61.8%	7.5%
Riverside	7,435.4	14,298.4	59.2%	92.3%	17.3%
San Bernardino	8,484.9	14,288.1	39.4%	68.4%	11.6%
Ventura	4,447.2	7,183.1	33.7%	61.5%	10.4%
Los Angeles Basin	**$90,306.4**	**$140,905.6**	**29.2%**	**56.0%**	**8.2%**
Alameda	$8,917.3	$13,418.5	24.6%	50.5%	-3.2%
Contra Costa	5,608.7	9,133.2	34.8%	62.8%	5.6%
Marin	1,939.3	2,871.0	22.6%	48.0%	-3.0%
Napa	669.6	1,205.7	49.1%	80.1%	5.2%
San Francisco	6,150.8	7,565.6	1.8%	23.0%	-13.5%
San Mateo	5,436.7	7,707.4	17.4%	41.8%	-10.3%
Santa Clara	12,175.3	16,218.3	10.3%	33.2%	-18.0%
Solano	2,134.9	3,593.4	39.4%	68.3%	13.0%
Sonoma	2,983.9	4,792.8	33.0%	60.6%	3.4%
San Francisco Bay Area	**$46,016.4**	**$66,505.9**	**19.7%**	**44.5%**	**-7.1%**
San Diego	$16,181.3	$27,460.0	40.5%	69.7%	10.0%
San Diego Region	**$16,181.3**	**$27,460.0**	**40.5%**	**69.7%**	**10.0%**
El Dorado	$654.0	$996.0	26.1%	52.3%	11.7%
Placer	1,757.7	4,213.4	98.5%	139.7%	24.5%
Sacramento	7,584.7	12,232.9	33.5%	61.3%	10.5%
Yolo	907.3	1,360.9	24.2%	50.0%	-0.8%
Sacramento Region	**$10,903.7**	**$18,803.2**	**42.8%**	**72.4%**	**12.5%**
Butte	$1,147.3	$1,680.5	21.3%	46.5%	10.6%
Colusa	99.4	134.9	12.4%	35.7%	4.7%
Glenn	108.8	147.5	12.2%	35.5%	17.2%
Shasta	1,047.6	1,614.4	27.6%	54.1%	15.0%
Sutter	497.4	842.2	40.2%	69.3%	18.9%
Tehama	260.6	388.6	23.5%	49.1%	16.0%
Yuba	221.6	259.5	-3.0%	17.1%	-3.5%
Sacramento Valley Region	**$3,382.6**	**$5,067.6**	**24.0%**	**49.8%**	**12.8%**

	1995	2002	% Change 1995-2002		2000-2002
			2002$	Current$	Current$
Monterey	$2,212.8	$3,486.2	30.4%	57.5%	4.2%
San Benito	161.4	297.3	52.5%	84.2%	5.1%
San Luis Obispo	1,321.8	2,370.1	48.5%	79.3%	13.9%
Santa Barbara	2,384.5	3,773.9	31.0%	58.3%	10.2%
Santa Cruz	1,392.8	2,109.3	25.4%	51.4%	-0.7%
Coastal Region	**$7,473.3**	**$12,036.8**	**33.4%**	**61.1%**	**6.9%**
Fresno	$4,426.7	$6,540.3	22.3%	47.7%	11.7%
Kern	3,305.4	5,041.3	26.3%	52.5%	13.1%
Kings	515.8	702.2	12.7%	36.1%	12.8%
Madera	447.1	619.3	14.7%	38.5%	6.4%
Merced	848.8	1,347.8	31.5%	58.8%	12.6%
San Joaquin	2,817.4	5,131.0	50.8%	82.1%	17.0%
Stanislaus	2,469.5	4,169.3	39.8%	68.8%	16.3%
Tulare	1,696.9	2,379.4	16.1%	40.2%	9.3%
San Joaquin Valley	**$16,527.6**	**$25,930.6**	**29.9%**	**56.9%**	**13.4%**
Del Norte	$94.8	$123.0	7.4%	29.7%	7.4%
Humboldt	720.3	986.8	13.4%	37.0%	5.9%
Lake	222.2	327.0	21.8%	47.2%	12.0%
Mendocino	486.2	754.3	28.4%	55.1%	6.9%
North Coast Region	**$1,523.5**	**$2,191.1**	**19.1%**	**43.8%**	**7.2%**
Alpine	$3.0	$3.9	9.2%	31.9%	-26.4%
Amador	178.9	297.3	37.6%	66.1%	11.7%
Calaveras	104.8	168.8	33.3%	61.0%	9.5%
Inyo	130.1	174.1	10.8%	33.8%	4.4%
Lassen	122.9	147.2	-0.8%	19.8%	4.5%
Mariposa	37.1	43.6	-2.8%	17.4%	5.3%
Modoc	35.9	47.2	8.8%	31.5%	13.5%
Mono	83.6	133.2	32.0%	59.4%	5.5%
Nevada	469.0	703.7	24.2%	50.0%	6.3%
Plumas	86.5	115.9	10.9%	33.9%	4.6%
Sierra	7.2	10.2	17.8%	42.3%	21.2%
Siskiyou	209.8	260.5	2.8%	24.1%	15.4%
Trinity	33.0	38.8	-2.6%	17.7%	3.2%
Tuolumne	260.9	411.1	30.5%	57.6%	13.0%
Mountain Region	**$1,762.7**	**$2,555.5**	**20.0%**	**45.0%**	**8.7%**
California	**$194,378.1**	**$301,873.9**	**28.6%**	**55.3%**	**5.2%**

Source: Board of Equalization - 2002 based on three quarters of data

The Impact of Inflation

The retail sales estimates and projections discussed above are measured in 2001 prices. The changes are, therefore, changes in real sales, i.e., excluding the impact of inflation. CCSCE projects that inflation will average 2.5% per year in the decade ahead. This compares with the 4.9% average inflation rate experienced in the 1980s and 2.6% between 1990 and 2000.

To convert the retail sales projected for 2010 to current dollars (i.e., including 2.5% yearly inflation), multiply by 1.2182. Total taxable sales in retail stores in California in 2010 for the moderate growth alternative are projected to be $475.1 billion measured in 2010 prices.

Measured in current dollars taxable retail sales in California increased from $94.2 billion in 1980 to $301.9 billion in 2002. This represents an annual growth rate of 5.4% including the impact of inflation.

Between 2002 and 2010 taxable sales will increase from $301.9 billion to $475.1 billion. This represents an average annual growth rate of 5.8%.

Large County Markets

Eight county markets had more than $10 billion in taxable retail sales in 2002 led by $74.6 billion in Los Angeles County. By 2010 that number will grow to ten with an additional nine counties having taxable retail sales above $5 billion. All of the ten largest county markets will remain in the Los Angeles, Bay Area, San Diego and Sacramento regions.

Ten Counties With Largest Taxable Retail Sales
1995-2010
(Billions of 2002$)

1995	(2002$)	2002	(2002$)	2010 Moderate	(2002$)
Los Angeles	$61.6	Los Angeles	$74.6	Los Angeles	$90.0
Orange	22.0	Orange	29.5	Orange	37.1
San Diego	19.5	San Diego	27.5	San Diego	36.1
Santa Clara	14.7	Santa Clara	16.2	Santa Clara	23.0
Alameda	10.8	Riverside	14.3	Riverside	22.4
San Bernardino	10.2	San Bernardino	14.3	San Bernardino	21.7
Sacramento	9.2	Alameda	13.4	Alameda	16.6
Riverside	9.0	Sacramento	12.2	Sacramento	16.6
San Francisco	7.4	Contra Costa	9.1	Contra Costa	11.1
Contra Costa	6.8	San Mateo	7.7	San Francisco	10.1
CALIFORNIA	$234.8	**CALIFORNIA**	$301.09	**CALIFORNIA**	$390.0

JOB GROWTH TRENDS

JOB GROWTH TRENDS

Job trends are analyzed for the 1994-2000, 2000-2003 and 1994-2003 time periods. This includes the strong economic growth period between 1994 and 2000, followed by the national recession and jobless recovery of 2000-2003.

All of the data is from the California Employment Development Department and is available online at www.calmis.cahwnet.gov.

There are three differences in this 2003 edition from the way job trends have been described in previous editions. One, EDD has not updated the job estimates for counties within metropolitan areas. So, for example, data is available for the Riverside–San Bernardino metropolitan area (MSA), but is not available until 12/12/03 for Riverside and San Bernardino counties separately.

Data for Alameda and Contra Costa counties are combined in the Oakland MSA; for Marin, San Francisco and San Mateo counties in the San Francisco MSA; for Napa and Solano counties in the Vallejo–Napa MSA; for El Dorado, Placer and Sacramento counties in the Sacramento MSA; for Sutter and Yuba counties in the Yuba City MSA; and for Fresno and Madera counties in the Fresno MSA.

Two, CCSCE chose to use September data instead of annual data in order to include job estimates for 2003. So, job estimates are provided for September 1994, 2000 and 2003.

Three, job estimates are now provided using the NAICS industry classifications instead of the SIC classifications. The change does not affect total wage and salary jobs but the definition of manufacturing jobs has changed in the NAICS industry structure. The number of total jobs in Manufacturing is lower in the NAICS-based estimates.

Total Wage and Salary Jobs

The San Diego and Sacramento regions led the state in job growth since 1994 with gains of 27.2% and 26.7% respectively. The Mountain region had the third highest rate of job growth (16.5%) for the 1994-2003 period. The Los Angeles Basin, recovering from the deep early 90s recession, experienced job gains of 15.2% – slightly below the state average, to rank fourth.

For the 1994–2000 sub-period, San Diego, Sacramento and the Bay Area were the growth leaders. The San Diego and Sacramento regions remained relatively strong in the 2000-2003 sub-period but job growth in the Bay Area fell to well below the state average as a result of the sharp downturn in 2001 and 2002.

The San Joaquin Valley posted below average job growth between 1994 and 2000 but has done better than average since 2000.

Total Wage and Salary Jobs By Economic Region September 1994-2003 (Percent Change)			
	1994-2000	**2000-2003**	**1994-2003**
San Diego Region	24.4%	2.3%	27.2%
Sacramento Region	23.6%	2.6%	26.7%
Mountain Region	13.0%	3.1%	16.5%
Los Angeles Basin	15.3%	-0.1%	15.2%
Coastal Region	15.7%	-0.7%	14.9%
San Joaquin Valley	10.9%	2.7%	13.9%
Sacramento Valley	13.4%	-0.7%	12.6%
San Francisco Bay Area	23.2%	-8.7%	12.5%
North Coast Region	9.8%	-1.4%	8.3%
California	**18.9%**	**-2.2%**	**16.4%**

County Job Trends

County job estimates for total wage and salary jobs are shown in Table 8.

Los Angeles Basin – Los Angeles County added the most jobs between September 1994 and September 2000 (368,600) and grew by 9.9%, still below the state average of 18.9%. Los Angeles County matched the statewide average job loss (2.2%) for 2000-2003. Orange County added 257,500 jobs and outpaced the state for the 1994-2000 period and showed a small job gain for 2000-2003.

The Riverside-San Bernardino metro area had the largest percentage job gain (40.5%) between 1994 and 2003. The metro area added nearly 315,000 jobs. The Inland Empire also had the largest percentage job gain (7.6%) between September 2000 and September 2003.

San Francisco Bay Area – Bay Area job gains disappeared in 2001 and 2002 after six strong years of tech-led growth. The Bay Area ended the 1994-2003 period with job growth of 12.5%, below the 16.4% statewide average.

Table 8
California, Economic Regions and Counties
TOTAL WAGE AND SALARY JOBS
1994 - 2003
(Thousands)

				Percent Change		
	Sept 1994	Sept 2000	Sept 2003	1994-2000	2000-2003	1994-2003
Imperial	43.9	47.8	47.1	8.9%	-1.5%	7.3%
Los Angeles	3,723.5	4,092.1	4,002.7	9.9%	-2.2%	7.5%
Orange	1,142.4	1,399.9	1,411.5	22.5%	0.8%	23.6%
Riverside	775.7	1,013.1	1,089.6	30.6%	7.6%	40.5%
San Bernardino						
Ventura	252.0	294.3	290.5	16.8%	-1.3%	15.3%
Los Angeles Basin	**5,937.5**	**6,847.2**	**6,841.4**	**15.3%**	**-0.1%**	**15.2%**
Alameda	883.6	1,057.2	1,045.3	19.6%	-1.1%	18.3%
Contra Costa						
Marin	909.2	1,094.2	975.5	20.3%	-10.8%	7.3%
San Francisco						
San Mateo						
Napa	150.2	184.9	195.5	23.1%	5.7%	30.2%
Solano						
Santa Clara	810.2	1,052.2	864.8	29.9%	-17.8%	6.7%
Sonoma	158.7	198.2	194.4	24.9%	-1.9%	22.5%
San Francisco Bay Area	**2,911.9**	**3,586.7**	**3,275.5**	**23.2%**	**-8.7%**	**12.5%**
San Diego	973.5	1,210.9	1,238.7	24.4%	2.3%	27.2%
San Diego Region	**973.5**	**1,210.9**	**1,238.7**	**24.4%**	**2.3%**	**27.2%**
El Dorado	578.2	721.6	742.9	24.8%	3.0%	28.5%
Placer						
Sacramento						
Yolo	81.3	93.3	92.8	14.8%	-0.5%	14.1%
Sacramento Region	**659.5**	**814.9**	**835.7**	**23.6%**	**2.6%**	**26.7%**
Butte	65.7	74.3	77.2	13.1%	3.9%	17.5%
Colusa	7.7	8.5	8.1	9.8%	-4.5%	4.9%
Glenn	8.0	8.2	7.8	2.1%	-5.4%	-3.4%
Shasta	54.4	61.8	64.0	13.6%	3.6%	17.6%
Tehama	14.7	17.3	14.7	17.8%	-15.0%	0.1%
Sutter	41.6	47.9	44.6	15.1%	-6.9%	7.2%
Yuba						
Sacramento Valley Region	**192.2**	**218.0**	**216.4**	**13.4%**	**-0.7%**	**12.6%**

				Percent Change		
	Sept 1994	Sept 2000	Sept 2003	1994-2000	2000-2003	1994-2003
Monterey	151.0	177.1	174.9	17.3%	-1.2%	15.8%
San Benito	13.3	16.2	16.0	21.9%	-1.2%	20.4%
San Luis Obispo	80.1	100.6	102.9	25.6%	2.3%	28.5%
Santa Barbara	157.9	181.3	178.7	14.8%	-1.4%	13.2%
Santa Cruz	102.5	108.8	107.5	6.1%	-1.2%	4.9%
Coastal Region	**504.8**	**584.0**	**580.0**	**15.7%**	**-0.7%**	**14.9%**
Fresno	366.5	401.2	402.2	9.5%	0.2%	9.7%
Kern						
Kings	219.4	242.1	258.5	10.3%	6.8%	17.8%
Madera	34.4	39.6	40.4	15.1%	1.9%	17.4%
Merced	64.8	68.0	71.7	4.9%	5.4%	10.6%
San Joaquin	181.9	211.5	215.2	16.3%	1.7%	18.3%
Stanislaus	148.7	168.6	175.3	13.4%	4.0%	17.9%
Tulare	128.4	137.6	140.0	7.2%	1.7%	9.0%
San Joaquin Valley	**1,144.1**	**1,268.6**	**1,303.3**	**10.9%**	**2.7%**	**13.9%**
Del Norte	7.7	8.2	8.0	6.2%	-2.3%	3.7%
Humboldt	47.1	50.6	50.4	7.4%	-0.4%	7.0%
Lake	14.0	14.6	15.5	4.3%	5.9%	10.5%
Mendocino	31.0	36.2	34.2	16.6%	-5.4%	10.3%
North Coast Region	**99.9**	**109.6**	**108.1**	**9.8%**	**-1.4%**	**8.3%**
Alpine	0.7	0.9	0.6	21.6%	-36.7%	-23.0%
Amador	9.6	11.6	13.0	20.4%	12.3%	35.2%
Calaveras	7.1	8.1	9.2	14.3%	13.5%	29.8%
Inyo	6.9	8.0	8.0	15.9%	-0.7%	15.0%
Lassen	9.2	9.8	10.5	7.1%	7.4%	15.1%
Mariposa	5.4	5.3	5.7	-2.0%	8.3%	6.1%
Modoc	3.0	2.8	3.4	-7.3%	20.0%	11.3%
Mono	5.1	6.2	6.0	22.2%	-3.5%	17.9%
Nevada	22.9	28.6	29.4	24.6%	2.8%	28.1%
Plumas	7.1	7.8	7.5	9.6%	-3.7%	5.5%
Sierra	1.1	1.1	0.9	1.8%	-19.8%	-18.3%
Siskiyou	14.3	15.1	14.7	5.5%	-2.5%	2.9%
Trinity	3.4	3.4	3.6	-1.2%	7.8%	6.5%
Tuolumne	14.9	16.5	16.6	10.5%	0.7%	11.2%
Mountain Region	**110.8**	**125.1**	**129.1**	**13.0%**	**3.1%**	**16.5%**
California	**12,728.4**	**15,137.2**	**14,809.5**	**18.9%**	**-2.2%**	**16.4%**

Source: California Employment Development Department

Santa Clara was the second-fastest growing county between 1994 and 2000 before leading the nation in job losses after 2000. The Napa-Solano metro area was the second-fastest growing area for the full 1994-2003 period, Sonoma ranked 8th and the Alameda-Contra Costa metro area ranked 10th. Napa-Solano was the 3rd ranked area for the 2000-2003 period.

San Diego – San Diego County ranked 6th throughout the 1994–2003 period. Above average gains in manufacturing jobs and the state's highest growth rate in foreign trade explain the region's growth leadership. Jobs grew by 24.8% between 1994 and 2000 compared to 18.9% for the state and by 2.3% for 2000-2003 compared with statewide losses of 2.2%.

Sacramento Region – The region ranked 2nd in job growth for 1994-2000 and 1994-2003 and third for 2000-2003. The Sacramento MSA was third in job growth for 1994-2003 with a gain of 28.5% compared with the 16.4% statewide average. When county data are released, they will show that El Dorado and Placer counties showed strong job growth.

Coastal Region – San Luis Obispo was the 4th fastest growing county for 1994–2003 led by modest gains in manufacturing and strong growth in retail and government jobs. San Benito had strong job gains on a very small job base and Monterey grew at near the statewide average.

San Joaquin Valley – Valley counties outperformed the state in the 2000-2003 recession period as they did a decade ago in the early 90s recession. San Joaquin County ranked 9th for the 1994-2003 period with a job gain of 18.3%. While Valley counties recorded positive job gains since 2000, they lagged in the strong growth environment of the late 1990s.

Sacramento Valley, North Coast and Mountain Regions – These regions ranked 7th, 9th and 3rd overall for job growth among the nine regional economies tracked by CCSCE. Nevada County (5th) was the only county from these regions ranked in the top ten overall. Mountain region counties had positive job growth for 2000-2003 and the Sacramento Valley and North Coast had smaller than average job losses.

Fastest Growing Counties

Only counties with more than 25,000 jobs in 2003 are ranked in the table below.

The Riverside-San Bernardino metro area led all counties in job growth for all three time periods. The Riverside-San Bernardino area had a 40.5% job growth for the 1994-2003 compared to 16.4% for California and a 7.6% job gain from September 2000 to September 2003 compared to a 2.2% job loss for the state.

The Napa-Solano metro area ranked 2nd in the 1994-2003 period followed by the Sacramento metro area, San Luis Obispo and Nevada counties. Eight of the ten fastest-growing areas were in the large urban regions – Los Angeles, San Francisco, San Diego and Sacramento. Only Nevada and San Luis Obispo were outside these regions.

The San Joaquin Valley had three counties in the top ten for the 2000-2003 period – Kern (2nd), Merced (4th) and Stanislaus (5th). Only four of the top ten areas in 2000-2003 were located in the four large urban regions.

Ten Fastest Growing Counties
Total Wage and Salary Jobs
(Counties with more than 25,000 jobs in 2003)
September 1994–2003

1994-2000	**Percent Change**	**2000-2003**	**Percent Change**	**1994-2003**	**Percent Change**
Riv-SB MSA	30.6%	Riv-SB MSA	7.6%	Riv-SB MSA	40.5%
Santa Clara	29.9%	Kern	6.8%	Napa-Solano MSA	30.2%
San Luis Obispo	25.6%	Napa-Solano MSA	5.7%	Sacramento MSA	28.5%
Sonoma	24.9%	Merced	5.4%	San Luis Obispo	28.5%
Sacramento MSA	24.8%	Stanislaus	4.0%	Nevada	28.1%
Nevada	24.6%	Butte	3.9%	San Diego	27.2%
San Diego	24.4%	Shasta	3.6%	Orange	23.6%
Napa-Solano MSA	23.1%	Sacramento MSA	3.0%	Sonoma	22.5%
Orange	22.5%	Nevada	2.8%	San Joaquin	18.3%
San Francisco MSA	20.3%	San Diego	2.3%	Ala-CC MSA	18.3%
CALIFORNIA	18.9%	**CALIFORNIA**	-2.2%	**CALIFORNIA**	16.4%

MANUFACTURING JOBS

Manufacturing job losses since 2000 outweighed job gains between 1994 and 2000 in both California and the United States. Still, California did better than the nation in that manufacturing job losses in California (6.8%) were far less than the national average (14.9%) for the September 1994-September 2003 period.

Only three regions had manufacturing job gains for the entire period and all were small. The San Joaquin Valley recorded a 5.3% gain followed by the San Diego and Sacramento regions.

The Bay Area recorded a 19.2% manufacturing job gain between 1994 and 2000 (2nd behind Sacramento) but had a 23.9% job loss between 2000 and 2003 to end with a 9.2% drop in manufacturing jobs for the 1994-2003 period to rank 5th in the state.

The Los Angeles Basin had a 10.4% manufacturing job loss to rank just behind San Francisco.

All regions except the North Coast did better than the nation in terms of manufacturing job growth.

Manufacturing Jobs
By Economic Region
September 1994-2003
(Percent Change)

	1994-2000	2000-2003	1994-2003
San Joaquin Valley	5.2%	0.1%	5.3%
San Diego Region	14.2%	-11.0%	1.6%
Sacramento Region	21.5%	-17.5%	0.2%
Sacramento Valley	4.3%	-6.2%	-2.1%
San Francisco Bay Area	19.2%	-23.9%	-9.2%
Los Angeles Basin	6.1%	-15.5%	-10.4%
Coastal Region	4.3%	-15.1%	-11.5%
Mountain Region	2.5%	-15.5%	-13.3%
North Coast Region	5.9%	-29.8%	-25.6%
California	**10.2%**	**-15.5%**	**-6.8%**
United States	**0.7%**	**-15.5%**	**-14.9%**

County Job Trends – County estimates for manufacturing jobs are shown in Table 9.

Los Angeles Basin – Los Angeles County continued to lose manufacturing jobs after 1994. Aerospace jobs declined further though more slowly than before 1994. Other manufacturing jobs rose and then fell back after 2000 as the national recession took effect. Los Angeles County lost 19.4% of its manufacturing jobs in the 1994-2003 period. On the other hand, the Inland Empire counties added more than 25,000 manufacturing jobs and, by 2003, Riverside and San Bernardino counties had nearly 115,000 manufacturing jobs and a 30.3% increase over 1994 job levels.

Manufacturing jobs in Orange County rose by 15.2% between 1994 and 2000 before declining in the tech downturn. Overall, manufacturing jobs fell by 8,500 (-4.5%) between 1994 and 2003. Ventura County ranked 6th statewide with a gain of 4,700 jobs (+14.6%), led by high tech.

San Francisco Bay Area – The Napa-Solano metro area ranked 1st in the state in manufacturing job growth since 1994 with a 35.6% gain on a small beginning base. Sonoma County ranked 7th statewide, led by gains in technology manufacturing. The Alameda –Contra Costa metro area was the 10th fastest growing county for manufacturing jobs, led by technology manufacturing as the East Bay has become an alternative to Silicon Valley for high-tech manufacturing. Santa Clara County added 43,400 manufacturing jobs between 1994 and 2000 but then lost 76,700 jobs in the next three years to end with a 15.4% manufacturing job loss since 1994 – close to the national average.

Sacramento Region – The Sacramento metro area added 9,900 manufacturing jobs between 1994 and 2000 and then lost 7,600 jobs in the next three years. Overall, the metro area posted a 6.5% manufacturing job gain in the 1994-2003 period – ranking 8th in the state. When the county-level data are published later in 2003, they will probably show that Placer County led the metro area in manufacturing job gains.

San Joaquin Valley – The region added 6,100 manufacturing jobs between 1994 and 2003. The good news was that food processing continued modest gains, especially in Kern County. In addition, the Valley does not have high concentrations of manufacturing sectors which declined in the 1990s. The bad news is, as yet, no major expansions of manufacturing activity have occurred from the coastal regions to the Valley.

Table 9
California, Economic Regions and Counties
MANUFACTURING JOBS
1994 - 2003
(Thousands)

	Sept 1994	Sept 2000	Sept 2003	Percent Change 1994-2000	Percent Change 2000-2003	Percent Change 1994-2003
Imperial	1.5	1.7	2.6	13.3%	52.9%	73.3%
Los Angeles	624.9	608.9	503.8	-2.6%	-17.3%	-19.4%
Orange	190.6	219.5	182.1	15.2%	-17.0%	-4.5%
Riverside	88.0	121.8	114.7	38.4%	-5.8%	30.3%
San Bernardino						
Ventura	32.1	42.0	36.8	30.8%	-12.4%	14.6%
Los Angeles Basin	**937.1**	**993.9**	**840.0**	**6.1%**	**-15.5%**	**-10.4%**
Alameda	96.7	118.1	98.0	22.1%	-17.0%	1.3%
Contra Costa						
Marin	62.0	60.8	48.1	-1.9%	-20.9%	-22.4%
San Francisco						
San Mateo						
Napa	16.0	21.8	21.7	36.3%	-0.5%	35.6%
Solano						
Santa Clara	215.7	259.1	182.4	20.1%	-29.6%	-15.4%
Sonoma	21.7	31.5	23.9	45.2%	-24.1%	10.1%
San Francisco Bay Area	**412.1**	**491.3**	**374.1**	**19.2%**	**-23.9%**	**-9.2%**
San Diego	106.6	121.7	108.3	14.2%	-11.0%	1.6%
San Diego Region	**106.6**	**121.7**	**108.3**	**14.2%**	**-11.0%**	**1.6%**
El Dorado	35.5	45.4	37.8	27.9%	-16.7%	6.5%
Placer						
Sacramento						
Yolo	7.3	6.6	5.1	-9.6%	-22.7%	-30.1%
Sacramento Region	**42.8**	**52.0**	**42.9**	**21.5%**	**-17.5%**	**0.2%**
Butte	5.2	4.6	5.1	-11.5%	10.9%	-1.9%
Colusa	0.8	1.3	1.0	60.5%	-23.1%	23.5%
Glenn	1.1	0.9	0.6	-10.5%	-33.0%	-40.0%
Shasta	3.5	3.7	3.2	5.7%	-13.5%	-8.6%
Tehama	2.7	2.4	2.2	-10.9%	-5.1%	-15.5%
Sutter	2.7	3.7	3.4	37.0%	-8.1%	25.9%
Yuba						
Sacramento Valley Region	**15.9**	**16.6**	**15.6**	**4.3%**	**-6.2%**	**-2.1%**

	Sept 1994	Sept 2000	Sept 2003	Percent Change		
				1994-2000	2000-2003	1994-2003
Monterey	9.7	8.8	8.0	-9.3%	-9.1%	-17.5%
San Benito	2.0	2.9	2.6	41.7%	-11.1%	26.0%
San Luis Obispo	5.5	7.6	7.3	38.2%	-3.9%	32.7%
Santa Barbara	15.6	16.1	13.0	3.2%	-19.3%	-16.7%
Santa Cruz	10.4	9.7	7.4	-6.7%	-23.7%	-28.8%
Coastal Region	**43.2**	**45.1**	**38.3**	**4.3%**	**-15.1%**	**-11.5%**
Fresno	29.7	32.2	34.5	8.4%	7.1%	16.2%
Kern						
Kings	9.5	10.9	11.1	14.7%	1.8%	16.8%
Madera	3.4	4.4	4.6	29.3%	4.8%	35.5%
Merced	10.4	10.9	12.4	4.8%	13.8%	19.2%
San Joaquin	25.7	27.6	22.7	7.4%	-17.8%	-11.7%
Stanislaus	27.8	26.6	28.0	-4.3%	5.3%	0.7%
Tulare	11.7	11.7	11.1	0.0%	-5.1%	-5.1%
San Joaquin Valley	**118.2**	**124.3**	**124.4**	**5.2%**	**0.1%**	**5.3%**
Del Norte	0.3	0.3	0.2	-12.1%	-44.8%	-51.5%
Humboldt	5.5	5.3	3.5	-3.6%	-34.0%	-36.4%
Lake	0.5	0.5	0.4	10.9%	-25.5%	-17.4%
Mendocino	4.2	5.1	3.8	19.1%	-25.0%	-10.6%
North Coast Region	**10.5**	**11.2**	**7.8**	**5.9%**	**-29.8%**	**-25.6%**
Alpine	NP	NP	NP			
Amador	1.0	0.8	0.8	-22.2%	-1.3%	-23.2%
Calaveras	0.2	0.4	0.4	85.7%	7.7%	100.0%
Inyo	0.3	0.4	0.3	40.0%	-22.9%	8.0%
Lassen	0.5	0.2	0.2	-56.0%	-4.5%	-58.0%
Mariposa	0.1	0.1	0.1	-7.7%	-8.3%	-15.4%
Modoc	0.0	0.0	0.0			
Mono	0.0	0.0	0.0			
Nevada	2.2	2.4	1.8	6.3%	-22.9%	-18.0%
Plumas	0.6	0.8	0.8	31.6%	0.0%	31.6%
Sierra	NP	NP	NP			
Siskiyou	0.9	1.0	0.6	12.6%	-41.8%	-34.5%
Trinity	0.2	0.2	0.2	-4.8%	20.0%	14.3%
Tuolumne	1.2	1.2	1.0	-0.8%	-12.0%	-12.7%
Mountain Region	**7.1**	**7.3**	**6.2**	**2.5%**	**-15.5%**	**-13.3%**
California	**1,691.4**	**1,864.5**	**1576.4**	**10.2%**	**-15.5%**	**-6.8%**

Source: California Empolyment Development Department

Fastest Growing Counties

The table below shows the ten fastest growing counties (with at least 7,500 manufacturing jobs in 2003) for 1994-2000, 2000-2003 and 1994–2003.

Ten Fastest Growing Counties
Manufacturing Jobs
1994-2003
(Counties with more than 7,500 manufacturing jobs in 2003)

1994-2000	Percent Change	2000-2003	Percent Change	1994-2003	Percent Change
Sonoma	45.2%	Merced	13.8%	Napa-Solano MSA	35.6%
Riv-SB MSA	38.4%	Fresno-Madera MSA	7.1%	Riv-SB MSA	30.3%
Napa-Solano MSA	36.3%	Stanislaus	5.3%	Merced	19.2%
Ventura	30.8%	Kern	1.8%	Kern	16.8%
Sacramento MSA	27.9%	Napa-Solano MSA	-0.5%	Fresno-Madera MSA	16.2%
Ala-CC MSA	22.1%	San Luis Obispo	-3.9%	Ventura	14.6%
Santa Clara	20.1%	Tulare	-5.1%	Sonoma	10.1%
Orange	15.2%	Riv-SB MSA	-5.8%	Sacramento MSA	6.5%
Kern	14.7%	Monterey	-9.1%	San Diego	1.6%
San Diego	14.2%	San Diego	-11.0%	Ala-CC MSA	1.3%
CALIFORNIA	10.2%	**CALIFORNIA**	-15.5%	**CALIFORNIA**	-6.8%

APPENDIX A

ANALYTICAL FRAMEWORK AND SOURCES OF MORE DETAILED INFORMATION

ECONOMIC REGIONS AND COUNTIES — AN ANALYTICAL FRAMEWORK

The county projections presented in this report were developed using an approach that links analyses at four geographical levels — United States, California, economic regions, and counties. The economic regions are a key element in the analysis because they (1) provide feedback to the derivation of statewide projections and (2) provide the basis for developing county projections within each economic region. Economic regions are defined to meet one or both of the following criteria:

- Economic regions represent commuting basins. There is substantial intra-regional commuting but very little commuting in and out of economic regions.

- Economic regions represent geographical areas with similar types of major economic activity, for example, agriculture.

Four of the nine economic regions in California (see the list on the next page) represent commuting basins. In these four regions — the five county Los Angeles Basin, nine county San Francisco Bay Area, the Sacramento Region, and San Diego County — nearly all of the residents both live and work within the region. These regions have the largest and most diversified economic bases in California.

The other five economic regions represent combinations of geographically connected counties with similar economic bases. In the San Joaquin Valley agriculture is the principal activity in the region's economic base. The San Joaquin Valley is also one of the major areas for spill out of diversified manufacturing activity from the metropolitan economic regions. Lumber and tourism predominate in the North Coast and Mountain Regions. Wood and related products and agriculture are the principal activities in the economic base of the Sacramento Valley. The Coastal Region is characterized by tourism and a beginning base in high tech manufacturing.

County projections are based on analysis of nine economic regions in California shown on the map on page iii. The nine regions and the constituent counties are:

Los Angeles Basin
- Imperial
- Los Angeles
- Orange
- Riverside
- San Bernardino
- Ventura

San Francisco Bay Area
- Alameda
- Contra Costa
- Marin
- Napa
- San Francisco
- San Mateo
- Santa Clara
- Solano
- Sonoma

San Diego Region
- San Diego

Sacramento Region
- El Dorado
- Placer
- Sacramento
- Yolo

Sacramento Valley Region
- Butte
- Colusa
- Glenn
- Shasta
- Sutter
- Tehama
- Yuba

Coastal Region
- Monterey
- San Benito
- San Luis Obispo
- Santa Barbara
- Santa Cruz

San Joaquin Valley
- Fresno
- Kern
- Kings
- Madera
- Merced
- San Joaquin
- Stanislaus
- Tulare

North Coast Region
- Del Norte
- Humboldt
- Lake
- Mendocino

Mountain Region
- Alpine
- Amador
- Calavaras
- Inyo
- Lassen
- Mariposa
- Modoc
- Mono
- Nevada
- Plumas
- Sierra
- Siskiyou
- Trinity
- Tuolumne

The objectives of the Center's approach to long term projections for California and substate geographical areas are to:

- Follow the principal hypotheses and major findings of regional economic theory.
- Develop projections of economic and demographic variables that are internally consistent and reflect the principal findings about each regional economy.
- Develop projections for California, economic regions, and sub-regional geographical areas (such as counties) that are internally consistent and reflect the principal findings about the long term economic and demographic outlook for the United States.

Development of Job Projections

The framework of the California Center Projection Model is shown on Chart A-1. The economies of the United States, California, and economic regions within California are linked through analysis of individual industries in each area's economic base. The principal hypothesis is that the projected change in the national economy is transmitted to smaller economic regions primarily through the decisions of firms to locate new facilities or expand existing facilities. Location decisions are the fundamental determinant of the number of new jobs in specific geographical areas of the nation.

Location decisions are analyzed in the context of individual industries in two ways: 1) in terms of their relative growth rates in the national economy and 2) in terms of the supply and demand determinants which affect the location of each industry.

Individual industries are classified into basic and non-basic analytical categories depending on whether the production of the industry is primarily a function of changes in national, international or regional (7 western states) markets or whether output and employment of the industry is a function of changes in specific state and local markets. Firms in basic industries are considered to have a choice among regions of the United States for location of facilities, while the growth of output and employment in non-basic industries is essentially determined by developments in state and local markets.

The latest CCSCE job projections and analysis are included in **California Economic Growth – 2003 Edition**, published in July 2003.

Chart A-1

CALIFORNIA CENTER PROJECTION MODEL

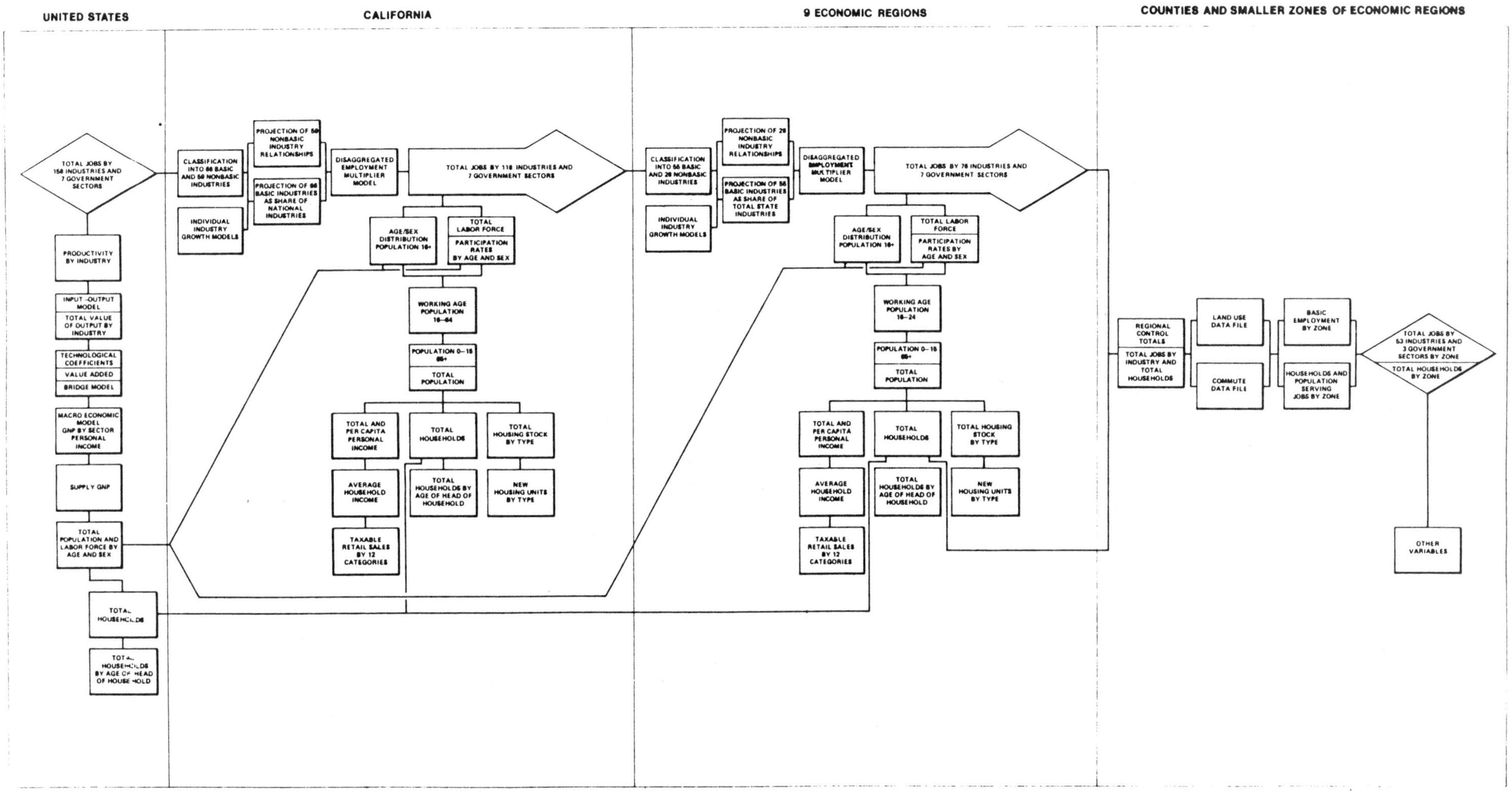

Development of Population and Household Projections

There is a major difference between the methodology for developing projections of population and households at the economic region level and at the sub-regional or county geographical level. At the regional level projections of population and households are related to projections of economic activity in a framework, shown on Chart A-2, that also includes analysis of fertility behavior and retirement migration.

While economic and demographic projections are strongly related at the regional level, they are not as interdependent at the county level within economic regions. The location of jobs and households within a particular region is dependent on land availability development. In addition, the possibility of commuting loosens the link between jobs and housing on a county by county basis within economic regions.

The county projections presented in this report were prepared in two stages. The regional projections were developed based on analysis of each regional economy in the context of projected state and national growth. The county projections in **County Projections – 2003 Edition** are based on the state and regional projections published in **California Economic Growth – 2003 Edition** in July 2003.

The county population and household projections are based on (1) the Center's regional projections; (2) the county level analysis and data bases of regional planning agencies, such as the Southern California Association of Governments (SCAG), Association of Bay Area Governments (ABAG) and Sacramento Area Council of Governments (SACOG), where available; and (3) analysis of historical county shares of regional growth. The Center's regional projections for population and households are allocated to counties based on these analyses.

See the box on page 3-29 for a further discussion of regional planning agency projections.

APPENDIX B

ALTERNATIVE MEASURES OF INCOME

ALTERNATIVE MEASURES OF HOUSEHOLD INCOME

Two different definitions of income are commonly reported by government agencies. These are 1) money income and 2) total personal income (TPI). As a result of differences in definitions and measurement techniques, income estimates for money income and total personal income are quite different. For example, average money income per household in California in 1999 was $65,978 according to the 2000 Census data while average household income based on the personal income definition was $86,704 – roughly 31% higher.

It is very important to note whether reported income estimates are for **median** income or **average** (mean) income. **Median** household income is the amount which divides households into two equal groups, one group (50%) having incomes above the median and another group (50%) having incomes below the median. **Average** (mean) household income is total income divided by the number of households.

Average household income was nearly 40% higher than median household income in 1999 according to 2000 Census data because the growing number of very high household incomes pulls the average income up.

Finally, it is important for users to realize that money income measures are acknowledged to underreport income by approximately 10%. Users should, therefore, increase reported money income estimates by 10% to get a more accurate reading.

The use of two definitions of income (money and total personal) and two measures (median and average) by public agencies and the reporting of both measures in the media (without differentiation or explanation) has led, understandably, to a great deal of confusion. The purpose of this appendix is to describe the alternative measures of income and help readers choose an income measure that best fits their needs.

A Wide Range of Income Estimates Exist for Any Year

Using 1999 as an example (Table B-1) it is easy to see that a wide range of household income estimates were reported.

The most often reported measure – median money income per household not adjusted for underreporting – is the lowest estimate. In 1999 unadjusted median household money income was $47,493 – roughly 28% below average household money income ($65,978) as measured by the U.S. Census Bureau in the 2000 Census.

Both measures were well below the $86,704 average household income measure defined as total personal. Income divided by the number of households.

Table B-1
California
Household Income
1999

Measure of Income	Average Income	Median Income
Money Income Per Household (From 2000 Census)	$65,978	$47,493
Money Income Per Household Adjusted for Underreporting	$74,555	$53,667
Total Personal Income Per Household	$86,704	$62,412

CCSCE's Use of Income Measures

CCSCE uses the total personal income definition in all our reports. There are two principal reasons:

1. Most major sources (e.g., California Department of Finance, U.S. Department of Commerce) use the total personal income definition in reporting per capita income. CCSCE prefers to use per capita and household income measures that are compatible.

   In 2000 per capita income in California was $32,831. With nearly three persons per household in California this produces an average household income estimate near $97,640 which is what CCSCE reports in Chapter 5.

2. The personal income measure includes fringe benefits. Since fringe benefits have risen as a share of compensation, including them gives a better measure of **changes** in average household income over time.

The remainder of Appendix B describes the definitions and differences between money income and total personal income and how these measures are reported in the media.

Definitions of Money Income and Personal Income

Money income is the measure of income used by the Bureau of the Census. Money income is used in the 1990 and 2000 Census reports and all publications based on Current Population Survey (CPS) data. Money income is the measure used in most published reports about housing affordability and in most media reports about trends in household income. (See Chart B-1)

Char B-1
Which Income Measure is Being Discussed

Topic	Discussed in	Income Measure
Average or median household income	Newspaper; other media	**Money** income (Census, CPS); Average household income was $65,978 in California in 1999. Median household money income was $47,493.
Housing affordability index	Newspaper; other media	Median household **money** income (Census, CPS)
Per capita income	Most media discussions; California Department of Finance publications	**Personal income** (U.S. Department of Commerce); Per capita personal income was $32,831 for California in 2002. Disposable income is approximately 85 percent of total income.
Total Personal Income – U.S., California, Counties	All sources	**Personal income** (U.S. Department of Commerce); Total personal income was $1,158.7 billion for California in 2002.

Money income is estimated by use of surveys. Both for the 2000 Census and annual CPS estimates, the basic data is gathered from a **sample** of individuals through a survey which asks respondents to recall last year's income in various categories. The definition of money income as used by the Bureau of the Census:

> "For each person in the sample 15 years old and over, questions were asked on the amount of money income received in the preceding calendar year from each of the following sources: 1) Earnings; 2) unemployment; 3) workers' compensation; 4) Social Security; 5) Supplemental Security income; 6) public assistance; 7) veterans' payments; 8) survivor benefits; 9) disability benefits; 10) pension or retirement income; 11) interest; 12) dividends; 13) rents, royalties, and estates and trusts; 14) educational assistance; 15)

alimony; 16) child support; 17) financial assistance from outside the household, 18) and other income."[1]

Total personal income (TPI) is the measure of income commonly used in reports of the Bureau of Economic Analysis of the U.S. Department of Commerce and the California Department of Finance (DOF) to describe trends in total and per capita income among states and counties. For example, the Department of Finance recently reported that total personal income in California reached $1,127.4 billion in 2001. The reports of total income and per capita income for California and counties produced by the California DOF use the total personal income based data produced by the U.S. Department of Commerce.

Thus one division of the U.S. Department of Commerce (the Bureau of the Census) regularly reports estimates of money income while another division (the Bureau of Economic Analysis) regularly reports estimates of total personal income.

Total personal income differs from money income in both concept and measurement. The measurement of total personal income is based on definitions of income used in producing national income accounts data, e.g., gross domestic product (GDP). Total personal income is a **broader definition** of income than is captured by the money income definition (See Table B-1). In addition, TPI is **measured from business and governmental records** such as employer's wage reports, records of payments to individuals from government agencies, and business records of dividends and interest paid.

Differences Between Money Income and Personal Income

There are two principal reasons for the large differences between estimates of average money income and average personal income per household. These differentiating factors are:

- Underreporting of money income in the surveys
- Inclusion in personal income of sources of income not included in the money income definition and vise versa

---

[1] **Money Income in the United States: 1996**, Bureau of the Census P60-197 September 1997, p A-1

Money Income Adjusted for Under Reporting

Underreporting of household money income in the Census and CPS surveys is acknowledged by the Bureau of the Census. Each year the Bureau of the Census and the Bureau of Economic Analysis reconcile their different measures of income. In recent years the BEA estimates that 10%-13% of money income is not reported. After adjusting for underreporting, average household money income in California was $74,555 in 1999 compared to the unadjusted estimates of $65,978 from the 2000 Census and total personal income per household of $86,704.

Definitional Differences

The major conceptual differences between the definition of money income and personal income are in the following sources of income included in personal income but not in money income:

In Personal Income, Not in Money Income

- Fringe Benefits
  - Health Insurance
  - Retirement Funding
- Imputed Income
  - Interest
  - Rent
- Direct Payments to Medical Providers by Governments

All of the above sources of income are included in total personal income as defined and measured by the U.S. Department of Commerce. The rationale for including these items is that the they represent real increases in the economic status of recipients. Income like fringe benefits, imputed interest and rent, and payments to medical providers (by Medicare and Medical) directly increase the spending potential of households by reducing expenditures that would otherwise have been made by the households.

For example, health insurance payments substitute for medical expenses; retirement programs substitute for a portion of personal savings requirements; and medical payments by the government substitute for medical payments by the households. The sources of imputed income, as explained below, also substitute for expenditures that would otherwise have been made.

A large portion of the increases in fringe benefits and imputed income appear as income because individuals, aware of the tax code, have chosen to arrange their income sources to reduce taxes. Much of the increase in fringe benefits, for example, has been requested in lieu of wage increases because the fringe benefit payments are not taxable to individuals.

Fringe benefits are the most rapidly growing component of total compensation (i.e., wages and fringe benefits). The largest monetary elements of fringe benefits are payments by employers for health insurance premiums and for retirement programs. Since these payments are part of total compensation, they are counted in total personal income by the U.S. Department of Commerce.

Fringe benefits account for half of the gap between money income and total personal income per household – health insurance premiums account for 30 percent of the gap and retirement funding accounts for an additional 20 percent.

Imputed interest and imputed rent account for another 30 percent of the gap. Imputed interest represents the excess of income received by financial intermediaries from funds entrusted to them by persons over income disbursed by these intermediaries to persons. Part of imputed interest reflects the value of financial services rendered persons by financial intermediaries without charge. The remainder is the property income withheld by life insurance companies and private non insured pension funds on the account of persons, such as the addition of income to policyholder reserve held by life insurance companies.

Imputed rent is the **excess** of rental value over payments (such as mortgage interest, taxes, and other ownership expenses) of individuals owning homes. In practice imputed rent income estimates the savings in rental or mortgage payments for households which have low out-of-pocket monthly home ownership costs – generally as a result of having an older, lower interest or paid down mortgage. Direct payments to medical providers from Medicare (for seniors) and from Medicaid (for households in poverty) programs accounts for the remaining major item in the gap between money income and total personal income per household.

In Money Income, Not Personal Income

There are two relatively large sources of income that are counted in money income but not in personal income. The largest amount is the employee paid portion of Social Security and Medicare contributions – the portion deducted from employee paychecks. The other source is child support payments.

Discretionary Income

Discretionary income is another measure of household economic status. Discretionary income varies in specific definition among users but is generally defined as disposable income minus income used for expenditures on "necessities" which are considered to be such items as food, clothing, housing, and transportation.

Other Difficulties in Interpreting Changes in Household Income

There is another difficulty in interpreting household income data. There is no typical or average household. One problem is that changes in household size affect household income. In the 1980s the number of adults per household increased even though divorce rates grew. This indicates that the number of households which include more than one family increased – for example, among recent immigrants. This could artificially raise household income without an increase in living standards.

The increase in multiple family households is one reason that average household income grew so rapidly in the 1980s. CCSCE expects that some of these families will "unbundle" in the 2000-2010 period and that the rate of household growth relative to population growth will increase. Thus average household income growth will be artificially reduced.

Household sizes also vary by type of household and by age. Thus changes in the share of single person households or single parent households – both of which have below average household incomes – can affect the trend for the average. Similarly changes in the mix of households by age group – different age groups have different average household incomes – can affect the calculated average or median.

APPENDIX C

GLOSSARY OF DEFINITIONS AND SOURCES

GLOSSARY OF DEFINITIONS AND SOURCES

Average Household Income — Total personal income divided by total households. Average household income for 2001 is total personal income for 2001 divided by total households as of January 1, 2002.

Note that the 2000 Census reports income estimates for the 1999 calendar year and uses a money income definition.

Household — The number of occupied housing units. Households may consist of more than one family or combinations of families and unrelated individuals. Historical estimates of total households by county are prepared by the Population Research Unit of the California Department of Finance (DOF) on a January 1 basis.

Money Income — The definition of income used by the Census Bureau in Census and Current Population Survey (CPS) estimates. See Appendix B.

Per Capita Income — Total personal income divided by population as of July 1. Per capita personal income for 2001 is total personal income for 2001 divided by July 1, 2001 population from estimates DOF.

Per capita income projections for 2010 were prepared by CCSCE.

Personal Income — The definition of income used by the U.S. Department of Commerce Regional Economic Measurement Unit in preparing estimate of total and per capita income for the U.S., states and counties. Used by CCSCE in **California County Projections**. See Appendix B.

The latest historical county estimates are for 2001. CCSCE prepared unofficial estimates of total, per capita and average household income for 2002.

Projections by CCSCE are annual averages for 2010.

Population — Total population residing in each county including military, college, prison, and other institutional population. Historical estimates of population for counties in California are prepared by DOF on a July 1 and January 1 basis. The latest DOF estimates are for July 1, 2002 and January 1, 2003.

Projections by CCSCE are for July 1, 2010.

Taxable Retail Sales — Sales of taxable items made in retail stores. Historical estimates are prepared by the State Board of Equalization. The latest annual estimates are for 2001. CCSCE prepared 2002 estimates based on three quarters of actual data.

Projections by CCSCE are annual averages for 2010.

Total Taxable Sales — sales of taxable items at retail stores and at other (non retail) establishments. Historical estimates are prepared by the State Board of Equalization. The latest annual estimates are for 2001. CCSCE prepared 2002 estimates based on three quarters of actual data.

Projections by CCSCE are annual averages for 2010.

APPENDIX D

2000 CENSUS DATA FROM SF 3

Census Data

The Census Bureau website – www.census.gov – now provides easy access to 2000 Census data.

The tables in Appendix D are repeated from last year for the convenience of new subscribers.

CCSCE recommends using the menu-driven Census Bureau query system to get the latest Census updates and revisions.

Table D-1
California and Counties
EDUCATIONAL ATTAINMENT AND COMMUTING

	Educational Attainment			Commuting To Work	
	Less Than 9th Grade	High School Grad or Higher	Bachelor Degree Or Higher	Car, Truck or Van - Drove Alone	Public Transp. Incl. Taxi
Imperial	23.8%	59.0%	10.3%	72.7%	1.7%
Los Angeles	16.2%	69.9%	24.9%	70.4%	6.6%
Orange	10.5%	79.5%	30.8%	76.5%	2.8%
Riverside	10.6%	75.0%	16.6%	73.4%	1.4%
San Bernardino	10.4%	74.2%	15.9%	73.6%	1.9%
Ventura	10.4%	80.1%	26.9%	75.9%	1.1%
Los Angeles Basin					
Alameda	8.0%	82.4%	34.9%	66.4%	10.6%
Contra Costa	5.2%	86.5%	31.6%	70.2%	9.0%
Marin	3.5%	91.2%	51.3%	65.5%	10.1%
Napa	9.6%	80.4%	26.4%	72.7%	1.4%
San Francisco	10.5%	81.2%	45.0%	40.5%	31.1%
San Mateo	7.2%	85.3%	39.0%	72.3%	7.4%
Santa Clara	8.0%	83.4%	40.5%	77.3%	3.5%
Solano	6.2%	83.8%	21.4%	73.3%	2.7%
Sonoma	6.7%	84.9%	28.5%	74.7%	2.4%
San Francisco Bay Area					
San Diego	7.9%	82.6%	29.5%	73.9%	3.4%
San Diego Region					
El Dorado	2.8%	89.1%	26.5%	75.8%	1.8%
Placer	3.1%	90.5%	30.3%	80.1%	1.0%
Sacramento	6.7%	83.3%	24.8%	75.4%	3.1%
Yolo	10.0%	79.8%	34.1%	67.2%	3.7%
Sacramento Region					
Butte	5.9%	82.3%	21.8%	74.3%	1.1%
Colusa	23.1%	64.0%	10.6%	67.9%	0.4%
Glenn	16.0%	68.5%	10.7%	71.3%	0.3%
Shasta	4.2%	83.3%	16.6%	79.7%	0.9%
Sutter	12.7%	73.0%	15.3%	78.2%	0.6%
Tehama	8.2%	75.7%	11.3%	75.4%	0.6%
Yuba	12.4%	71.8%	10.3%	73.2%	0.7%
Sacramento Valley					

	Educational Attainment			Commuting To Work	
	Less Than 9th Grade	High School Grad or Higher	Bachelor Degree Or Higher	Car, Truck or Van - Drove Alone	Public Transp. Incl. Taxi
Monterey	18.9%	68.4%	22.5%	68.7%	2.2%
San Benito	13.2%	74.9%	17.1%	73.1%	1.3%
San Luis Obispo	4.9%	85.6%	26.7%	73.9%	1.0%
Santa Barbara	10.9%	79.2%	29.4%	69.4%	2.4%
Santa Cruz	9.7%	83.2%	34.2%	69.5%	3.3%
Coastal Region					
Fresno	18.3%	67.5%	17.5%	74.2%	1.7%
Kern	15.0%	68.5%	13.5%	73.8%	1.4%
Kings	15.7%	68.8%	10.4%	73.5%	1.6%
Madera	18.4%	65.4%	12.0%	73.1%	0.7%
Merced	21.6%	63.8%	11.0%	72.9%	0.7%
San Joaquin	13.3%	71.2%	14.5%	74.6%	1.4%
Stanislaus	13.7%	70.4%	14.1%	76.9%	1.0%
Tulare	23.0%	61.7%	11.5%	72.2%	0.9%
San Joaquin Valley					
Del Norte	6.7%	71.6%	11.0%	73.9%	1.3%
Humboldt	4.0%	84.9%	23.0%	71.6%	1.0%
Lake	6.3%	77.3%	12.1%	72.2%	0.4%
Mendocino	6.7%	80.8%	20.2%	71.6%	0.6%
North Coast Region					
Alpine	2.6%	88.3%	28.2%	51.9%	0.5%
Amador	3.9%	84.0%	16.6%	76.8%	0.3%
Calaveras	2.9%	85.7%	17.1%	73.9%	0.3%
Inyo	4.3%	82.3%	17.1%	70.4%	0.7%
Lassen	4.2%	79.6%	10.7%	76.7%	0.5%
Mariposa	3.7%	85.1%	20.2%	63.5%	1.4%
Modoc	7.4%	77.1%	12.4%	72.8%	0.1%
Mono	4.8%	87.9%	28.9%	62.4%	3.0%
Nevada	1.8%	90.3%	26.1%	75.4%	0.7%
Plumas	2.9%	88.0%	17.5%	74.3%	0.3%
Sierra	4.8%	85.2%	17.2%	68.6%	0.0%
Siskiyou	5.0%	83.8%	17.7%	70.2%	0.6%
Trinity	3.4%	81.0%	15.5%	69.9%	0.3%
Tuolumne	3.2%	84.3%	16.1%	77.4%	0.6%
Mountain Region					
California	11.5%	76.8%	26.6%	71.8%	5.1%

Source: 2000 Census

Table D-2
California and Counties
NATIONALITY AND LANGUAGE

	Nationality		Language Spoken at Home	
	Foreign Born	Not A Citizen	Spanish	Asian and Pacific Island
Imperial	32.2%	19.6%	65.3%	1.7%
Los Angeles	36.2%	22.5%	37.9%	10.0%
Orange	29.9%	18.5%	25.3%	11.3%
Riverside	19.0%	12.1%	27.7%	2.6%
San Bernardino	18.6%	11.6%	27.7%	3.7%
Ventura	20.7%	12.5%	26.2%	3.6%
Los Angeles Basin				
Alameda	27.2%	15.4%	14.3%	15.2%
Contra Costa	19.0%	10.3%	13.1%	7.5%
Marin	16.6%	9.7%	9.5%	2.9%
Napa	18.1%	12.3%	19.3%	2.3%
San Francisco	36.8%	15.7%	12.0%	26.1%
San Mateo	32.3%	16.5%	18.1%	15.5%
Santa Clara	34.1%	20.0%	17.6%	19.5%
Solano	16.9%	7.9%	12.1%	9.3%
Sonoma	14.3%	9.5%	13.8%	2.2%
San Francisco Bay Area				
San Diego	21.5%	12.7%	21.9%	7.1%
San Diego Region				
El Dorado	7.2%	4.2%	6.4%	1.2%
Placer	7.1%	3.7%	5.9%	1.6%
Sacramento	16.1%	9.3%	10.0%	8.2%
Yolo	20.3%	13.2%	19.4%	6.2%
Sacramento Region				
Butte	7.7%	4.8%	7.8%	2.6%
Colusa	27.6%	21.0%	39.8%	0.5%
Glenn	17.8%	13.4%	26.7%	3.0%
Shasta	4.0%	2.1%	3.3%	1.7%
Sutter	19.3%	12.5%	17.7%	1.4%
Tehama	7.9%	5.4%	13.0%	0.3%
Yuba	13.2%	8.9%	13.1%	6.7%
Sacramento Valley				

	Nationality		Language Spoken at Home	
	Foreign Born	**Not A Citizen**	**Spanish**	**Asian and Pacific Island**
Monterey	29.0%	20.7%	39.5%	4.3%
San Benito	18.8%	12.7%	35.0%	1.2%
San Luis Obispo	8.9%	5.3%	10.7%	1.7%
Santa Barbara	21.2%	14.4%	26.5%	2.7%
Santa Cruz	18.2%	12.5%	22.2%	2.0%
Coastal Region				
Fresno	21.1%	14.9%	31.5%	6.2%
Kern	16.9%	11.8%	29.0%	2.6%
Kings	16.0%	11.2%	30.7%	3.8%
Madera	20.1%	15.2%	33.4%	0.8%
Merced	24.8%	16.8%	35.1%	5.2%
San Joaquin	19.5%	12.5%	21.2%	8.7%
Stanislaus	18.3%	11.4%	23.6%	2.8%
Tulare	22.6%	16.7%	38.8%	2.7%
San Joaquin Valley				
Del Norte	5.7%	4.1%	6.1%	1.6%
Humboldt	4.5%	2.4%	4.6%	1.1%
Lake	6.6%	3.6%	7.7%	0.6%
Mendocino	10.2%	7.4%	13.1%	0.7%
North Coast Region				
Alpine	3.2%	1.7%	3.5%	0.3%
Amador	3.4%	1.3%	5.0%	0.7%
Calaveras	3.0%	1.2%	4.0%	0.2%
Inyo	7.6%	4.7%	9.2%	0.6%
Lassen	2.3%	1.0%	10.1%	2.0%
Mariposa	2.8%	0.9%	3.4%	0.4%
Modoc	5.9%	4.1%	8.6%	0.4%
Mono	12.4%	9.4%	14.8%	0.6%
Nevada	4.4%	2.2%	4.2%	0.3%
Plumas	2.5%	1.2%	3.6%	0.4%
Sierra	3.0%	1.5%	3.2%	0.3%
Siskiyou	5.4%	3.0%	5.6%	1.1%
Trinity	1.6%	0.8%	1.8%	0.3%
Tuolumne	3.2%	1.2%	3.5%	0.5%
Mountain Region				
California	26.2%	15.9%	25.8%	8.6%

Source: 2000 Census

Table D-3
California and Counties
OCCUPATIONS AND POVERTY STATUS

	Occupations			Poverty Status	
	Mgmt., Prof. & Related Occ.	Contruction, Extraction & Maintenance	Production, Transptatn & Material Mvg	Individuals	Related Children Under 18
Imperial	24.7%	9.0%	11.7%	22.6%	28.7%
Los Angeles	34.3%	7.8%	15.5%	17.9%	24.2%
Orange	38.1%	7.3%	12.5%	10.3%	13.2%
Riverside	27.8%	11.8%	14.3%	14.2%	18.5%
San Bernardino	28.1%	11.3%	17.0%	15.8%	20.6%
Ventura	36.5%	8.2%	11.5%	9.2%	11.6%
Los Angeles Basin					
Alameda	42.3%	7.5%	11.8%	11.0%	13.5%
Contra Costa	41.0%	8.9%	8.5%	7.6%	9.8%
Marin	52.5%	6.0%	4.5%	6.6%	6.9%
Napa	34.6%	9.3%	11.4%	8.3%	10.6%
San Francisco	48.3%	4.2%	7.5%	11.3%	13.5%
San Mateo	42.7%	7.5%	8.6%	5.8%	6.0%
Santa Clara	48.5%	6.6%	11.2%	7.5%	8.4%
Solano	30.9%	11.0%	13.0%	8.3%	10.3%
Sonoma	35.0%	10.2%	11.4%	8.1%	8.4%
San Francisco Bay Area					
San Diego	37.7%	8.7%	9.9%	12.4%	16.5%
San Diego Region					
El Dorado	37.3%	10.4%	7.6%	7.1%	7.6%
Placer	39.7%	9.9%	8.7%	5.8%	6.3%
Sacramento	36.3%	8.7%	10.2%	14.1%	20.2%
Yolo	41.4%	7.1%	10.9%	18.4%	16.0%
Sacramento Region					
Butte	31.7%	9.3%	11.6%	19.8%	23.8%
Colusa	22.9%	9.6%	14.0%	16.1%	19.5%
Glenn	24.4%	28.4%	15.6%	18.1%	26.3%
Shasta	30.4%	9.8%	12.3%	15.4%	21.0%
Sutter	28.5%	11.0%	15.5%	15.5%	21.3%
Tehama	25.3%	9.3%	19.7%	17.3%	24.0%
Yuba	23.0%	12.5%	16.6%	20.8%	27.6%
Sacramento Valley					

	Occupations			Poverty Status	
	Mgmt., Prof. & Related Occ.	Contruction, Extraction & Maintenance	Production, Transptatn & Material Mvg	Individuals	Related Children Under 18
Monterey	29.2%	8.5%	11.1%	13.5%	17.4%
San Benito	30.2%	12.0%	13.3%	10.0%	11.4%
San Luis Obispo	34.3%	9.8%	9.8%	12.8%	11.4%
Santa Barbara	35.4%	7.7%	9.6%	14.3%	16.3%
Santa Cruz	40.3%	8.9%	8.9%	11.9%	12.5%
Coastal Region					
Fresno	29.5%	8.5%	13.3%	22.9%	31.7%
Kern	27.0%	11.0%	13.5%	20.8%	27.8%
Kings	25.9%	8.5%	13.7%	19.5%	25.9%
Madera	24.7%	10.2%	15.2%	21.4%	28.6%
Merced	25.6%	10.5%	17.4%	21.7%	28.4%
San Joaquin	27.1%	10.2%	16.8%	17.7%	23.7%
Stanislaus	26.5%	11.4%	17.5%	16.0%	20.5%
Tulare	25.3%	8.4%	14.2%	23.9%	32.6%
San Joaquin Valley					
Del Norte	24.3%	8.8%	9.4%	20.2%	26.7%
Humboldt	31.5%	8.8%	12.6%	19.5%	22.5%
Lake	27.2%	13.8%	11.3%	17.6%	22.8%
Mendocino	29.6%	10.9%	12.9%	15.9%	21.5%
North Coast Region					
Alpine	26.6%	9.9%	9.1%	19.5%	27.4%
Amador	30.0%	11.2%	11.1%	9.2%	13.1%
Calaveras	31.1%	14.5%	11.5%	11.8%	15.6%
Inyo	27.6%	12.0%	10.8%	12.6%	16.0%
Lassen	30.0%	10.0%	9.0%	14.0%	16.1%
Mariposa	25.1%	12.0%	12.0%	14.8%	16.5%
Modoc	29.9%	8.5%	10.7%	21.5%	29.7%
Mono	35.4%	13.0%	6.7%	11.5%	12.2%
Nevada	34.3%	12.3%	9.5%	8.1%	9.5%
Plumas	30.0%	12.2%	13.5%	13.1%	16.7%
Sierra	34.7%	13.9%	12.1%	11.3%	14.3%
Siskiyou	30.8%	9.1%	11.7%	18.6%	26.6%
Trinity	28.3%	10.8%	13.9%	18.7%	26.2%
Tuolumne	29.7%	12.1%	11.3%	11.4%	16.2%
Mountain Region					
California	36.0%	8.4%	12.7%	14.2%	19.0%

Source: 2000 Census: Poverty Data for 1999

Table D-4
California and Counties
HOUSING COSTS

	Owner Occupied Units		Renter Occupied Units	
	Median Price	**Median Monthly Mortgage**	**Paying 30%+ of Household Income**	**Median Rent**
Imperial	$100,000	$1,026	28.7%	$504
Los Angeles	$209,300	$1,514	34.5%	$704
Orange	$270,000	$1,620	31.6%	$923
Riverside	$146,500	$1,268	22.0%	$660
San Bernardino	$131,500	$1,202	31.0%	$648
Ventura	$248,700	$1,595	32.0%	$892
Los Angeles Basin				
Alameda	$303,100	$1,625	30.6%	$852
Contra Costa	$267,800	$1,614	29.9%	$898
Marin	$514,600	$1,922	32.3%	$1,162
Napa	$251,300	$1,523	28.5%	$818
San Francisco	$396,400	$1,693	39.5%	$928
San Mateo	$469,200	$1,820	31.3%	$1,144
Santa Clara	$446,400	$1,780	28.9%	$1,185
Solano	$178,300	$1,453	30.2%	$797
Sonoma	$273,200	$1,535	31.5%	$864
San Francisco Bay Area				
San Diego	$227,200	$1,523	31.8%	$761
San Diego Region				
El Dorado	$194,400	$1,444	31.5%	$702
Placer	$213,900	$1,512	28.6%	$780
Sacramento	$144,200	$1,223	26.7%	$659
Yolo	$169,800	$1,351	26.7%	$687
Sacramento Region				
Butte	$129,800	$1,002	26.2%	$563
Colusa	$107,500	$921	25.2%	$494
Glenn	$94,900	$836	23.2%	$458
Shasta	$120,800	$1,025	29.7%	$563
Sutter	$120,700	$1,051	26.7%	$506
Tehama	$103,100	$873	25.7%	$486
Yuba	$89,700	$867	27.8%	$488
Sacramento Valley				

	Owner Occupied Units		Renter Occupied Units	
	Median Price	Median Monthly Mortgage	Paying 30%+ of Household Income	Median Rent
Monterey	$265,800	$1,506	33.0%	$776
San Benito	$284,000	$1,615	36.3%	$765
San Luis Obispo	$230,000	$1,390	31.7%	$719
Santa Barbara	$293,000	$1,508	32.3%	$830
Santa Cruz	$377,500	$1,661	34.1%	$924
Coastal Region				
Fresno	$104,900	$1,047	28.6%	$534
Kern	$93,300	$986	27.2%	$518
Kings	$97,600	$979	24.8%	$533
Madera	$118,800	$933	30.6%	$562
Merced	$111,100	$1,016	29.7%	$518
San Joaquin	$142,400	$1,235	28.8%	$617
Stanislaus	$125,300	$1,112	28.5%	$611
Tulare	$97,800	$943	28.5%	$516
San Joaquin Valley				
Del Norte	$121,100	$968	22.6%	$519
Humboldt	$133,500	$980	24.4%	$537
Lake	$122,600	$974	30.6%	$567
Mendocino	$170,200	$1,128	20.9%	$600
North Coast Region				
Alpine	$184,200	$1,223	24.9%	$659
Amador	$153,600	$1,140	24.9%	$685
Calaveras	$156,900	$1,131	31.8%	$599
Inyo	$161,300	$1,098	19.2%	$516
Lassen	$106,700	$962	21.8%	$561
Mariposa	$141,900	$1,005	27.7%	$502
Modoc	$69,100	$669	18.3%	$429
Mono	$236,300	$1,462	37.9%	$682
Nevada	$205,700	$1,328	31.8%	$746
Plumas	$137,900	$1,001	23.7%	$525
Sierra	$128,600	$897	22.9%	$513
Siskiyou	$100,300	$812	22.8%	$471
Trinity	$112,000	$850	26.9%	$487
Tuolumne	$149,800	$1,088	26.4%	$611
Mountain Region				
California	$211,500	$1,478	31%	$747

Source: 200 Census; Rent and mortgage data for 1999